PATHWAYS

SECOND EDITION

Reading, Writing, and Critical Thinking

LAURIE BLASS

MARI VARGO

4

D1157526

NATIONAL GEOGRAPHIC
LEARNING

Australia • Brazil • Mexico • Singapore • United Kingdom • United States

NATIONAL GEOGRAPHIC
L E A R N I N G

Pathways
Reading, Writing, and Critical Thinking 4,
Second Edition

Laurie Blass and Mari Vargo

Publisher: Andrew Robinson

Executive Editor: Sean Bermingham

Development Editor: Christopher Street

Director of Global Marketing: Ian Martin

Product Marketing Manager: Tracy Bailie

Media Researcher: Leila Hishmeh

Senior IP Analyst: Alexandra Ricciardi

IP Project Manager: Carissa Poweleit

Senior Director of Production: Michael Burggren

Senior Production Controller: Tan Jin Hock

Manufacturing Planner: Mary Beth Hennebury

Art Director: Brenda Carmichael

Compositor: MPS North America LLC

Cover Photo: An explorer traverses a glacier cave in Gornergrat, Switzerland: © Robbie Shone/National Geographic Creative

For product information and technology assistance, contact us at
Cengage Learning Customer & Sales Support, cengage.com/contact
For permission to use material from this text or product,
submit all requests online at **cengage.com/permissions**
Further permissions questions can be emailed to
permissionrequest@cengage.com

Student Book:
ISBN-13: 978-1-337-40780-9

Student Book with Online Workbook:
ISBN-13: 978-1-337-62513-5

National Geographic Learning
20 Channel Center Street
Boston, MA 02210
USA

National Geographic Learning, a Cengage Learning Company, has a mission to bring the world to the classroom and the classroom to life. With our English language programs, students learn about their world by experiencing it. Through our partnerships with National Geographic and TED Talks, they develop the language and skills they need to be successful global citizens and leaders.

Locate your local office at **international.cengage.com/region**

Visit National Geographic Learning online at **NGL.Cengage.com/ELT**
Visit our corporate website at **www.cengage.com**

Printed in China

Print Number: 01 Print Year: 2018

Contents

Scope and Sequence iv
Introduction to *Pathways* viii

1 CHANGING THE PLANET 1

2 ON THE EDGE 25

3 BEAUTY AND PERCEPTION 47

4 RETHINKING BUSINESS 71

5 WORKING TOGETHER 93

6 LANGUAGE AND CULTURE 117

7 RESOURCES AND DEVELOPMENT 139

8 LIVING LONGER 163

9 TRUTH AND DECEPTION 187

10 IMAGINING THE FUTURE 207

Vocabulary Extension 231
Independent Student Handbook 241
Acknowledgments and Credits 258
Index of Exam Skills and Tasks 262

Scope and Sequence

	Unit Title and Theme	Reading Texts and Video	ACADEMIC SKILLS Reading
	1 **CHANGING THE PLANET** *page 1* ACADEMIC TRACK: Environmental Studies	**Reading** The Human Age *by Elizabeth Kolbert* (argumentative essay) **VIDEO** Trees of Life	**Focus** Understanding Cohesion Understanding Main Ideas and Details, Understanding Infographics
	2 **ON THE EDGE** *page 25* ACADEMIC TRACK: Life Science/Conservation	**Reading** A Cry for the Tiger *by Caroline Alexander* (explanatory/persuasive report) **VIDEO** Tigers in the Snow	**Focus** Understanding Appositives Understanding Main Ideas and Details, Identifying Problems, Reasons and Solutions
	3 **BEAUTY AND PERCEPTION** *page 47* ACADEMIC TRACK: Art/Sociology	**Reading** Images of Beauty *by Annie Griffiths* (expository/classification article) **VIDEO** Photo Contest	**Focus** Using a Concept Map Understanding Main Ideas and Details
	4 **RETHINKING BUSINESS** *page 71* ACADEMIC TRACK: Fashion/Business Studies	**Reading** Changing Fashion *by Mike W. Peng* (case study article) **VIDEO** Behind the Brand	**Focus** Understanding Sentences with Initial Phrases Understanding Main Ideas and Supporting Ideas
	5 **WORKING TOGETHER** *page 93* ACADEMIC TRACK: Life Science/Sociology	**Reading** The Smart Swarm *by Peter Miller* (explanatory article) **VIDEO** Ant Teamwork	**Focus** Understanding Complex Sentences Understanding Main Ideas, Understanding Purpose, Summarizing

Critical Thinking	Writing	Vocabulary Extension
Focus Analyzing Evidence Evaluating, Synthesizing, Guessing Meaning from Context	**Language for Writing** Using cohesive devices **Writing Skill** Reviewing essay writing **Writing Goal** Writing a cause-effect essay	**Word Forms** Adjectives ending in -ic **Word Partners** *dramatic* + noun
Focus Analyzing Text Organization Personalizing, Making Inferences, Synthesizing, Guessing Meaning from Context	**Language for Writing** Using appositives **Writing Skill** Reviewing the thesis statement **Writing Goal** Writing a persuasive essay	**Word Partners** Adjective/verb + *priority*
Focus Applying Ideas Inferring Meaning, Synthesizing, Guessing Meaning from Context	**Language for Writing** Using restrictive and nonrestrictive adjective clauses **Writing Skill** Supporting a thesis **Writing Goal** Writing an evaluative essay	**Word Forms** Nouns, verbs, adjectives, and adverbs
Focus Understanding Multi-word Units Understanding Visual Data, Inferring Meaning, Synthesizing	**Language for Writing** Using sentences with initial phrases **Writing Skill** Organizing a comparative essay **Writing Goal** Writing a comparative essay	**Word Web** Business words and antonyms **Word Forms** Adjectives with -ive
Focus Evaluating Sources Analyzing, Synthesizing, Guessing Meaning from Context	**Language for Writing** Avoiding plagiarism (I) — Paraphrasing **Writing Skill** Writing a summary **Writing Goal** Writing a summary essay	**Word Link** *co-, com-, col-*

Scope and Sequence

Unit Title and Theme	Reading Texts and Video	ACADEMIC SKILLS Reading
6 **LANGUAGE AND CULTURE** *page 117* ACADEMIC TRACK: Anthropology/Linguistics	**Reading** The Secret Language *by Daisy Zamora* (autobiographical essay) **VIDEO** Culture Shock	**Focus** Understanding Verbal Phrases Understanding Main Ideas and Details
7 **RESOURCES AND DEVELOPMENT** *page 139* ACADEMIC TRACK: History/Economics	**Reading** The Shape of Africa *by Jared Diamond* (expository/persuasive essay) **VIDEO** Honey and Pepper	**Focus** Annotating a Text Understanding Main Ideas and Details
8 **LIVING LONGER** *page 163* ACADEMIC TRACK: Health/Medicine	**Reading** Beyond 100 *by Stephen S. Hall* (explanatory/scientific article) **VIDEO** Longevity Village	**Focus** Asking Questions as You Read Understanding Main Ideas and Details, Identifying Supporting Examples
9 **TRUTH AND DECEPTION** *page 187* ACADEMIC TRACK: Psychology	**Reading** Why We Lie *by Yudhijit Bhattacharjee* (explanatory article/research summary) **VIDEO** Learning to Lie	**Focus** Understanding a Research Summary Understanding Main Ideas, Identifying Supporting Details
10 **IMAGINING THE FUTURE** *page 207* ACADEMIC TRACK: Interdisciplinary	**Reading** My Mars/Sci-fi novel excerpts *by Ray Bradbury/H. G. Wells* (autobiographical essay/ fiction extracts) **VIDEO** Mission: Mars	**Focus** Identifying Literary Elements Understanding Main Ideas and Details

Critical Thinking	Writing	Vocabulary Extension
Focus Inferring an Author's Attitude Recognizing Levels of Formality, Guessing Meaning from Context	**Language for Writing** Adding information with verbal phrases **Writing Skill** Writing introductions and conclusions **Writing Goal** Writing an opinion essay	**Word Link** *ir-, im-, il-*
Focus Analyzing Point of View Understanding Chronology, Guessing Meaning from Context	**Language for Writing** Avoiding plagiarism (II) — Referring to sources **Writing Skill** Researching and note-taking **Writing Goal** Writing an expository essay	**Word Link** adjective + *economy* **Word Partners** *distinct* + noun
Focus Interpreting Visual Data Personalizing, Synthesizing, Guessing Meaning from Context	**Language for Writing** Explaining the significance of evidence **Writing Skill** Planning an argumentative research paper **Writing Goal** Writing an argumentative essay	**Word Partners** Words and phrases with *life* **Word Link** *re-*
Focus Evaluating Research Interpreting, Relating, Guessing Meaning from Context	**Language for Writing** Introducing results and describing data **Writing Skill** Summarizing research **Writing Goal** Writing a research summary	**Word Forms** Forming nouns with *-ance* and *-ence* **Word Forms** Word forms of *deceit*
Focus Reading Literature Critically Interpreting Figurative Language, Making Inferences, Applying, Guessing Meaning from Context	**Language for Writing** Using a variety of sentence types **Writing Skill** Writing an analysis of literature **Writing Goal** Writing an analytical essay	**Word Web** Words for describing literature **Word Web** Phrasal verbs with *down*

Vocabulary Extension 231   Independent Student Handbook 241   Index of Exam Skills and Tasks 262

Pathways Reading, Writing, and Critical Thinking, Second Edition uses National Geographic stories, photos, video, and infographics to bring the world to the classroom. Authentic, relevant content and carefully sequenced lessons engage learners while equipping them with the skills needed for academic success. Each level of the second edition features **NEW** and **UPDATED** content.

Academic skills are clearly ▶ labeled at the beginning of each unit.

ACADEMIC SKILLS

READING	Understanding cohesion
WRITING	Writing a cause-effect essay
GRAMMAR	Using cohesive devices
CRITICAL THINKING	Analyzing evidence

NEW AND UPDATED ▶ reading passages incorporate a variety of text types, charts, and infographics to inform and inspire learners.

Explicit reading skill instruction ▶ includes main ideas, details, inference, prediction, note-taking, sequencing, and vocabulary development.

▼ **Critical thinking activities** are integrated throughout each unit, and help develop learner independence.

CRITICAL THINKING   **Applying ideas** from a reading to other contexts can help you evaluate the information. For example, applying an author's opinion to your own experience can help you decide how far you agree with it.

PHOTO CONTEST

BEFORE VIEWING

A How would you rate the photo above? Consider Griffiths's six criteria and discuss in a small group.

DISCUSSION

_____

_____

B Read the information. Then answer the questions.

LEARNING ABOUT THE TOPIC

Each year, National Geographic invites amateur photographers to enter their photographs into a competition. In 2014, people from more than 150 countries submitted photos representing three categories: people, places, and nature. Over 9,000 photos were submitted, but only a handful were chosen as winners. The winning entries all had one thing in common: they told a story. The grand prize winner, Brian Yen, received $10,000 and a trip to National Geographic headquarters. When asked why he takes pictures, he explained, "Photography to me is like going on an archaeological dig: It offers me a tool to interpret reality by dusting away the uninteresting bits to reveal the gem underneath. It's an exciting, creative, and exploratory process."

1. What story does Yen's photo tell?

_____

2. Why does Yen compare taking pictures to archaeology?

_____

Brian Yen's winning photo from the 2014 National Geographic Photography Contest

BEAUTY AND PERCEPTION **61**

◀ **NEW AND UPDATED *Video*** sections use National Geographic video clips to expand on the unit's reading passage and to give learners ideas and language for the unit's writing task.

◀ **NEW** An additional short reading passage provides integrated skills practice.

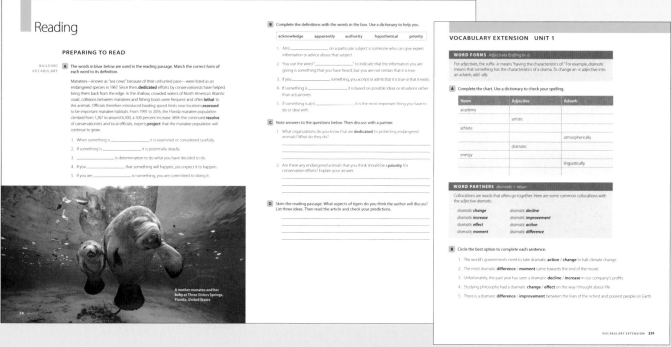

▲ **Key academic and thematic vocabulary** is practiced, and expanded throughout each unit.

▲ **NEW Vocabulary extension activities** cover word forms, word webs, collocations, affixes, and more, to boost learners' reading and writing fluency.

Pathways' approach to writing guides students through the writing process and develops learners' confidence in planning, drafting, revising, and editing.

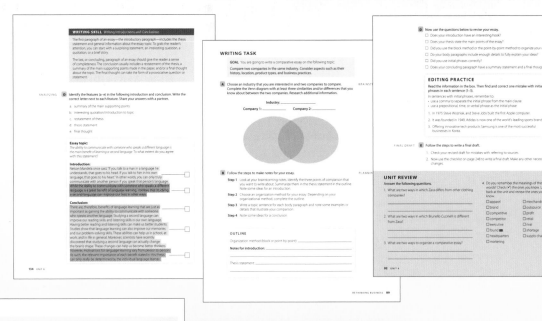

WRITING TASK

GOAL You are going to write a comparative essay on the following topic:

Compare two companies in the same industry. Consider aspects such as their history, location, product types, and business practices.

Writing Goals and **Language for Writing** ▶ sections provide the focus and scaffolding needed for learners to become successful writers.

LANGUAGE FOR WRITING Adding information with Verbal Phrases

You can use a present or past participle verbal phrase to add extra information to a sentence, or to combine two sentences that have the same subject. Look at the examples below.

Jack apologized to his sister. He was feeling terrible about what he'd done.
Jack apologized to his sister, feeling terrible about what he'd done.
present participle

Carrie was published in 1973. It was Stephen King's first novel.
Published in 1973, *Carrie* was Stephen King's first novel.
past participle

Verbal phrases can be used at the start, middle, or end of sentences.

Jack apologized to his sister, feeling terrible about what he'd done.
Jack, feeling terrible about what he'd done, apologized to his sister.
Feeling terrible about what he'd done, Jack apologized to his sister.

UPDATED Revising ▶ **Practice** sections incorporate realistic model essays and help learners refine their writing.

▼ An **online workbook**, powered by MyELT, includes video clips and automatically graded activities for learners to practice the skills taught in the Student Books.

NEW Guided online writing ▶ **practice** provides reinforcement and consolidation of language skills, helping learners to become stronger and more confident writers.

CHANGING THE PLANET

1

A residential suburb in Arizona, United States

ACADEMIC SKILLS

READING Understanding cohesion

WRITING Writing a cause-effect essay

GRAMMAR Using cohesive devices

THINK AND DISCUSS

1 In what ways have humans changed the planet?

2 What are some of the positive and negative effects of the changes humans have made on the planet?

A Look at the maps and answer the questions.

1. What four types of human impact does the main map show?

2. Which regions experience the most deforestation, desertification, and pollution?

3. What are some causes of air pollution, deforestation, and desertification?

B Match the correct form of the words in blue to their definitions.

_____ (n) the layer of gases around a planet

_____ (n) a substance used by farmers to help crops grow

_____ (n) gradual destruction by natural causes such as the weather, the sea, and rivers

Deforestation

Loss of forest cover contributes to a buildup of carbon dioxide (a greenhouse gas) in the **atmosphere**. It also causes soil **erosion** and a loss of soil nutrients.

THE HUMAN IMPACT

Around the world, natural environments are under pressure from the release of air and water pollutants, and by the removal of vegetation to extract mineral resources or to create land for farming.

In more developed countries, industries create waste and pollution; farmers use **fertilizers** and pesticides that run off into water supplies; and motor vehicles release exhaust fumes into the air.

In less developed countries, forests are cut down for fuel or to clear land for farming; grasslands are turned into deserts as farmers and herders overuse the land; and expanding urban areas face problems of water quality and sanitation.

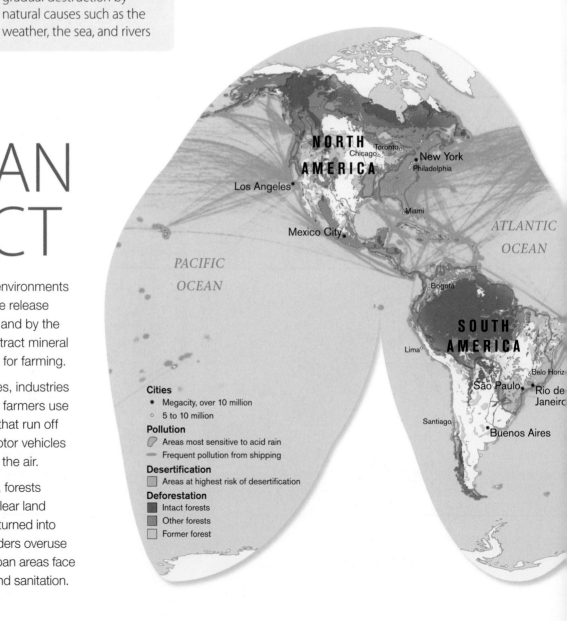

Cities
- Megacity, over 10 million
- ○ 5 to 10 million

Pollution
- Areas most sensitive to acid rain
- Frequent pollution from shipping

Desertification
- Areas at highest risk of desertification

Deforestation
- Intact forests
- Other forests
- Former forest

Desertification

In semiarid and arid areas—which receive limited rainfall—land that is overgrazed or overcultivated can become desertlike.

Pollution

Poor air quality is a serious environmental problem in many parts of the world. Smoke from industrial plants may contain particles that contribute to acid rain.

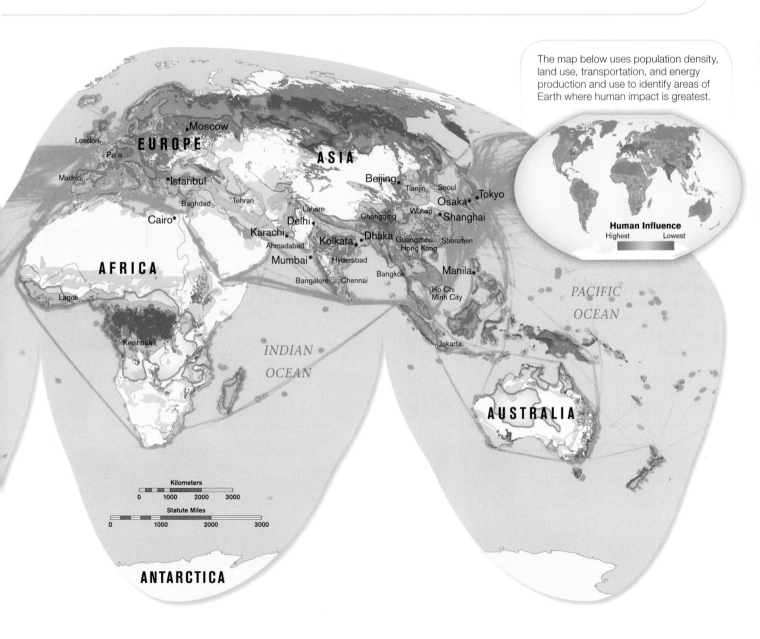

The map below uses population density, land use, transportation, and energy production and use to identify areas of Earth where human impact is greatest.

Human Influence
Highest — Lowest

EUROPE
London
Paris
Madrid
Moscow

ASIA
Istanbul
Baghdad
Tehran
Cairo
Delhi
Karachi
Ahmadabad
Lahore
Beijing
Tianjin
Seoul
Osaka Tokyo
Chongqing Wuhan
Shanghai
Mumbai
Hyderabad
Kolkata
Dhaka
Guangzhou
Hong Kong
Shenzhen
Bangalore Chennai
Bangkok
Manila
Ho Chi Minh City

AFRICA
Lagos
Kinshasa

INDIAN OCEAN

PACIFIC OCEAN

Jakarta

AUSTRALIA

ANTARCTICA

Kilometers
0 1000 2000 3000

Statute Miles
0 1000 2000 3000

Reading

PREPARING TO READ

BUILDING VOCABULARY

A The words in **blue** below are used in the reading passage. Match the correct form of each word to its definition.

Diplomats and scientists from around the world met to discuss climate issues at the 2016 United Nations Climate Change Conference in Marrakech, Morocco. The conference was **devoted to** discussing the reduction of global carbon emissions, which contribute to global warming. The dominant **perspective** on global warming is that it is a **consequence** of human activities. A **dramatic** increase in carbon emissions in the last several years has had a **profound** effect on the global climate. While most experts agree that it is impossible to completely **eliminate** carbon emissions, they do believe it is possible to cool down the planet.

1. _____ (adj) very noticeable; sudden and surprising

2. _____ (adj) focused only on one thing

3. _____ (v) to remove completely

4. _____ (n) a way of thinking about something

5. _____ (adj) very great

6. _____ (n) the effect or result of an action

▶ **Participants pose for a photo at the opening ceremony of the 2016 United Nations Climate Change Conference in Marrakech, Morocco.**

B Complete the sentences with the words in the box. Use a dictionary to help you.

| concept | criteria | current | essentially | satisfy | transform |

1. One of the _____ for naming a new animal species is that the name must be easy to remember.

2. A basic scientific _____ is cause and effect: the idea that an event is caused by or affected by another event.

3. Coal is _____ the remains of prehistoric plants. Over time, physical and chemical changes _____ ancient plant material into a substance that could be used as fuel.

4. Most animal species _____ the basic needs of their young until their offspring reach a certain age and can take care of themselves.

5. If our _____ efforts to lower carbon emissions are not significant enough to stop climate change, global warming may become worse in the future.

C Note answers to the questions below. Then discuss with a partner.

1. What are some of the **consequences** of human existence on the planet?

   _____

2. What do you think is the most **dramatic** consequence?

   _____

3. What are some **current** efforts to deal with these consequences?

   _____

D How do we know what Earth was like in the past? How do we know about plants or animals that existed in the past? Note your ideas below. Then discuss with a partner.

_____

_____

E Look at the photos and infographics in the reading and read the captions. Read the title and the first sentence of each paragraph. Circle your answers to the questions.

1. What do you think this reading is about? Circle your answer (a–c).

   It's an explanation of how _____ on the planet is changing the way people in the future might describe the current geological period.
   a. the effect of global warming
   b. the overall human impact
   c. the increasing population

2. What time period do you think *Anthropocene* describes?
   a. an ancient period   b. the current period   c. a future period

3. What area of science is this passage mainly about?
   a. biology   b. climatology   c. geology

THE HUMAN AGE

by Elizabeth Kolbert

Western Minnesota: Vast wheat fields and long train lines have created a distinctive human landscape in the Midwestern United States.

> Human beings have altered the planet so much in just the past century or two that we now have a new name for a new epoch: the Anthropocene.

[🎧 1.1]

A   **The word *Anthropocene*** was coined by Dutch chemist Paul Crutzen in 2002. Crutzen, who shared a Nobel Prize for discovering the effects of ozone-depleting compounds, was sitting at a scientific conference one day. The conference chairman kept referring to the Holocene, the epoch that began 11,500 years ago, at the end of the last ice age, and that—officially, at least—continues to this day.

B   "Let's stop it," Crutzen recalls blurting out. "We are no longer in the Holocene. We are in the Anthropocene." It was quiet in the room for a while. When the group took a coffee break, the Anthropocene was the main topic of conversation.

C   Way back in the 1870s, an Italian geologist named Antonio Stoppani proposed that people had introduced a new era, which he labeled the Anthropozoic. Stoppani's proposal was ignored; other scientists found it unscientific. The Anthropocene, by contrast, struck a chord. The human impact on the world has become a lot more obvious since Stoppani's day, in part because the size of the population has roughly quadrupled,[1] to nearly seven billion.

D   When Crutzen wrote up the Anthropocene idea in the journal *Nature*, the concept was immediately picked up by researchers working in a wide range of disciplines. Soon, it began to appear regularly in the scientific press. At first, most of the scientists using the new geologic term were not geologists. Jan Zalasiewicz, a British geologist, found the discussions intriguing. "I noticed that Crutzen's term was appearing in the serious literature, without quotation marks and without a sense of irony," he says.

E   In 2007, Zalasiewicz was serving as chairman of the Geological Society of London's Stratigraphy[2] Commission. At a meeting, he decided to ask his fellow stratigraphers what they thought of the Anthropocene. Twenty-one of twenty-two thought the concept had merit. The group agreed to look at it as a formal problem in geology. Would the Anthropocene satisfy the criteria used for naming a new epoch?

F   The rock record of the present doesn't exist yet, of course. So the question was: When it does, will human impacts show up as "stratigraphically significant"? The answer, Zalasiewicz's group decided, is yes—though not necessarily for the reasons you would expect.

---

[1] If something **quadruples**, it increases by a factor of four.
[2] **Stratigraphy** is a branch of geology concerned with the study of rock layers.

Earth's Geological Timeline

start of the Anthropocene?

Era	Period		Epoch	Millions of Years
Cenozoic	Quaternary		Holocene	
			Pleistocene	
	Neogene		Pliocene	1.5
			Miocene	
	Paleogene		Oligocene	2.3
			Eocene	
			Paleocene	
Mesozoic	Cretaceous			65
	Jurassic			
	Triassic			
Paleozoic	Permian			250
	Carboniferous	Pennsylvanian		
		Mississippian		
	Devonian			
	Silurian			
	Ordovician			
	Cambrian			
Precambrian	Proterozoic			540
	Archean			2500
	Hadean			3800
				4600

In geology, epochs are relatively short time spans, though they can extend for tens of millions of years. Periods, such as the Ordovician and the Cretaceous, last much longer, and eras, like the Mesozoic, longer still. The boundaries between epochs are defined by changes preserved in sedimentary rocks[3] —for example, the emergence of one type of commonly fossilized organism, or the disappearance of another.

G   PROBABLY THE MOST OBVIOUS way humans are altering the planet is by building cities, which are essentially vast stretches of man-made materials—steel, glass, concrete, and brick. But it turns out most cities are not good candidates for long-term preservation: they're built on land, and on land the forces of erosion tend to win out over those of sedimentation. From a geologic perspective, the most plainly visible human effects on the landscape today "may in some ways be the most transient,[4]" Zalasiewicz observes.

H   Humans have also transformed the world through farming; something like 38 percent of the planet's ice-free land is now devoted to agriculture. Here again, some of the effects that seem most significant today—runoff from the use of fertilizers on fields, for example—will leave behind only subtle traces at best. Future geologists are most likely to grasp the scale of 21st-century industrial agriculture from the pollen[5] record— from the monochrome[6] stretches of corn, wheat, and soy pollen that will have replaced the varied record left behind by rain forests or prairies.

[3] Sedimentary rocks are formed from sediment—solid material that settles at the bottom of a liquid.
[4] Transient describes a situation that lasts only a short time or is constantly changing.
[5] Pollen is a powder produced by flowers that fertilizes other flowers of the same species.
[6] If something is monochrome, it is all one color.

The leveling of the world's forests will send at least two coded signals to future stratigraphers, though deciphering the first may be tricky. Massive soil erosion is causing increasing sedimentation[7] in some parts of the world—but at the same time, the dams we've built on most of the world's major rivers are holding back sediment that would otherwise be washed to sea. The second signal of deforestation should come through clearer. Loss of forest habitat is a major cause of extinctions, which are now happening at a rate hundreds or even thousands of times higher than during most of the past half billion years. If current trends continue, the rate may soon be tens of thousands of times higher.

Probably the most significant change, from a geologic perspective, is one that's invisible to us—the change in the composition of the atmosphere. Carbon dioxide emissions are colorless, odorless, and—in an immediate sense—harmless. But their warming effects could easily push global temperatures to levels that have not been seen for millions of years. Some plants and animals are already shifting their ranges toward the Poles, and those shifts will leave traces in the fossil record. Some species will not survive the warming at all. Meanwhile, rising temperatures could eventually raise sea levels 20 feet or more.

Long after our cars, cities, and factories have turned to dust, the consequences of burning billions of tons' worth of coal and oil are likely to be clearly discernible. As carbon dioxide warms the planet, it also seeps into the oceans and acidifies them. Sometime this century, they may become acidified to the point that corals can no longer construct reefs, which would register in the geologic record as a "reef gap." Reef gaps have marked each of the past five major mass extinctions. The most recent one—which is believed to have been caused by the impact of an asteroid—took place 65 million years ago, at the end of the Cretaceous period; it eliminated not just the dinosaurs but also the plesiosaurs, pterosaurs, and ammonites.[8] Since then, there has been nothing to match the scale of the changes that we are now seeing in our oceans. To future geologists, Zalasiewicz says, our impact may look as sudden and profound as that of an asteroid.

---

[7] **Sedimentation** is the process by which solid material—especially earth and pieces of rock—settles at the bottom of a liquid.
[8] **Plesiosaurs**, **pterosaurs**, and **ammonites** are extinct prehistoric organisms.

Colorado River Delta, Mexico:
Aerial photography can illustrate the human impact on Earth's landscape.

> " Do we decide the Anthropocene's here, or do we wait 20 years and things will be even worse? "

IF WE HAVE INDEED entered a new epoch, then when exactly did it begin? When did human impacts rise to the level of geologic significance?

William Ruddiman, a paleoclimatologist at the University of Virginia, has proposed that the invention of agriculture some 8,000 years ago—and the deforestation that resulted—led to an increase in atmospheric CO_2 just large enough to stave off what otherwise would have been the start of a new ice age. In his view, humans have

Trotternish, Isle of Skye: Millions of years of history are recorded in the rocks of Scotland. Are we creating a new chapter in Earth's geological history?

been the dominant force on the planet practically since the start of the Holocene. Crutzen has suggested that the Anthropocene began in the late 18th century, when, ice cores show, carbon dioxide levels began what has since proved to be an uninterrupted rise. Other scientists put the beginning of the new epoch in the middle of the 20th century, when the rates of both population growth and consumption accelerated rapidly.

Zalasiewicz now heads a working group of the International Commission on Stratigraphy (ICS) that is tasked with officially determining whether the Anthropocene deserves to be incorporated into the geologic timescale. A final decision will require votes by both the ICS and its parent organization, the International Union of Geological Sciences. The process is likely to take years. As it drags on, the decision may well become easier. Some scientists argue that we've not yet reached the start of the Anthropocene— not because we haven't had a **dramatic** impact on the planet, but because the next several decades are likely to prove even more stratigraphically significant than the past few centuries. "Do we decide the Anthropocene's here, or do we wait 20 years and things will be even worse?" says Mark Williams, a geologist and colleague of Zalasiewicz's at the University of Leicester in England.

Crutzen, who started the debate, thinks its real value won't lie in revisions to geology textbooks. His purpose is broader: He wants to focus our attention on the consequences of our collective action—and on how we might still avert the worst. "What I hope," he says, "is that the term *Anthropocene* will be a warning to the world."

Adapted from "The Age of Man," by Elizabeth Kolbert: National Geographic Magazine, March 2011

National Magazine Award winner Elizabeth Kolbert has written extensively about environmental issues for *National Geographic Magazine, The New Yorker,* and other publications. Her book *The Sixth Extinction* won the 2015 Pulitzer Prize for general nonfiction.

UNDERSTANDING THE READING

UNDERSTANDING
MAIN IDEAS

A Note answers to the questions below.

1. What is the purpose of Kolbert's article? Complete the main idea.

   Kolbert's purpose is to present the idea of a new _____ and to show how our human impact will be noted in the future.

2. What does "Anthropocene" mean? Explain it in your own words.

   _____

   _____

3. What four main areas does Kolbert examine for signs of human impact?

   cities, _____

UNDERSTANDING
MAIN IDEAS

B The reading passage has three main parts. Where could you place each of these section heads? Write paragraph letters: **A**, **G**, and **L**.

Section Head	Before Paragraph …
How We Are Changing the Planet	_____
Tracing the Origins of the Anthropocene	_____
A New Perspective on Earth's History	_____

UNDERSTANDING
DETAILS

C Note answers to the questions below. Then discuss with a partner.

1. When was the idea of a new era first proposed? What was it called? Why did people not take it seriously?

   _____

   _____

   _____

2. Why did Crutzen's ideas gain more support than Stoppani's?

   _____

   _____

   _____

3. What are two effects of cutting down forests?

   _____

   _____

   _____

4. How does climate change affect plants and animals? How is it affecting the oceans?

   _____

   _____

   _____

   _____

D Complete the chart summarizing the human impact on our planet. Then discuss this question in a small group: Of the four kinds of human impact, which do you think will leave the most obvious record in the future? Why?

	The Human Impact	Will It Leave a Trace? Why, or Why Not?
Cities	building structures made of 1 _____	No—structures built on land; 2 _____ may make them disappear
Farming	farming 3 _____ percent of the available land	4 _____—but only from the 5 _____ record of the shift from a variety of plants to a few types
Forests	6 _____ trees	Maybe—sedimentation and 7 _____ may be noticed
Atmosphere	8 _____ the atmosphere	Most likely—shifts in habitat range will leave traces in 9 _____; the world's 10 _____ will become acidified and coral will no longer be able to construct reefs

E Look at the timeline on page 8 and note answers to the questions below. Then discuss your ideas with a partner.

1. What era, period, and epoch are we currently living in?

   Era: _____   Period: _____
   Epoch: _____ or _____

2. When did the current era begin?

   _____

3. How do scientists decide when one epoch ends and another one begins?

   _____
   _____

The acidification of the ocean, caused by high levels of carbon dioxide in the atmosphere, could cause coral reefs to die out.

CRITICAL THINKING:
ANALYZING EVIDENCE

F In the reading passage, what evidence does the writer present in support of either side of the main argument? Take notes in the chart. Then discuss answers to the questions below with a partner.

Argument: Humans are having such a great impact on the planet that the Holocene epoch is over, and we are now living in a new epoch: the Anthropocene.	
Evidence For	**Evidence Against**

1. Is the evidence on both sides balanced, or is there more evidence for one side than the other?
2. Do the facts and opinions come from reliable sources? Is the information relevant and up to date?

CRITICAL THINKING:
GUESSING MEANING
FROM CONTEXT

G Find and underline the following words and expressions in the reading passage. Use context to guess their meanings. Then match the sentence parts.

1. Para A: If a word is **coined by** someone, ____
2. Para C: If an idea **struck a chord**, ____
3. Para I: If you **decipher** something, ____
4. Para K: If a consequence is **discernible**, ____
5. Para M: If you **stave off** an event, ____
6. Para N: When something **drags on**, ____

a. it continues for a long time.
b. you can detect it.
c. you figure out the meaning of it.
d. you prevent it from happening.
e. it was invented by that person.
f. other people thought it sounded logical.

DEVELOPING READING SKILLS

Cohesion refers to the way that ideas are linked in a text. Writers use certain techniques (sometimes called "cohesive devices") to refer to ideas mentioned elsewhere in the passage. Some of these techniques include pronouns (*one*[s], *another*, *the other*), demonstratives (*this*, *that*, *these*, *those*), and synonyms.

Look at these examples from "The Human Age."

> In 2002, when Crutzen wrote up <u>the Anthropocene idea</u> in the journal Nature, <u>the concept</u> was immediately picked up by researchers working in a wide range of disciplines.

The writer uses a synonym, *the concept*, to refer to *the idea* in the first part of the sentence.

> Wilson calculates that human <u>biomass</u> is already a hundred times larger than <u>that</u> of any other large animal species that has ever walked the Earth.

In this example, the writer uses *that* to refer to *biomass*.

Note: The referent—the word or idea that is referred to—is not always close to the cohesive device. It may be in a different part of the sentence, or in a different sentence or section of the text.

A Circle the word or idea that each underlined word in these extracts refers to.   ANALYZING

1. Paragraph D: When Crutzen wrote up the Anthropocene idea in the journal *Nature*, the concept was immediately picked up by researchers working in a wide range of disciplines. Soon, <u>it</u> began to appear regularly in the scientific press.

   a. the researchers   b. the journal   c. the concept

2. Paragraph G: But it turns out most cities are not good candidates for long-term preservation for the simple reason that they're built on land, and on land the forces of erosion tend to win out over <u>those</u> of sedimentation.

   a. forces   b. cities   c. candidates

B Find the following excerpts in "The Human Age." Write the words or ideas that each   ANALYZING
underlined word or phrase refers to.

1. Paragraph D: At first, most of the scientists using <u>the new geologic term</u> were not geologists. _____

2. Sidebar: The boundaries between epochs are defined by changes preserved in sedimentary rocks—for example, the emergence of one type of commonly fossilized organism, or the disappearance of <u>another</u>. _____

3. Paragraph J: Probably the most significant change, from a geologic perspective, is <u>one</u> that's invisible to us—the change in the composition of the atmosphere. _____

4. Paragraph K: The most recent <u>one</u>—which is believed to have been caused by the impact of an asteroid—took place 65 million years ago, at the end of the Cretaceous period. _____

TREES OF LIFE

Deforestation threatens the habitats of many species of animals.

BEFORE VIEWING

DISCUSSION

A How does deforestation affect our planet? Note your ideas below. Then discuss with a partner.

_____

_____

LEARNING ABOUT THE TOPIC

B Read the information. Then answer the questions.

Rain forests provide habitats for thousands of species of animals. However, they also provide humans with many useful resources such as fruits and spices. Perhaps the most valuable rain forest resources, however, are medicinal plants. Scientists use rain forest plants to create drugs for many serious health problems. The bark of the cinchona tree, for example, is used to make quinine—a medication used to treat malaria. It is thought that scientists have analyzed less than one percent of rain forest plants, so there are probably hundreds, if not thousands, of medicinal plants that remain undiscovered.

1. What benefits of rain forests are mentioned in the paragraph above?

_____

2. How do you think deforestation would affect our ability to treat serious illnesses?

_____

C Read these extracts from the video. Match the correct form of each **bold** word to its definition.

VOCABULARY IN CONTEXT

> "At the current rate of **destruction**, the world's rain forests will completely disappear within a hundred years."
>
> "Forests are also destroyed as a result of growing urban sprawl, as land is developed for **dwellings**."
>
> "And while some plant and animal species are gone forever, **combatting** deforestation can help prevent further loss of biodiversity."

1. _____ (v) to fight against

2. _____ (n) a house or home

3. _____ (n) the act of damaging something completely

WHILE VIEWING

A ▶ Read the sentences below. Watch the video. Circle **T** for true or **F** for false.

UNDERSTANDING MAIN IDEAS

a. Transportation produces more greenhouse gases than forestry and agriculture.　　　　　**T**　**F**

b. Over 80 percent of land animals live in forests.　　　　　**T**　**F**

c. Increases in the size of urban areas is the primary cause of deforestation.　**T**　**F**

B ▶ Watch the video again. Complete the notes below.

UNDERSTANDING CAUSES AND EFFECTS

DEFORESTATION	
Effects	**Causes**
1. Increases greenhouse gases in two ways: 　• [1]_____ releases CO_2 　• Forests help to [2]_____ 2. Destroys [3]_____ Also effects people who use forests for [4]_____	1. [5]_____ is the main cause. 2. Logging for [6]_____ industries 3. Increasing [7]_____

AFTER VIEWING

A What are two signs of deforestation that future stratigraphers will notice? Look again at the reading passage for ideas. Note your answer below. Then discuss with a partner.

CRITICAL THINKING: SYNTHESIZING

_____

_____

Writing

EXPLORING WRITTEN ENGLISH

VOCABULARY FOR WRITING **A** The following words and phrases can be useful when writing about the human impact on the planet. Find them in the reading passage. Use the context to guess their meanings. Then complete each definition.

> **preservation** (paragraph G) **relatively** (sidebar) **subtle** (paragraph H)
>
> **tasked with** (paragraph N) **determine** (paragraph N) **avert** (paragraph O)

1. To _____ something is to prevent it from happening.

2. If you _____ something, you figure it out.

3. If a person or group is _____ a duty, it is their responsibility to do it.

4. _____ refers to the protection of something over time.

5. If something is _____ big, it is big in comparison to something else.

6. If something is _____, it is not very noticeable.

NOTICING **B** Read the sentences. Circle the words that the underlined words refer to.

1. Crutzen, who started the debate, thinks <u>its</u> real value won't lie in revisions to geology textbooks.

2. The process is likely to take years. As <u>it</u> drags on, the decision may well become easier.

3. Crutzen has suggested that the Anthropocene began in the late 18th century … Other scientists put the beginning of <u>the new epoch</u> in the middle of the 20th century …

4. As carbon dioxide warms the planet, <u>it</u> also seeps into the oceans and acidifies <u>them</u>.

5. To future geologists, Zalasiewicz says, our impact may look as sudden and profound as <u>that</u> of an asteroid.

Flower fields in California, United States

Writers use cohesive devices to emphasize key concepts they have already mentioned and to avoid repetition. Cohesive devices include reference words such as *it*, *these*, *those*, and *that*. They also include synonyms and word forms.

Reference Words and Synonyms:

In 2002, when Crutzen wrote up <u>the Anthropocene idea</u> in the journal *Nature*, **the concept** was immediately picked up by researchers working in a wide range of disciplines. Soon it began to appear regularly in the scientific press.

The writer uses *the concept* and *it* to refer to *the Anthropocene idea*.

Word Forms:

Way back in the 1870s, an Italian geologist named Antonio Stoppani <u>proposed</u> that people had introduced a new era, which he labeled the Anthropozoic. Stoppani's **proposal** was ignored; other scientists found it unscientific.

The writer uses *proposal* to refer to what Stoppani *proposed*.

C Use the cues to complete the second sentence in each pair below. Use reference words, synonyms, or word forms for the underlined words in the first sentence.

USING COHESIVE
DEVICES

1. Cities are filled with structures made of <u>glass, steel, and concrete</u>. Many people might think that _____ are indestructible materials. (reference word)

2. <u>Farming</u> has had a huge impact on the world's landscapes. Around 38 percent of our planet's ice-free land is now used solely for _____. (synonym)

3. Humans <u>have destroyed forests</u>, <u>built over animal habitats</u>, and <u>heated up the atmosphere</u> with CO_2 emissions. Of all these _____, the changes in the atmosphere may leave the most lasting traces. (synonym)

4. By creating pedestrian-only streets in city centers, planners <u>are reducing</u> the amount of time people spend in cars. This _____ in car use will have a positive impact on the environment. (word form)

5. Chemicals used in pesticides may <u>harm</u> people and animals. These _____ compounds can have a negative impact on the soil and water as well. (word form)

WRITING SKILL Reviewing Essay Writing

An essay is a short piece of writing that includes an **introduction**, a **body**, and a **conclusion**. The introduction presents general information on the topic, and usually includes a **thesis statement**. The thesis statement presents the main idea of the entire essay. The body paragraphs support the thesis with facts, details, explanations, and other information. **Transitions** between paragraphs help the reader follow the essay. The conclusion restates the thesis and leaves the reader with a final thought on the topic.

You usually write an essay in response to an **essay prompt**. The prompt might be an instruction (*Describe/Explain . . .*), or it might be a question (*Why . . . ? To what extent . . . ? How . . . ?*). When you respond to a prompt, think about your position on the topic (which will become your thesis statement) and ways to support or explain your position (which may become the topic sentences of your body paragraphs).

CRITICAL THINKING:
EVALUATING

D Read the following essay prompt. Circle the best thesis statement for it. Why is it the best? Discuss your answer with a partner.

What are some ways that people can help heal the planet through their food choices?

a. People can make much better food choices.

b. People can help heal the planet by making environmentally friendly food choices.

c. It's important that we start caring about the future of the planet right now.

CRITICAL THINKING:
EVALUATING

E Think about ways to support or explain the thesis statement. Assume you are going to write three body paragraphs. Check (✓) the three best supporting ideas from the list below.

Make food choices that _____.

☐ a. are cheap

☐ b. promote health

☐ c. don't contribute to pollution

☐ d. preserve endangered species

☐ e. use fewer resources such as water

APPLYING

F Complete topic sentences for three body paragraphs based on the ideas you chose in exercise **E**.

One way that our food choices can help heal the planet is _____

_____

Another way is _____

_____

Finally, _____

_____

DISCUSSION

G Discuss the following essay prompt. Think of a good thesis statement and at least three possible ideas to support it. Share your ideas with a partner.

Describe new policies that would improve the quality of life at your college or school.

WRITING TASK

> **GOAL** You are going to write an essay on the following topic:
>
> Describe how the activities of a charity or a nonprofit organization are having a positive impact on the planet.

A Choose a charity or a nonprofit organization that you want to write about. Then think about how its activities are having a positive impact on the planet. Write as many activities and impacts in the chart as you can. Share your ideas with a partner.

BRAINSTORMING

Organization: _____

Activities	Impacts (Effects)
e.g., cleans plastic out of the ocean	e.g., protects marine life habitats

B Follow the steps to make notes for your essay.

PLANNING

Step 1 Write a thesis statement in the outline below.

Step 2 Write a topic sentence about each of the organization's activities for each body paragraph. Then write two or three examples, details, or facts that explain how each activity affects the planet.

Step 3 Note some ideas for an introduction and a conclusion for your essay.

OUTLINE

Thesis statement: _____

_____

Notes for Introduction: _____

_____

Body Paragraph 1: Topic sentence: _____

_____

Details: _____

_____

Body Paragraph 2: Topic sentence: _____

_____

Details: _____

_____

Body Paragraph 3: Topic sentence: _____

_____

Details: _____

_____

Notes for Conclusion: _____

_____

REVISING PRACTICE

The draft below is a model of the essay you are writing. Follow the steps to create a better second draft.

1. Add the sentences (a–c) in the most suitable spaces.

   a. This reduces energy use as well as cost.
   b. By instituting these and other methods to make cities more livable and environmentally friendly, we can look forward to a happy and healthy future as our cities grow.
   c. Green spaces have a positive impact on a community.

2. Now fix the following problems (a–c) with the essay.

   a. Replace the **bold** word in paragraph B with a cohesive device.
   b. Replace the **bold** word in paragraph C with a cohesive device.
   c. Cross out one sentence that does not relate to the topic of the essay in paragraph D.

A

Cities are growing in size and in population. Will they have a harmful impact on the environment as they grow? Not necessarily. Many city planners have solutions to make cities and the people who live in them healthier and happier, while at the same time having a positive impact on the environment. Three ways to improve cities include creating green spaces, developing mixed-use areas, and encouraging building owners to transform their rooftops into gardens.

B

_____ **Green spaces** are protected areas that remain undeveloped, such as parks or other open areas. Increasing the number of them in a city has several advantages. Green spaces make a city more attractive, as plants and other features—such as streams and rocks—are left in their natural state. They also provide peaceful recreation areas for city dwellers. People can walk, hike, bicycle, and picnic in these areas away from the hustle and bustle of city life. Trees also shelter the area from the noise and traffic of the city while improving the air quality.

C

Another way to improve the quality of life in cities is the development of mixed-use areas. **Mixed-use** areas combine several purposes in one space. One of these areas, for example, may contain offices and businesses, apartments, and entertainment facilities. Ideally, mixed-use developments attract people who want to live and work in the same area. The benefits to the community are significant because these developments allow people to reduce the amount of time they spend in cars— driving to work and running errands—which in turn reduces air pollution. Creating mixed-use areas with pedestrian- and bicycle-only streets further lessens the impact on the environment, and it can also encourage better health and fitness as citizens spend less time in cars.

D

Finally, encouraging building owners to convert their rooftops into high-rise gardens and farms can bring about dramatic changes to city life and improve the environment at the same time. Rooftop gardens insulate buildings. For example, in areas that have hot summer weather, rooftop gardens can cool buildings so that they don't require as much air conditioning. _____ Gardens that are used to grow organic fruits and vegetables—as opposed to those grown with chemical compounds—can also improve the quality of life for city dwellers, especially if they live in areas where access to fresh produce is limited. Organic fruits and vegetables are increasingly available in many cities. Limiting the use of harmful pesticides through organic gardening is good for the planet and for human health, too.

E

Green spaces, mixed-use areas, and rooftop gardens are just a few of the ways that we can lessen the impact of cities on the planet. _____

D Now use the questions below to revise your essay.

REVISED DRAFT

☐ Does your introduction provide relevant background information on the topic?

☐ Does your thesis state the main points of the essay?

☐ Do your body paragraphs include enough details to fully explain your ideas?

☐ Did you use cohesive devices to avoid repetition?

☐ Do all your sentences relate to the main idea?

☐ Does your concluding paragraph have a summary statement and a final thought?

▼ **A chef picks bay leaves from the roof garden of a hotel in Vancouver, Canada.**

EDITING PRACTICE

Read the information below. Then edit the sentences (1–3) to make them clearer.

When using cohesive devices, remember to:

- use pronouns that match the referent in gender and number.

- make sure a pronoun clearly refers to a specific word or idea. Sometimes it's better to repeat words or use synonyms for clarity.

- choose the correct synonym when using a dictionary or thesaurus.

1. One reason to limit the use of pesticides is that it contains harmful compounds.

2. Some people are installing rooftop gardens and using solar panels in their homes. It can save money and resources.

3. Many fish species have become extinct and, as a result, there is less biodiversity in our oceans. They are a problem, because they upset the natural balance of the oceans' ecosystems.

FINAL DRAFT **E** Follow these steps to write a final draft.

1. Check your revised draft for mistakes with cohesive devices.

2. Now use the checklist on page 248 to write a final draft. Make any other necessary changes.

UNIT REVIEW

Answer the following questions.

1. What are three examples of the human impact on our planet?

_____

_____

2. Why are forests important to our planet?

_____

_____

3. What is an example of a cohesive device?

_____

_____

4. Do you remember the meanings of these words? Check (✓) the ones you know. Look back at the unit and review the ones you don't know.

☐ atmosphere   ☐ erosion **AWL**

☐ concept **AWL**   ☐ essentially

☐ consequence **AWL**   ☐ fertilizer

☐ criteria **AWL**   ☐ perspective **AWL**

☐ current   ☐ profound

☐ devoted to **AWL**   ☐ satisfy

☐ dramatic **AWL**   ☐ transform **AWL**

☐ eliminate **AWL**

ON THE EDGE

2

A two-week-old rescued orphan elephant with her keeper in Nairobi National Park, Kenya

ACADEMIC SKILLS

READING Understanding appositives
WRITING Writing a persuasive essay
GRAMMAR Using appositives
CRITICAL THINKING Analyzing text organization

THINK AND DISCUSS

1 What endangered species are you aware of?
2 What are some reasons these animals are endangered?

A **Look at the information on these pages and answer the questions.**

   1. Which big cat on these pages do you think is most in danger? Why?

   2. Why do you think conservationists think it is important to protect these animals?

B **Match the words in blue to their definitions.**

_____ (n) animals that kill and eat other animals

_____ (n) the animals that another animal eats for food

_____ (n) the illegal catching and/or killing of animals

_____ (adj) possible and practical to do or achieve

_____ (adj) hiding your feelings or actions from others

BIG CATS IN CRISIS

Snow Leopard

The **secretive** snow leopard is known as the "ghost of the mountains." Its home is in the Himalayas and surrounding ranges of Central Asia.

Estimated wild population: 4,000 to 8,700

Population in zoos: 414

Status: Vulnerable

The big cats on these pages are all in danger of disappearing from the wild. A major reason is loss of habitat resulting from human population growth in the areas where they live. Additional threats are posed by illegal **poaching** for skins and other body parts, and killing by ranchers when the cats eat their livestock. Conservationists, however, believe it is still **feasible** to save these **predators**.

Lion

Lions once roamed across Africa and into Asia; today, the largest lion population is in Tanzania.

Estimated wild population: 20,000 to 30,000
Population in zoos: 1,888
Status: Vulnerable

Cheetah

The cheetah uses its incredible speed to chase down its **prey**. It is found mainly in east and southwest Africa; another 70–110 live in Iran.

Estimated wild population: 7,000 to 10,000
Population in zoos: 1,015
Status: Vulnerable

Tiger

The biggest cat, with some males weighing over 600 pounds (270 kilograms). Three tiger subspecies have gone extinct since the 1930s; four or five other subspecies survive in Asia.

Estimated wild population: Fewer than 4,000
Population in zoos: 1,660
Status: Endangered

Reading

PREPARING TO READ

BUILDING
VOCABULARY

A The words in **blue** below are used in the reading passage. Match the correct form of each word to its definition.

Manatees—known as "sea cows" because of their unhurried pace—were listed as an endangered species in 1967. Since then, **dedicated** efforts by conservationists have helped bring them back from the edge. In the shallow, crowded waters of North America's Atlantic coast, collisions between manatees and fishing boats were frequent and often **lethal** to the animals. Officials therefore introduced boating speed limits near locations **assessed** to be important manatee habitats. From 1991 to 2016, the Florida manatee population climbed from 1,267 to around 6,300, a 500 percent increase. With the continued **resolve** of conservationists and local officials, experts **project** that the manatee population will continue to grow.

1. When something is _____, it is examined or considered carefully.

2. If something is _____, it is potentially deadly.

3. _____ is determination to do what you have decided to do.

4. If you _____ that something will happen, you expect it to happen.

5. If you are _____ to something, you are committed to doing it.

A mother manatee and her baby at Three Sisters Springs, Florida, United States

B Complete the definitions with the words in the box. Use a dictionary to help you.

| acknowledge | apparently | authority | hypothetical | priority |

1. A(n) _____ on a particular subject is someone who can give expert information or advice about that subject.

2. You use the word "_____" to indicate that the information you are giving is something that you have heard, but you are not certain that it is true.

3. If you _____ something, you accept or admit that it is true or that it exists.

4. If something is _____, it is based on possible ideas or situations rather than actual ones.

5. If something is a(n) _____, it is the most important thing you have to do or deal with.

C Note answers to the questions below. Then discuss with a partner.

1. What organizations do you know that are **dedicated** to protecting endangered animals? What do they do?

_____
_____
_____

2. Are there any endangered animals that you think should be a **priority** for conservation efforts? Explain your answer.

_____
_____
_____

D Skim the reading passage. What aspects of tigers do you think the author will discuss? List three ideas. Then read the article and check your predictions.

_____
_____
_____
_____

A CRY FOR THE TIGER

by Caroline Alexander

A lone tiger hunts in the forests of northern Sumatra, Indonesia.

> We have the means to save the mightiest cat
>
> on Earth. But do we have the will?

🎧 1.2

Dawn, and mist covers the forest. Only a short stretch of red dirt track can be seen. Suddenly—emerging from the red-gold haze of dust and misted light—a tigress walks into view. First, she stops to rub her right-side whiskers against a roadside tree. Then she crosses the road and rubs her left-side whiskers. Then she turns to regard us with a look of bored indifference.

Consider the tiger, how she is formed. The claws of a tiger are up to four inches long and retractable,[1] like those of a domestic cat; her teeth can shatter bone. While able to achieve bursts above 35 miles an hour, the tiger is a **predator** built for strength, not sustained speed. Short, powerful legs propel her **lethal** attacks. The eye of the tiger is backlit by a membrane, a thin piece of skin that reflects light through the retina—the secret of the animal's famous night vision and glowing night eyes. The roar of the tiger—*Aaaaauuuunnnn!*—can carry more than a mile.

For weeks, I had been traveling through some of the best tiger habitats in Asia, but never before had I seen a tiger. Partly this was because of the animal's legendarily **secretive** nature. The tiger is powerful enough to kill and drag **prey** five times its weight, yet it can move through high grass, forest, and even water in unnerving silence. Those who have witnessed—or survived—an attack commonly report that the tiger "came from nowhere."

But the other reason for the lack of sightings is that the ideal tiger landscapes have very few tigers. The tiger has been a threatened species for most of my lifetime, and its rareness has come to be regarded—like its dramatic coloring—as a defining attribute. The common view that the tiger will continue to be "rare" or "threatened" is no longer tenable.[3] In the early 21st century, tigers in the wild face complete annihilation. "This is about making decisions as if we're in an emergency room," says Tom Kaplan, co-founder of Panthera, an organization **dedicated** to big cats. "This is it."

The tiger's enemies are well-known. Loss of habitat is exacerbated by exploding human populations. Poverty contributes to the **poaching** of prey animals. Above all, there is the dark threat of a black market for tiger parts. Less **acknowledged** are decades of botched conservation strategies. The tiger population, dispersed among Asia's 13 tiger countries, is estimated at fewer than 4,000 animals, though many conservationists believe there are hundreds less than that. To put this number in perspective: Global alarm for the species was first sounded in 1969, and early in the 1980s it was estimated that some 8,000 tigers remained in the wild. So decades of concern for tigers—not to mention millions of dollars donated by well-meaning individuals—has failed to prevent the loss of perhaps half of an already threatened population.

---

[1] If something is **retractable**, it can be moved in and out or back and forth.
[2] The **retina** is the area at the back of the eye.

[3] If an argument is **tenable**, it is reasonable and can be successfully defended against criticism.

> **" If the core breeding grounds are lost, you will have tiger landscapes with no tigers. "**

My determination to see a wild tiger in my lifetime brought me to Ranthambore Tiger Reserve, one of 40 in India. India is home to some 50 percent of the world's wild tigers. The 2010 census reported a maximum estimate of 1,909 in the country—up 20 percent from the previous estimate. While this is welcome news, most authorities regard the new figure as reflecting better census methods rather than growth of the tiger population: Tiger counts, in India or elsewhere, are still at best only estimates. A modest 41 of these tigers were living in Ranthambore.

Reserves such as Ranthambore exist as islands of fragile habitat in a vast sea of humanity, yet tigers can range over a hundred miles, seeking prey, mates, and territory. An unwelcome revelation of the new census is that nearly a third of India's tigers live outside tiger reserves, a situation that is dangerous for both humans and animals. Prey and tigers can only disperse if there are recognized corridors[4] of land between protected areas to allow safe passage. No less critical, such passages would serve as genetic corridors, essential to the long-term survival of the species.

It is a heady[5] experience to see an idealistic map of Asia's tiger landscapes linked by these not-yet-existent corridors. A spiderweb of green lines weaves among core tiger populations, forming a network that includes breathtaking extremes of habitat—Himalayan foothills, jungle, swamp, forest, grasslands. However, close examination breaks the spell. The places that have actual tigers—here-and-now,

[4]**Corridors** are strips of land that connect one place to another.
[5]A **heady** experience strongly affects your senses, such as, by making you feel excited.

Tiger cubs at a water hole in Bandhavgarh National Park, India

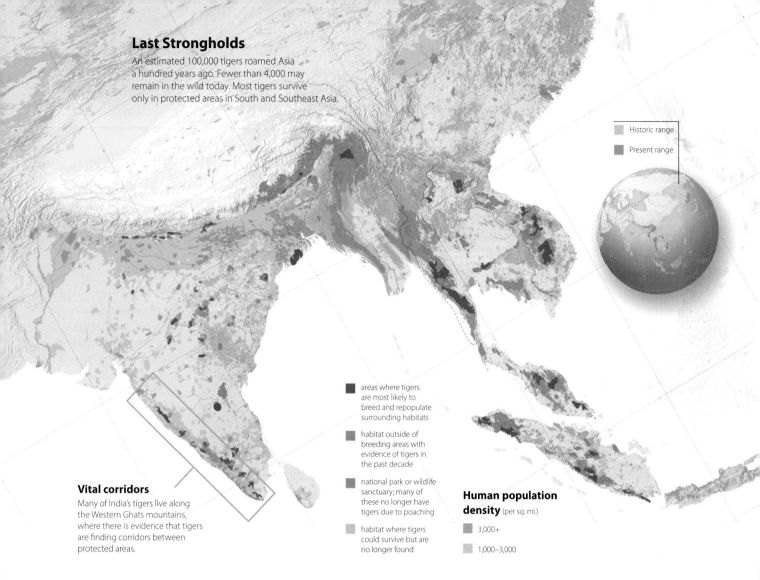

Last Strongholds

An estimated 100,000 tigers roamed Asia a hundred years ago. Fewer than 4,000 may remain in the wild today. Most tigers survive only in protected areas in South and Southeast Asia.

Historic range

Present range

areas where tigers are most likely to breed and repopulate surrounding habitats

habitat outside of breeding areas with evidence of tigers in the past decade

national park or wildlife sanctuary; many of these no longer have tigers due to poaching

habitat where tigers could survive but are no longer found

Vital corridors
Many of India's tigers live along the Western Ghats mountains, where there is evidence that tigers are finding corridors between protected areas.

Human population density (per sq. mi.)

3,000+

1,000–3,000

flesh-and-blood tigers—as opposed to hypothetical ones, are represented by a scattering of brown-colored spots. The master plan is ambitious, but is it feasible? Over the next decade, infrastructure projects—the kind of development that often destroys habitat— are projected to average some $750 billion a year in Asia.

"I've never met a head of state who says, 'Look, we're a poor country, if it comes between tigers and people, you just have to write off tigers,'" said Alan Rabinowitz, an authority on tigers and the CEO of Panthera. "The governments don't want to lose their most majestic animal. They consider it part of what makes their country what it is, part of the cultural heritage. They won't sacrifice a lot to save it, but if they can see a way to save it, they will usually do it."

Seeing a way has proved difficult due to the variety of tiger strategies, programs, and initiatives competing for attention—and funding. Long-term conservation must focus on all aspects of a tiger landscape: core breeding populations, sanctuaries, wildlife corridors, and the surrounding human communities. In an ideal world, all would be funded; as it is, different agencies adopt different strategies for different components.

With time running out, tough priorities must be set. "Since the 1990s, there has been what I would sum up as mission drift," said Ullas Karanth of the Wildlife Conservation Society, who is one of the world's most respected tiger biologists. Apparently, the drift toward tiger conservation activities like eco-development and social programs—which possibly have greater fund-raising appeal than antipoaching patrols—

takes away funds and energy from the single most vital task: safeguarding core breeding populations of tigers. "If these are lost," Karanth said, "you will have tiger landscapes with no tigers."

Decades of experience and failures have yielded a conservation strategy that, according to Rabinowitz, "allows any site or landscape to increase its tigers if followed correctly." Central to this approach is the need for systematic patrolling and monitoring of sites assessed as harboring defensible core tiger populations. In this way, a population of a mere half dozen breeding females can rebound.[6]

For now, the essential task is to save the few tigers that actually exist. In November 2010—the Year of the Tiger—the world's 13 tiger countries came together at the Global Tiger Summit in St. Petersburg, Russia. Together, they agreed on the need "to double the number of wild tigers across their range by 2022." Most authorities believe that the fight to save the tiger can be won—but that it must be fought with tireless professional focus that keeps to a proven strategy. It will require the human species to display not merely resolve but outright zealotry.[7]

[6]If something **rebounds**, it successfully goes back to a previous state or level.
[7]If someone displays **zealotry**, they display very extreme views and behavior.

Adapted from "A Cry for the Tiger," by Caroline Alexander: National Geographic Magazine, December 2011.

Caroline Alexander is the author of several best-selling books, including *The Bounty: The True Story of the Mutiny on the Bounty* (2004), for which she was nominated for the National Book Critic's Circle Award.

A Bengal tiger in the Sundarbans, India, pauses in a river to listen to another tiger's roar.

UNDERSTANDING THE READING

A Check (✓) three statements that best summarize the writer's main ideas.

UNDERSTANDING
MAIN IDEAS

☐ 1. Safeguarding main breeding areas should be a top priority for tiger conservation.

☐ 2. It is a positive sign that tigers have been spotted outside of tiger reserves in India.

☐ 3. We should not accept the idea the tiger will continue to be a rare species; it might die out completely.

☐ 4. Patrolling and monitoring core tiger areas can help to increase tiger populations.

☐ 5. The last few decades of tiger conservation strategies have generally been successful.

☐ 6. Establishing land corridors for Indian tigers is probably unrealistic as a long-term strategy.

B Match each question with the correct answer. Three items are extra.

UNDERSTANDING
DETAILS

1. When did the world first realize that tigers were endangered? _____

2. How many tigers were estimated to be alive in the early 1980s? _____

3. What percentage of the world's tigers lives in India? _____

4. How many tigers are in Ranthambore? _____

5. Approximately how many tigers in India live outside of tiger reserves? _____

6. What year was the St. Petersburg Global Tiger Summit? _____

7. How many countries have natural tiger habitats? _____

a. 2010

b. 41

c. the 1990s

d. 4,000

e. 1969

f. 1/3

g. 8,000

h. 20 percent

i. 50 percent

j. 13

C Complete the chart with information from the reading.

IDENTIFYING
PROBLEMS, REASONS,
AND SOLUTIONS

Problem: Tigers are endangered	
Possible Reasons	**Possible Solutions**
Past conservation efforts were not effective	
Growth of human populations	

CRITICAL THINKING   Writers **organize their texts** in specific ways in order to reveal certain information at specific times. Identifying and understanding the organizational structure of a text can help with reading comprehension. The organizational structure can reveal a writer's purpose and point of view. The reader can also anticipate what kind of information might be coming next.

CRITICAL THINKING:
ANALYZING TEXT
ORGANIZATION

D How does the writer organize the article? Number the ideas in the correct order (1–5).

_____ a. reasons for why tigers have become rare

_____ b. an outline of a variety of global initiatives to save the tiger

_____ c. a description of the power and mystery of tigers

_____ d. a detailed explanation of how one country is trying to protect tiger habitats

_____ e. a description of how urgent it is to save the last remaining tigers

CRITICAL THINKING:
ANALYZING TEXT
ORGANIZATION

E Discuss the questions with a partner.

1. Do you think the opening of the article is effective? Why or why not?

2. How else could the writer have organized the article?

CRITICAL THINKING:
GUESSING MEANING
FROM CONTEXT

F Find and underline the following words and phrases in the reading passage. Use the context to help you identify the meaning of each word or phrase. Then match each word or phrase with its definition.

1. Paragraph A: **indifference** _____
2. Paragraph C: **unnerving** _____
3. Paragraph D: **defining attribute** _____
4. Paragraph D: **annihilation** _____
5. Paragraph E: **botched** _____
6. Paragraph E: **dispersed** _____
7. Paragraph G: **unwelcome revelation** _____
8. Paragraph L: **harboring** _____

a. an unpleasant and surprising discovery
b. a key characteristic to someone's identity
c. lack of interest or concern
d. total defeat or destruction
e. spread over a wide area
f. failed; mismanaged
g. giving a safe home or shelter to (something)
h. making (someone) lose courage or confidence

CRITICAL THINKING:
PERSONALIZING

G How important do you think it is to protect endangered animals? Note your ideas below. Then discuss with a partner.

_____

_____

_____

DEVELOPING READING SKILLS

An appositive is a noun or a noun phrase that explains, defines, or gives more information about another noun or noun phrase that is close to it. Writers use commas, dashes, or colons to separate appositives from the nouns that they describe. For example, the underlined phrases in the sentences below are appositives. The double-underlined words are the nouns that they describe.

"I've never met a head of state who says, 'Look, we're a poor country. If it comes between tigers and people, you just have to write off tigers,'" said <u>Alan Rabinowitz, an authority on tigers and the CEO of Panthera</u>.

A spiderweb of green lines weaves among core tiger populations, forming a network that includes breathtaking <u>extremes of habitat—Himalayan foothills, jungle, swamp, forest, grasslands</u>.

Long-term conservation must focus on all aspects of <u>a tiger landscape: core breeding populations, sanctuaries, wildlife corridors, and the surrounding human communities</u>.

A In each of these sentences from the passage, underline the appositive and circle the noun or noun phrase that it refers to. One sentence has two noun phrase appositives that refer to two different nouns.

UNDERSTANDING APPOSITIVES

1. My determination to see a wild tiger in my lifetime brought me to Ranthambore Tiger Reserve, one of 40 in India.

2. "This is about making decisions as if we're in an emergency room," says Tom Kaplan, co-founder of Panthera, an organization dedicated to big cats.

3. The places that have actual tigers—here-and-now, flesh-and-blood tigers—as opposed to hypothetical ones, are represented by a scattering of brown-colored spots.

4. Over the next decade, infrastructure projects—the kind of development that often destroys habitat—are projected to average some $750 billion a year in Asia.

5. In November 2010—the Year of the Tiger—the world's 13 tiger countries came together at the Global Tiger Summit in St. Petersburg, Russia.

B Scan for and underline other examples of appositives in the reading passage in Unit 1. Share your answers with a partner.

APPLYING

A pair of Siberian tiger cubs

TIGERS IN THE SNOW

BEFORE VIEWING

DISCUSSION **A** What threats to tigers do you remember from the reading? Make a list.

_____

_____

LEARNING ABOUT THE TOPIC **B** Read the information. Then answer the questions.

Siberian (or Amur) tigers live mainly in the forests of Russia's far east, though some still exist in China and North Korea. The climates that these tigers live in are harsh—temperatures in some areas can drop to –40°C—but this also offers some advantages. These cold northern forests offer the lowest human density of any tiger habitat, allowing the tigers far more room to move around. However, the Siberian tiger, like other tiger species, is endangered. Estimates suggest that there are fewer than 500 individuals left in Russia.

1. In what kind of areas do Siberian tigers live? What advantages do these areas offer the tigers?

_____

_____

2. Why do you think Siberian tigers might be endangered?

_____

C Read these extracts from the video. Match the correct form of each **bold** word to its definition.

VOCABULARY IN CONTEXT

"Once the kill has been made, it's clear the male is the **dominant** partner. He won't allow the female to get near until he's had enough."

"They are at the top of their **food chain**, but the tigers are still endangered."

"It is thought its fragile population has been **stabilized** for the moment."

1. _____ (v) to get to a state in which there aren't any more big problems or changes

2. _____ (adj) more powerful, successful, influential, or noticeable than others

3. _____ (n) the process by which one living thing is eaten by another, which is then eaten by another, and so on

WHILE VIEWING

A ▶ Watch the video. Check the main idea.

UNDERSTANDING MAIN IDEAS

☐ a. Siberian tigers are in danger, but their populations are currently remaining steady.

☐ b. Siberian tigers are in danger, and their populations are decreasing very quickly.

☐ c. Siberian tigers were endangered, but their populations are now getting bigger.

B ▶ Watch the video again. Then answer the questions below.

UNDERSTANDING DETAILS

1. How is a Siberian tiger different from other tigers?

_____

2. How big does a Siberian tiger's territory have to be?

Female: _____   Male: _____

3. According to the video, what are the two main threats to Siberian tigers?

_____

4. How has the Siberian tiger's decline changed since the mid-1990s?

_____

AFTER VIEWING

A Why do you think male tigers need such a large home range? Note your ideas below. Then discuss with a partner.

CRITICAL THINKING: MAKING INFERENCES

_____

B How does the Siberian tiger's situation compare with the challenges facing other tigers? Note your ideas below. Then discuss with a partner.

CRITICAL THINKING: SYNTHESIZING

_____

_____

Writing

EXPLORING WRITTEN ENGLISH

VOCABULARY FOR
WRITING

A The following words and expressions can be useful when writing about problems and solutions. Use the words to complete the definitions.

> **threatened** (paragraph D) **exacerbated** (paragraph E) **sacrifice** (paragraph I)
>
> **initiatives** (paragraph J) **funding** (paragraph J) **components** (paragraph J)
>
> **safeguarding** (paragraph K) **strategy** (paragraph L)

1. _____ is money that a government or organization provides for a particular purpose.

2. If an animal species is _____, it is likely to become endangered.

3. _____ are parts or elements of a larger whole.

4. If something _____ a problem or bad situation, it made it worse.

5. _____ are important actions that are intended to solve a particular problem.

6. _____ something is keeping it from harm or danger.

7. A(n) _____ is a plan of action designed to achieve a long-term or overall aim.

8. If you _____ something that is valuable or important, you give it up, usually to obtain something else for yourself or for other people.

**A critically endangered
female Sumatran tiger and
her five-month-old cub**

B Read the information in the box. Then use appositives to combine the sentence pairs (1–5).

> **LANGUAGE FOR WRITING** Using Appositives
>
> As you saw in the Reading Skill section, writers use appositives to give more information about a noun. Appositives help writers avoid redundancy and short, choppy sentences. You can separate appositives with commas, dashes, or colons.
>
> **With an appositive:**
> *"I've never met a head of state who says, 'Look, we're a poor country. If it comes between tigers and people, you just have to write off tigers,'" said Alan Rabinowitz, <u>a renowned authority on tigers and the CEO of Panthera</u>.*
>
> **Without an appositive:**
> *"I've never met a head of state who says, 'Look, we're a poor country. If it comes between tigers and people, you just have to write off tigers,'" said Alan Rabinowitz. Rabinowitz is a renowned authority on tigers and the CEO of Panthera.*

1. The Bengal tiger is one of India's most popular attractions. The Bengal tiger is India's national animal.

   _____

   _____

2. In addition to tigers, other animals live in Ranthambore. Monkeys, deer, wild boars, owls, and parakeets live in Ranthambore.

   _____

   _____

3. Ranthambore is home to 41 tigers. Ranthambore is a former private hunting estate.

   _____

   _____

4. Fateh Singh Rathore used to work at Ranthambore when it was a hunting estate. Fateh Singh Rathore is the assistant field director of the reserve.

   _____

   _____

5. Zaw Win Khaing once saw a tiger in 2002. Zaw Win Khaing is the head ranger of a tiger reserve in Myanmar.

   _____

   _____

WRITING SKILL Reviewing the Thesis Statement

Individual paragraphs have main ideas. Similarly, essays have main ideas. A **thesis statement** is a statement that expresses the main idea of an entire essay. A good thesis statement has the following characteristics:

- It presents your position or opinion on the topic.

- It includes a reference to the reasons for your opinion or position on the topic.

- It expresses only the ideas that you can easily explain in your body paragraphs.

CRITICAL THINKING:
EVALUATING

C Read the following pairs of thesis statements. Check (✓) the statement in each pair that you think is better. Then share your answers with a partner.

1. a. ☐ Palisades Park should be protected for three main reasons: It is the only park in the city, it is a gathering place for families, and it is a safe place for children to play after school.

   b. ☐ Palisades Park is a beautiful place for parents to spend time with their children and for people in the community to gather for events.

2. a. ☐ The Bloodroot plant (*Sanguinaria Canadensis*) is endangered and should be protected because it can cure dozens of ailments, from skin disorders to cancer.

   b. ☐ The Bloodroot plant (*Sanguinaria Canadensis*), an endangered plant found in the forests of North America, can be used to cure diseases.

A bloodroot plant

CRITICAL THINKING:
EVALUATING

D Read the question below about tiger conservation. Write your opinion and two reasons. Then use your opinion and your reasons to write a thesis statement.

Should governments spend more money to protect tigers?

My opinion: _____

_____

Reason 1: _____

_____

Reason 2: _____

_____

Thesis statement: _____

_____

_____

WRITING TASK

GOAL You are going to write an essay on the following topic:

Describe an animal, a habitat, or a natural place that people are working to protect. Explain why it should be protected.

A Make a list of animals, habitats, or natural places that people are trying to protect. If you need more ideas, go online and research.

BRAINSTORMING

B Follow the steps to make notes for your essay.

PLANNING

Step 1 Choose one idea to write about from your brainstorming list.

Step 2 Complete the outline below with notes about the idea. Go online to do some research if you need more information.

OUTLINE

Introduction

Information about the animal/habitat/place: _____

_____

_____

How is it valuable? _____

Why is it in danger? _____

Thesis statement: We need to protect _____

because _____ and _____.

Body paragraph 1

Topic sentence: (Reason 1) _____

Supporting detail: _____

Supporting detail: _____

Body paragraph 2

Topic sentence: (Reason 2) _____

_____

Supporting detail: _____

Supporting detail: _____

Conclusion

What can be done to protect it? _____

_____

_____

REVISING PRACTICE

The draft below is a model of the essay you are writing. Follow the steps to create a better second draft.

1. Add the sentences (a–c) in the most suitable spaces.

   a. With a combination of international and local efforts, Borneo may be saved from destruction.

   b. so that we can save all the different forms of life that live on the island.

   c. because it is home to so many different species and because the rain forest helps reverse damage from climate change.

2. Now fix the following problems (a–c) with the essay.

   a. Cross out one sentence that doesn't relate to the topic of the essay in paragraph B.

   b. Use an appositive to revise the first two sentences in paragraph C.

   c. Use an appositive to revise sentences five and six in paragraph D.

A

The rain forest island of Borneo, the world's third largest island, is about the size of the state of Texas in the United States. The island is one of the most biodiverse places in the world. It is home to endangered animals such as the Sumatran tiger, the Sumatran rhinoceros, the pygmy elephant, and the Bornean orangutan. And nearly 400 new species have been discovered in 10 years. Sadly, this island's diverse and beautiful rain forest is in danger. In the past 20 years, 80 percent of the rain forest has been destroyed because of illegal logging, forest fires, and development. At the same time, people are capturing and selling some of the wildlife, particularly the orangutans. We need to protect Borneo _____

B

It's important to protect Borneo _____. Visitors to Borneo can enjoy its beautiful beaches and mountains. Thousands of species of plants, animals, and insects live on Borneo. Many, like the pygmy elephant, cannot be found anywhere else on Earth. In addition, scientists continue to find new species of plants and animals. Some of these might provide medicines for diseases or teach us more about biology.

C

We also need to protect Borneo in order to protect the globe from climate change. Borneo is home of one of the world's remaining rain forests. Carbon dioxide, a greenhouse gas, is heating up Earth's atmosphere and causing a number of problems such as extreme weather and melting polar ice. Rain forests absorb carbon dioxide and create more oxygen. They also help produce rain all around the world. If we lose rain forests, we will lose one of our best weapons against global warming.

D

So, what can be done to protect Borneo? Both international and local communities are involved in saving the island. An organization called the World Wildlife Fund (WWF) is working to create safety corridors and protect the 220,000-square-kilometer (85,000-square-mile) area from destruction. The organization is raising funds to help make this happen. The Borneo Project is an international organization. The Borneo Project provides support to local communities. These communities protect the rain forests of Borneo in various ways: They stop loggers from cutting down trees, they educate the local community about the need to save the rain forest, and they block developers from building on the land. _____

D   Now use the questions below to revise your essay.

REVISED DRAFT

☐ Does your introduction have an interesting hook?

☐ Does your thesis state your position on the topic?

☐ Do your body paragraphs include enough details to fully explain your ideas?

☐ Did you use appositives to avoid redundancy and short, choppy sentences?

☐ Do all your sentences relate to the main idea?

☐ Does your concluding paragraph have a summary statement and a final thought?

Orangutans in a Borneo forest sanctuary

EDITING PRACTICE

Read the information below. Then find and correct one mistake with appositives in each of the sentences (1–5).

In sentences with appositives, remember that an appositive must:
- be a noun or a noun phrase.
- come right after a noun or noun phrase.
- be separated by commas, dashes, or colons.

1. Tigers, they are an endangered species, live throughout Asia.

2. Ranthambore, a tiger reserve is in India.

3. Tiger conservationists—people who protect tigers, are looking for new solutions.

4. Corridors, are paths for safe travel, may help tigers survive in wild areas.

5. There are fewer than 4,000 tigers. The biggest cat in the world.

FINAL DRAFT **E** Follow the steps to write a final draft.

1. Check your revised draft for mistakes with appositives.

2. Now use the checklist on page 248 to write a final draft. Make any other necessary changes.

UNIT REVIEW

Answer the following questions.

1. What are two reasons tigers are endangered?

_____

_____

2. What are two ways we can help protect tigers?

_____

_____

3. What are two things a thesis statement should include?

_____

_____

4. Do you remember the meanings of these words? Check (✓) the ones you know. Look back at the unit and review the ones you don't know.

☐ acknowledge AWL   ☐ poaching
☐ apparently AWL   ☐ predator
☐ assess AWL   ☐ prey
☐ authority AWL   ☐ priority AWL
☐ dedicated   ☐ project AWL
☐ feasible   ☐ resolve AWL
☐ hypothetical AWL   ☐ secretive
☐ lethal

BEAUTY AND PERCEPTION 3

A visitor looks at artwork during an art festival at the Dubai World Trade Center.

ACADEMIC SKILLS

READING   Using a concept map to identify supporting details

WRITING   Writing an evaluative essay

GRAMMAR   Using restrictive and nonrestrictive adjective clauses

CRITICAL THINKING   Applying ideas

THINK AND DISCUSS

1 What do you think makes certain things—for example, landscapes, buildings, or images—beautiful?

2 What is the most beautiful thing you have ever seen? Why is it beautiful?

A **Look at the information on these pages and answer the questions.**

1. What is *aesthetics*?
2. According to the text, what factors affect aesthetic principles?
3. Is the image on the opposite page beautiful, in your opinion? If so, what makes it beautiful?

B **Match the correct form of the words in blue to their definitions.**

_____ (n) the basic rules or laws of a particular theory

_____ (n) the size of something or its size in relation to other things

_____ (adj) relating to patterns and shapes with regular lines

WHAT IS BEAUTY?

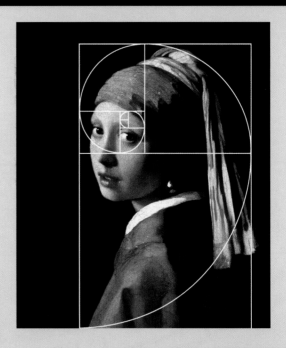

Aesthetics is a branch of philosophy concerned with the study of beauty. Aesthetic **principles** provide a set of criteria for creating and evaluating artistic objects such as sculptures and paintings, as well as music, film, and other art forms.

Aesthetic principles have existed almost as long as people have been producing art. Aesthetics were especially important to the ancient Greeks, whose principles have had a great influence on Western art. The Greeks believed that beautiful objects were intrinsically beautiful; that is, their beauty did not depend on people's interpretation of them. Concepts such as **proportion**, symmetry, and order made objects beautiful.

For example, the "golden spiral," applied here to a painting by Johannes Vermeer (1632–1675), is thought to illustrate the **geometric** proportions that people find aesthetically pleasing.

Today, however, most people would agree that aesthetic principles are culturally influenced and are not universal. Ideas on how the human form is represented, for example, vary widely. In traditional African art, sculpture is often abstract and stylized rather than realistically representing particular individuals.

Johannes Vermeer's
Girl with a Pearl Earring

Reading

PREPARING TO READ

BUILDING
VOCABULARY

A The words in **blue** below are used in the reading passage. Match the correct form of each word to its definition (1–8).

The time and place in which a work of art is created often influence its aesthetic value. Therefore, understanding the historical and social **context** of a work of art can help you to appreciate it better and give you **insight** into its significance. For example, many works of European and American art during the mid- to late 19th century have Asian—or more specifically, Japanese—influences.

Artists such as Vincent van Gogh and James McNeill Whistler incorporated into their own work the subjects, colors, and **composition** of Japanese prints. They were **exposed to** Japanese art partly because Japan opened up to the West in the mid-1800s. As a result, European exhibitions started showing art objects from Japan. Artists who were looking for new styles were especially influenced by Japanese woodblock prints, which **violated** the rules of traditional Western art. To Western eyes, objects in Japanese woodblock prints look flat instead of three-dimensional. Scenes do not have perspective, as in Western paintings.

There were other **crucial** elements that pointed to the differences in Western and Asian **notions** of beauty. For example, the arrangement of objects in Japanese prints is often irregular and asymmetrical, and the focal point—the central object in a print—is often off center, not in the middle as in a Western painting. Some artists were so inspired by these new ideas that they even moved to Japan during the late 19th century in order to **pursue** their interest in Asian art.

▶ *Sudden Shower Over Shin-Ohashi Bridge and Atake,* **by Hiroshige (left), and** *Bridge in the Rain (after Hiroshige),* **by Vincent Van Gogh**

1. _____ (v) to follow

2. _____ (v) to bring into contact with

3. _____ (adj) extremely important

4. _____ (n) the general situation that an idea or an event relates to

5. _____ (n) an accurate and deep understanding of something

6. _____ (v) to break or to fail to comply with

7. _____ (n) ideas or beliefs about something

8. _____ (n) the way in which the parts of something are arranged

B Complete the sentences with the words in the box. Use a dictionary to help you.

BUILDING VOCABULARY

balance	depression	ethics	imperfect

1. _____ is a mental state in which you are sad and feel that you cannot enjoy anything.

2. _____ are ideas or moral beliefs that influence the behavior, attitudes, or philosophy of a group of people.

3. If something has _____, elements in it are treated equally in terms of strength or importance.

4. If a thing is _____, it has faults; it is missing certain possible desirable qualities or characteristics.

C Discuss these questions with a partner.

USING VOCABULARY

1. What skills do you think are **crucial** if you want to be a professional artist?

2. Would you encourage someone with artistic talent to **pursue** a career in art? Why or why not?

D Discuss your answer to this question in small groups: Look at the everyday items around you. Can you see anything beautiful? What makes it beautiful to you?

BRAINSTORMING

_____

_____

E Look at the photos in the reading passage and read the first sentence of each paragraph. What are some of the aspects of photography that the reading passage discusses? Note your ideas below. Then read the passage to check your answers.

PREVIEWING

_____

_____

_____

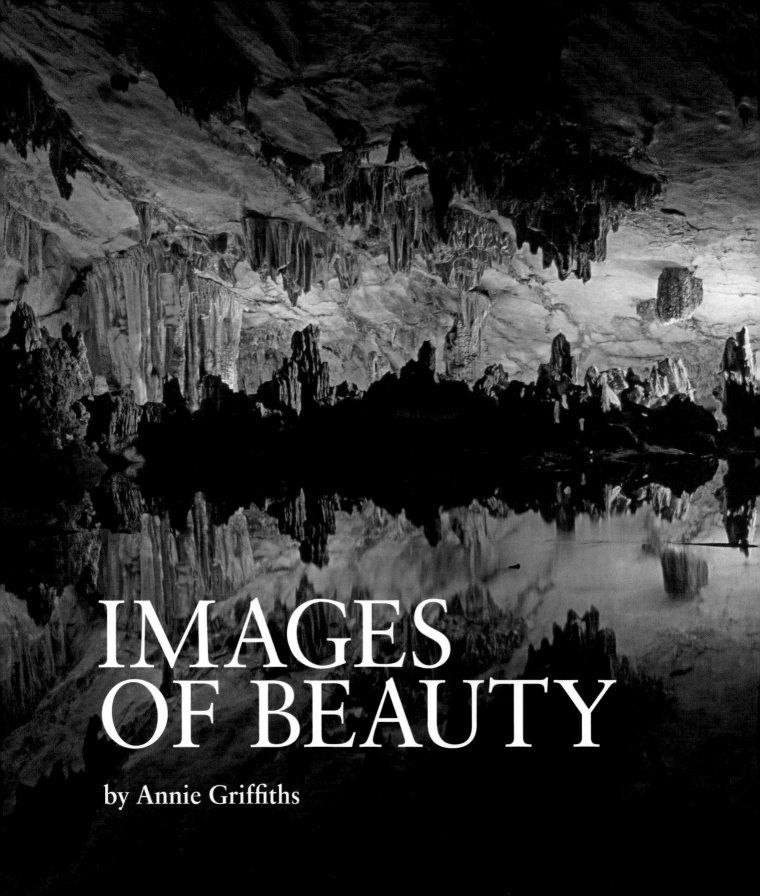

IMAGES OF BEAUTY

by Annie Griffiths

Reed Flute Cave, China,
by Raymond Gehman

> Some photographs rise above the others. These are photos that catch a moment of emotion or light that make them ignite a deeper response in the viewer.

🎧 1.3

A Photography has opened our eyes to a multitude of beauties, things we literally could not have seen before the advent of the frozen image. It has greatly expanded our **notion** of what is beautiful, what is aesthetically pleasing. Items formerly considered trivial, and not worth an artist's paint, have been revealed and honored by photographs: things as pedestrian as a fence post, a chair, a vegetable. And as technology has developed, photographers have explored completely new points of view: those of the microscope, the eagle, the cosmos.

What is it that delights the human eye and allows us to proclaim that a photograph is beautiful? Photography depends on three **principles**: light, **composition**, and moment. Light literally makes the recording of an image B possible, but in the right hands, light in a photograph can make the image soar. The same is true with composition. What the photographer chooses to keep in or out of the frame is all that we will ever see—but that combination is vital. And the moment that the shutter is pressed, when an instant is frozen in time, endows[1] the whole image with meaning. When the three—light, composition, and moment—are in concert, there is visual magic.

Let us begin with light. Light literally reveals the subject. Without light, there is nothing: no sight, no color, no form. How light is **pursued** and captured is the photographer's constant challenge and constant joy. We watch it dance across a landscape or a face, and we prepare for the moment when it illuminates or softens or ignites the subject before us. Light is rarely interesting when it is flawless. Photographers may be the only people at the beach or on the C mountaintop praying for clouds, because nothing condemns a photograph more than a blazingly bright sky. Light is usually best when it is fleeting or dappled,[2] razor sharp or threatening, or atmospheric. On a physiological level, we are all solar powered. Scientific studies have proved that our moods are profoundly affected by the amount of light we are **exposed to**. Lack of sun has been linked to loss of energy and even **depression**. Light in a photograph sets an emotional expectation. It can be soft or harsh, broad or delicate, but the mood that light sets is

---

[1]If you **endow** something with a particular feature or quality, you provide it with that feature or quality.

[2]**Dappled** light is a combination of dark and light patches on the object or person that is being illuminated.

a preface to the whole image. Consider the light in a stunning scene by Sam Abell (below). It is the quality of light through morning fog that blesses this image and turns a forest into a field of light, shadow, and color, where every tree takes on a personality.

Composition represents the structural choices the photographer makes within the photographic frame. Everything in the photo can either contribute or distract. Ironically, the definition of what makes a picture aesthetically pleasing often comes down to mathematics: the geometric **proportions** of objects and their placements within the frame. When we look at a beautiful photograph with an objective eye, we can often

D find serpentine[3] lines, figure eights, and triangular arrangements formed by the objects. The **balance**, or mathematical proportion, of the objects makes up the picture's composition: a key element in any beautiful image. Look closely at photographer James Stanfield's charming composition of a child jumping for joy in a doorway at the Louvre (right). It is the moment that draws us in, but that moment is set in a striking composition of the doorway and the architecture beyond. The

[3]Something that is **serpentine** is curving and winding in shape, like a snake.

geometric composition of the photograph makes the child look small, and even more appealing.

The third **crucial** element in a photograph is the moment when the shutter is pressed. The moment captured in a beautiful image is the storytelling part of the photograph.

E Whether a small gesture or a grand climax, it is the moment within a picture that draws us in and makes us care. It may be the photographer's most important choice. If a special moment is caught, it endows the whole image with meaning. Often, waiting for that moment involves excruciating patience, as the photographer anticipates that something miraculous is about to happen. At other times, it's an almost electric reaction that seems to bypass the thought process entirely and fire straight to instinct. Capturing that perfect moment may be a photographer's biggest challenge, because most important moments are fleeting. Hands touch. The ball drops. A smile flashes. Miss the moment and it is gone forever.

Light, composition, and moment are the basic elements in any beautiful photograph. But there

F are three other elements that draw the viewer in and encourage an emotional response. These are palette, time, and wonder.

Morning fog at Kelly's Ford, Virginia, United States, by Sam Abell

re, Paris,
ield

Palette refers to the selection of colors in a photograph that create a visual **context**. Colors can range from neon to a simple gradation of grays in a black-and-white photograph. Even in the abstract, colors can make us feel elated or sad. The chosen palette sets up the mood of the whole image. It can invite or repel, soothe or agitate. We feel calm in a palette of pastels. Icy blues can make us shiver. Oranges and reds tend to energize.

Other images stand out because of the freezing or blurring of time. There are the lovely images of raindrops falling, lightning flashing, and athletes frozen in midair. There are also time exposures[4] that allow us to see a choreography of movement within the still frame. The laundry flutters, the traffic merges, the water flows. In a photograph of a bird in flight, the high-speed exposure allows us to see things that our eyes literally cannot: every feather supporting the bird's flight, the arc of the wings, the light in the bird's eye. High-speed photography has been a gift to both art and science.

[4]A **time exposure** is a photograph that results when the camera's shutter is left open for a long time.

Wonder refers to the measure of human response when the photograph reveals something extraordinary—something never seen before, or seen in a fresh, new way. Wonder is about **insight** and curiosity. It is an expression of the child inside every one of us. Some photographers, following their childlike sense of wonder, have literally given their lives in pursuit of images so wonderful that they must be seen.

Light, composition, and moment come together in a photograph to bring us the ultimate reality: a view of the world unknown before the invention of the camera. Before photography, the basic artistic rules of painting were rarely **violated**. Images were made to please, not to capture reality. But as photography evolved, painterly[5] rules were often rejected in the pursuit of fresh vision. Photographers became interested in the real world, warts and all, and it was the accidental detail that was celebrated. Photography invited the world to see with new eyes—to see photographically—and all of the arts benefited from this new point of view.

[5]**Painterly** means relating to or characteristic of painting or painters.

An aerial view of the towering Kronotsky volcano, Kamchatka, Russia, by Michael Melford

Time exposure of cars speeding past a cowboy on horseback, Badlands, United States, by Annie Griffiths

Painters, sculptors, designers, weavers, and dancers all expanded their vision of beauty by embracing the photographer's love of reality. And when the photographer is creative with the basic elements in a photograph, the resulting image has greater appeal. A surprising truth about photography is that each element is most effective not when it captures perfection but rather when it reveals the imperfect. Photographs are most eloquent when they impart a new way of seeing. What is more wonderful than the imperfect moment, when a simple scene turns sublime[6] because a cat entered the room, the mirror caught a reflection, or a shaft of light came through the window? And real beauty depends upon how the image moves us: A photograph can make us care, understand, react, emote,[7] and empathize with the wider world by humanizing and honoring the unknown.

K

Photographs have created a new ethic of seeing. They have greatly expanded our notion of what is beautiful. It is to photography's credit that it has found beauty in the most humble places, and that it has ushered in a new democracy of vision. People from all walks of life are able to feast their eyes on subjects remote and grand. Photographs have given us visual proof that the world is grander than we imagined, that there is beauty, often overlooked, in nearly everything.

Adapted from "Simply Beautiful Photographs" by Annie Griffiths: National Geographic Books, 2010

[6]If you describe something as **sublime**, you mean that it has a wonderful quality that affects you deeply.
[7]To **emote** is to express emotion in an intense way.

Photographer and writer Annie Griffiths has documented the lives of people in nearly 150 countries around the world. She has received awards from the National Press Photographers Association, the Associated Press, and the White House News Photographers Association.

UNDERSTANDING THE READING

A Note answers to the questions below.

1. What are the three main elements that make a photograph beautiful?

   _____

2. What additional elements make a photograph beautiful?

   _____

3. The passage is divided into two main parts. Which paragraph begins the second part?

   _____

B Note answers to the questions below. Then discuss with a partner.

1. How has photography changed our notion of beauty?

   _____

   _____

2. Write a definition for each of the main elements you listed in exercise A, question 1.

   _____

   _____

   _____

3. What is the effect of color in a photograph, according to Griffiths?

   _____

   _____

4. What kinds of things do time exposures help us to see in a photograph?

   _____

   _____

5. What is wonder as it applies to a photograph, according to Griffiths? Explain it in your own words.

   _____

   _____

6. How has photography affected other art forms?

   _____

   _____

> **CRITICAL THINKING** **Applying ideas** from a reading to other contexts can help you evaluate the information. For example, applying an author's opinion to your own experience can help you decide how far you agree with it.

C Find the following quotes in paragraph J of the reading passage. Note answers to the questions. Then discuss with a partner.

1. "Before photography, the basic artistic rules of painting were rarely violated. Images were made to please, not to capture reality." Can you think of any famous paintings or types of artwork that are examples of this idea?

   _____

   _____

2. "A surprising truth about photography is that each element is most effective not when it captures perfection but rather when it reveals the imperfect." Can you find a picture in this book that is an example of this? Do you agree with the writer?

   _____

   _____

D Find and underline the *italicized* words below in the passage. Use the context to help you understand the meaning. Then circle the correct words to complete the definitions.

1. Paragraph A: If something is *pedestrian*, it's **ordinary** / **extraordinary**.

2. Paragraph B: You use *in concert* when you're talking about things that **work well together** / **are not coordinated**.

3. Paragraph D: If an idea *comes down to* something in particular, it means it is an **essential** / **unimportant** part of it.

4. Paragraph E: If a moment is *fleeting*, it goes by very **slowly** / **quickly**.

5. Paragraph J: If a photograph shows images of real life, *warts and all*, then it is showing us **just the positive** / **both the positive and the negative** aspects of reality.

6. Paragraph K: If something has *ushered in* a thing, such as a new era or way of thinking, it has **ended it** / **brought it into being**.

7. Paragraph K: People from *all walks of life* are people who come from **similar** / **different** backgrounds.

E What is your opinion of the photograph below? Consider the elements of a beautiful photograph mentioned in the reading passage. Discuss with a partner.

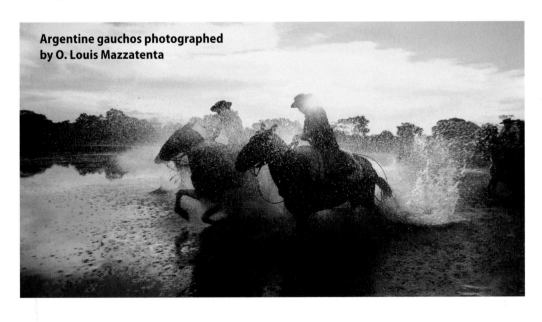

Argentine gauchos photographed by O. Louis Mazzatenta

DEVELOPING READING SKILLS

READING SKILL Using a Concept Map to Identify Supporting Details

A **concept map** is a type of graphic organizer. It helps you see how main ideas and details in a reading passage relate to each other. Taking notes in a concept map can help you understand and remember information so you can use it later in a discussion, a writing assignment, or a test.

When you take notes in any kind of graphic organizer, be as brief as possible. Use abbreviations and leave out unimportant or repeated information.

USING A
CONCEPT MAP

A Complete the concept map using information from the reading passage.

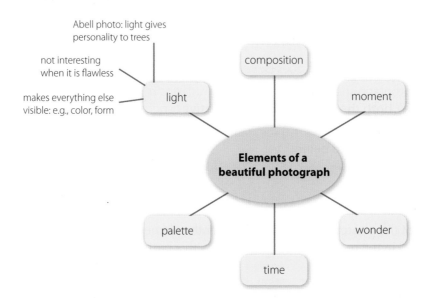

USING A
CONCEPT MAP

B Now look back at the reading passage in Unit 1. Create a concept map to summarize the key ideas relating to the Anthropocene.

Video

PHOTO CONTEST

"A Node in the Dark,"
by Brian Yen

BEFORE VIEWING

A How would you rate the photo above? Consider Griffiths's six criteria and discuss in a small group.

DISCUSSION

_____

_____

B Read the information. Then answer the questions.

LEARNING ABOUT
THE TOPIC

Each year, National Geographic invites amateur photographers to enter their photographs into a competition. In 2014, people from more than 150 countries submitted photos representing three categories: people, places, and nature. Over 9,000 photos were submitted, but only a handful were chosen as winners. The winning entries all had one thing in common: they told a story. The grand prize winner, Brian Yen, received $10,000 and a trip to National Geographic headquarters. When asked why he takes pictures, he explained, "Photography to me is like going on an archaeological dig: It offers me a tool to interpret reality by dusting away the uninteresting bits to reveal the gem underneath. It's an exciting, creative, and exploratory process."

1. What story does Yen's photo tell?

   _____

2. Why does Yen compare taking pictures to archaeology?

   _____

C Read these extracts from the video. Match the correct form of each **bold** word to its definition.

> "Everyone looks really peaceful but at the same time it just looks really **surreal** and something, you know, otherworldly."
>
> "The overall **tone** of it was just very relaxing in what was a very **chaotic** scene."
>
> "A photograph like this has got to be like a chessboard, where everything is there and there's no **foreground**."

1. _____ (adj) strange; dreamlike

2. _____ (adj) not having any order or organization

3. _____ (n) the front part of a picture

4. _____ (v) the general character or feeling of something, for example a place or piece of writing

WHILE VIEWING

A ▶ Watch the video about judging the 2014 National Geographic Photo Contest. What criteria for judging the photos do the judges mention?

A winning photo …
- ☐ a. should have just one main element.
- ☑ b. touches the viewer emotionally.
- ☑ c. must be good technically.
- ☐ d. must have good composition.
- ☐ e. needs to look natural.
- ☑ f. has good use of color and light.
- ☑ g. shows something new and unusual.

B ▶ Watch the video again. Match each image from the video (a–e) with a statement.

a. the swimming pool   b. the owl   c. the wildebeest   d. the train   e. the basketball game

1. It took time for the judges to appreciate it. _____

2. The judges had divided opinions about it. _____

3. A judge felt that it offered a new perspective. _____

4. The judges felt it had a calming effect on them. _____

5. It was rejected by the judging panel. _____

AFTER VIEWING

A What do you think the judge means when he refers to a "gut reaction"? Discuss with a partner.

B Considering the elements of a good photo described earlier, which photo in the video do you think was best? Discuss your choice with a partner.

_____

_____

Writing

EXPLORING WRITTEN ENGLISH

A The following words and expressions can be useful when writing about visual art forms. Find the words in this unit's reading passage. Use the context to guess their meanings. Then use the words to complete the definitions.

VOCABULARY FOR WRITING

aesthetically pleasing (paragraph A)	**within the frame** (paragraph D)
illuminate (paragraph C)	**gradation** (paragraph G)
atmospheric (paragraph C)	**pastels** (paragraph G)

1. If a scene is _____, it creates a pleasant mood or feeling.

2. If a work of art is _____, it is beautiful.

3. In a photograph, things that are _____ are the things that the photographer has chosen to include in the image.

4. To _____ something means to shine light on it.

5. A(n) _____ is a small change in something, such as a slight change from one color to another.

6. _____ are pale colors.

B Read the sentences (a–e) below. Then answer the questions (1–3).

NOTICING

a. The winning photo was taken by Brian Yen, <u>who lives in Hong Kong</u>.

b. My personal favorite was the photo <u>that came in second place</u>.

c. Yen's photo, <u>which is called "A Node Glows in the Dark,"</u> uses an interesting balance of light and dark.

d. Yen, <u>whose image shows people on a train at night</u>, mostly takes photos after dark.

e. The central focus of the image is on the woman <u>who is using her cellphone</u>.

1. What is the purpose of the underlined clauses?

_____

2. What words are used to introduce the underlined clauses?

_____

3. If you take away the underlined clauses, which sentences still make sense? Why?

_____

Writers use adjective clauses to give more information about nouns. An adjective clause has a subject and a verb.

> Palette is a term **that** _refers to the selection of colors in a photograph_.

> My father was someone **who** _was interested in photography from a young age_.

As in the examples above, restrictive adjective clauses give essential information about a noun. In other words, if you take away the clause, the sentence no longer makes sense. Nonrestrictive adjective clauses give nonessential information:

> Our concept of beauty has been influenced by photography, **which** _is a relatively recent art form_.

> Annie Griffiths, **who** _is a professional photographer_, is the executive director of an organization that empowers women in developing countries.

> Annie Leibovitz, **whose** _photographs have been published in several magazines_, is famous for her use of light and color.

Adjective clauses are a good way to add details to your writing. They help vary your sentence types and make your sentences more interesting.

Note: Remember to use commas in nonrestrictive adjective clauses. Use one comma before a nonrestrictive adjective clause that appears at the end of a sentence. Use commas before and after a nonrestrictive adjective clause when it appears in the middle of a sentence. Use _which_ (not _that_) for objects in nonrestrictive adjective clauses.

C Read the pairs of sentences below. Join them into a single sentence using a restrictive or nonrestrictive adjective clause.

1. Vivian Maier was a photographer. Her work was only discovered after her death.

   _____

   _____

2. Ansel Adams was an American photographer. He was most known for his images of the Californian wilderness.

   _____

   _____

3. Aesthetics were important to the ancient Greeks. They believed beautiful objects were intrinsically beautiful.

   _____

   _____

4. Vincent van Gogh was influenced by Japanese art. He made a copy of Hiroshige's print _Sudden Storm Over Shin-Ohashi Bridge and Atake_.

   _____

   _____

D Write three sentences about photographs in this unit using nonrestrictive or restrictive adjective clauses.

- _____

  _____

- _____

  _____

- _____

  _____

WRITING SKILL Supporting a Thesis

As you saw in Unit 2, a thesis statement expresses the main idea of an entire essay. Each body paragraph in an essay then provides details for and explanation of the main idea. To effectively support a thesis statement, make sure you do the following:

- Describe one key point of your thesis in the topic sentence of each body paragraph.
- Order your body paragraphs to match the order of ideas mentioned in your thesis statement.
- Provide adequate details (facts and examples) that develop the idea of each topic sentence.

E Read this excerpt from an introduction to an essay on Frank Lloyd Wright's famous building, Fallingwater. Underline the key concepts in the thesis statement. Then answer the questions.

CRITICAL THINKING: ANALYZING

The term *organic architecture*, which was coined by the American architect Frank Lloyd Wright, applies to structures that create a sense of harmony with the natural world. Fallingwater, the western Pennsylvania house designed by Wright, is a perfect example of the organic approach to architecture due to its surroundings and its materials.

— Thesis Statement

1. How many body paragraphs do you think the essay will have? _____

2. What ideas do you think will appear in the body paragraphs?

_____

_____

_____

_____

F Read the topic sentences below for the essay about Fallingwater. Underline the ideas in the topic sentences that match the main points of the thesis statement.

Body paragraph 1:

Topic sentence: The way Fallingwater is assimilated into its natural environment is an example of organic architecture.

Body paragraph 2:

Topic sentence: The organic approach is also shown in the natural materials Wright used to build Fallingwater.

APPLYING

G Now read some notes for the essay. Which body paragraph from exercise **F** does each note best support? Match a paragraph (1–2) with each note.

Notes:

_____ a.   exterior color matches color of leaves on surrounding plants

_____ b.   natural spring drips water into house

_____ c.   built from stones found in local area

_____ d.   living room fireplace incorporates boulders from a nearby building site

_____ e.   house is built around a tree

_____ f.   large window in living room overlooks a waterfall

Fallingwater, designed by Frank Lloyd Wright

WRITING TASK

GOAL In this lesson, you are going to write an essay on the following topic:

Choose an example of a visual art form (e.g., a painting, a photograph, a piece of sculpture) and evaluate it using aesthetic criteria.

A Choose a type of visual art (painting, drawing, photography, sculpture). Think of three criteria to judge it.

BRAINSTORMING

Type of art: _____

Criteria: 1. _____   2. _____   3. _____

Now pick one example of your chosen type of visual art. Describe it, and evaluate it based on your criteria.

Name of piece of art: _____

Description	Evaluation
	1.
	2.
	3.

B Follow the steps to make notes for your essay.

PLANNING

Step 1 In the outline on the next page, write a thesis statement and note some ideas for your introduction.

Step 2 Write a topic sentence and two or three details for each body paragraph.

Step 3 Note some ideas for your conclusion.

OUTLINE

Notes for introduction: _____

_____

Thesis statement: _____

_____

Body paragraph 1: Topic sentence: _____

_____

Details: _____

_____

_____

Body paragraph 2: Topic sentence: _____

_____

Details: _____

_____

_____

Body paragraph 3: Topic sentence: _____

Details: _____

_____

_____

Notes for conclusion: _____

_____

FIRST DRAFT **C** Use the information in your outline to write a first draft of your essay.

REVISING PRACTICE

The draft on the next page is an essay that uses a set of criteria to evaluate a building. Follow the steps to create a better second draft.

1. Write the sentences (a–c) in the correct spaces.

   a. For example, it has large double doors that are at street level; there are no stairs at the entrance.
   b. The copper color offers an interesting contrast to the light gray color of the granite structure, and the contrast will remain as the copper ages.
   c. For example, it is resistant to acid rain.

2. Now fix the following problems (a–c) with the essay.

   a. Fix a problem with a nonrestrictive clause in paragraph B.
   b. Fix a problem with a nonrestrictive clause in paragraph D.
   c. Delete an unrelated idea in paragraph D.

A

What makes a work of architecture great? Most people would say that aesthetics are most important. For example, many people agree that the Eiffel Tower in Paris and the Blue Mosque in Istanbul are beautiful structures. It is true that aesthetics are important; however, according to the Roman architect Marcus Vitruvius Pollio, there are two additional principles that we should consider when judging a structure. They are durability—how strong and long-lasting a structure is designed to be—and function— how well the structure serves its intended purpose. The new Rostonville Library in my city is a good example of Vitruvius's principles because it is durable, functional, and aesthetically pleasing.

B

The Rostonville Library which is built entirely of granite—a hard and very tough stone—is an example of durability. Granite is likely to remain strong and unaffected by environmental pollution. _____ Granite structures are stable and resistant to vibrations, so the Rostonville Library will likely be able to withstand an earthquake. The Rostonville Library is also durable in terms of sustainability, because it uses solar energy for heating, and a rooftop garden provides insulation that keeps the building cool in hot weather.

C

Designed to provide free access for members of the community to a variety of print and digital information, the Rostonville Library is also an example of Vitruvius's principle of functionality. The Rostonville Library conveys a feeling of openness and accessibility. _____ Furthermore, the entire library is on one level, and it has an open design—there are no interior walls or dividers. In addition, large windows let in plenty of natural light, so it's easy to see and get to each department within the library.

D

Finally, the Rostonville Library is beautiful. Aesthetically pleasing details make it attractive, both inside and out. The large windows are framed in copper. _____ Growth from the rooftop garden, that cascades down the sides of the building, adds to the aesthetics of the building. It softens the lines of the structure and helps it to blend into its natural surroundings. The library was built on the edge of the city park, which was designed using only native plants.

E

Durability, functionality, and beauty make the Rostonville Library a great structure. Architects and designers who follow Vitruvius's principles help to make urban environments more pleasant places to live. Structures that exemplify these criteria provide peace of mind as well as beauty for the people who use them.

D **Now use the questions below to revise your essay.**

REVISED DRAFT

- ☐ Does your introduction provide relevant background information on the topic?
- ☐ Does your thesis state the main points of the essay?
- ☐ Do your body paragraphs include enough details to fully explain your ideas?
- ☐ Did you use restrictive and nonrestrictive adjective clauses correctly?
- ☐ Do all your sentences relate to the main idea?
- ☐ Does your concluding paragraph have a summary statement and a final thought?

EDITING PRACTICE

Read the information below. Then find and correct one mistake with nonrestrictive adjective clauses in each of the sentences (1–4).

When using nonrestrictive adjective clauses, remember to:

- use one comma before a nonrestrictive adjective clause that appears at the end of a sentence. Use two commas, one before and one after, when the nonrestrictive adjective clause appears in the middle of a sentence.

- use *which* (not *that*) for objects in nonrestrictive adjective clauses.

1. This image is an excellent example of composition which is the way objects are arranged in a photograph.

2. That photograph, that I like best of all, is Berenice Abbott's *Pennsylvania Station*.

3. Another important element is light, that illuminates the objects in a photograph.

4. Moment which captures time in a photograph helps to tell the image's story.

FINAL DRAFT **E** Follow the steps to write a final draft.

1. Check your revised draft for mistakes with adjective clauses.

2. Now use the checklist on page 248 to write a final draft. Make any other necessary changes

UNIT REVIEW

Answer the following questions.

1. What are three important elements of a good photograph?

_____

_____

2. What do you think is the most important element in a beautiful photograph?

_____

_____

3. What is the purpose of a nonrestrictive clause?

_____

_____

4. Do you remember the meanings of these words? Check (✓) the ones you know. Look back at the unit and review the ones you don't know.

☐ balance   ☐ imperfect
☐ composition   ☐ insight AWL
☐ context AWL   ☐ notion AWL
☐ crucial AWL   ☐ principle AWL
☐ depression AWL   ☐ proportion AWL
☐ ethics AWL   ☐ pursue AWL
☐ expose to AWL   ☐ violate AWL
☐ geometric

RETHINKING BUSINESS 4

A "break out space" designed to encourage creativity among staff at Google's London office

A Look at the information on these pages and answer the questions.

1. Which country exports the most clothing? In which country do people spend the most on clothing?

2. Which of the facts below is most interesting? Why?

B Match the correct form of the words in blue to their definitions.

_____ (n) clothing

_____ (n) the sale of goods to the public

_____ (n) the financial gain a company or a person makes

_____ (n) a person or business that you are competing with

FASHION FACTS

Fashion is big business. The global **apparel** market is valued at around 2.4 trillion dollars and accounts for 2 percent of the world's Gross Domestic Product (GDP).

These are the three largest fashion companies in the world—each making billions of dollars of **profits** each year. Nike's closest **rival** in the sportswear business, Adidas, is ranked number 5, after the fashion **retail** outlet, TJ Maxx.

1 Dior $43.6 billion in sales

2 Nike $33.8 billion in sales

3 Inditex $25.7 billion in sales

There are **24.8 million** people in the world working to make clothes. China, the world's largest exporter of cloth and clothing, has over 10 million people working in the industry. They can make over 40 billion items of clothing in a year.

On average, Australians spend the most money on clothing.

**Total Yearly Spending on Apparel
Per Capita* (in US$) (2015):**

1. Australia	$1,050
2. Canada	$831
3. Japan	$814

The fashion industry has a huge impact on the environment. For example, it takes **2,700** liters of water to make just one cotton shirt. That's enough water for a person to drink for two and a half years!

A model showcases the hanbok, a form of traditional Korean dress. The traditional outfit has seen a growth in popularity in recent years. Hanbok purchases by women in South Korea increased by 80 percent between 2013 and 2016.

Reading

PREPARING TO READ

BUILDING
VOCABULARY

A The words in blue below are used in the reading passage. Match the correct form of each word to its definition.

Nearly 80 years ago, a woman named Yoon Dokjeong began selling hand-pressed camellia oil as a hair treatment in her home of Kaesong, in what is now North Korea.

As a boy, her son Suh Sunghwan worked alongside his mother as she taught him how to make skincare products from natural materials. In 1945, Suh Sunghwan **founded** the South Korean cosmetics company AmorePacific. The company has its **headquarters** in Seoul, South Korea, and owns 30 cosmetic **brands**, including Laneige and Annick Goutal. Today, Yoon Dokjeong's grandson, Suh Kyungbae, is the company's CEO (chief **executive** officer). A great success in a very **competitive** industry, AmorePacific earned a profit of 811.5 billion won (US$707.2 million) in 2016.

1. _____ (adj) describing a situation or activity in which people or companies are trying to be more successful than others

2. _____ (v) to start a company, institution, or other organization

3. _____ (n) a senior-level employee who is responsible for making important decisions for the company

4. _____ (n) a product (or group of products) with its own name

5. _____ (n) an organization or company's main offices or center of control

▶ **Suh Kyungbae speaks to the media during AmorePacific's 70th anniversary conference.**

B Complete each sentence with the correct form of a word or phrase in the box. Use a dictionary to help you.

competitor	marketing	merchandise
outsource	shortage	supply chain

1. _____ is the activity of promoting and advertising goods or services in order to encourage people to buy them.

2. A company's _____ is someone who is trying to sell similar goods or services to the same people.

3. When a company _____ something, it pays workers from outside the company to do the work or supply the things it needs or sells.

4. If there is a _____ of something, there is not enough of it.

5. The things or goods a person or company sells is their _____.

6. A(n) _____ is the process involved in moving a product from supplier to customer.

C Discuss these questions with a partner.

1. What famous clothing **brands** do you know? Make a list below.

_____

_____

2. What do you know about the companies that make your favorite clothing brands? When were they **founded**? Where are their **headquarters**?

D Look back at your list of clothing brands in **C**. What makes each brand special? Note your ideas below. Then discuss with a partner.

_____

_____

E Skim the reading passage. What is it mainly about? Circle the correct option. Then read the passage to check your answers.

a. It describes the challenges of starting a clothing company.

b. It compares one company with other similar companies.

c. It explains how clothing is designed and manufactured.

CHANGING FASHION

by Mike W. Peng

> In the world of fast fashion, rather than only releasing a few new collections each year, companies like Zara sell a never-ending cycle of trend-led clothing, all year round.

🎧 1.4

Zara is now one of the world's hottest fashion chains. **Founded** in 1975, its parent company,[1] Inditex, has become a leading global **apparel** retailer. Since its initial public offering (IPO)[2] in 2001, Inditex, which owns eight fashion **brands**, has doubled the number of its stores. It has quadrupled its sales to US$25.7 billion, and its **profits** have risen to over US$3 billion. Zara contributes two-thirds of Inditex's total sales. In this intensely **competitive** industry, the secret to Zara's success is that Zara excels in **supply chain** management. In fact, Zara succeeds by first breaking and then rewriting industry rules.

Industry rule number one: *The origins of a fashion house usually carry a certain cachet.*[3] This is why most European fashion houses have their **headquarters** in Paris or Milan. However, Zara does not hail from Italy or France—it is from Spain. Even within Spain, Zara is not based in a cosmopolitan city like Barcelona or Madrid. Its headquarters are in Arteixo, a town of only 25,000 people in a remote corner of northwestern Spain. Yet Zara is active not only throughout Europe, but also in Asia and North America. Currently, it has more than 5,000 stores in 88 countries, and these stores can be found in some truly pricey locations: the Champs-Elysees in Paris, Fifth Avenue in New York, Galleria in Dallas, Ginza in Tokyo, Queen's Road Central in Hong Kong, and Huaihai Road in Shanghai.

---

[1] A **parent company** is a company that owns smaller businesses.
[2] When a company has an **initial public offering**, it sells its stock to the public for the very first time.
[3] If something has a certain **cachet**, it has a quality that makes people admire it.

Rule number two: *Avoid stock-outs* (running out of in-demand items). From Zara's point of view, stock-outs are a good thing, since occasional **shortages** contribute to a shopper's urge to "buy now." At Zara, items sell out fast, with new products arriving at **retail** outlets twice a week. "If you see something and don't buy it," said one shopper, "you can forget about coming back for it because it will be gone." By giving just a short window of opportunity to purchase a limited quantity of **merchandise**, Zara's customers are motivated to visit the stores more frequently. In London, shoppers visit the average store four times a year, but frequent Zara 17 times. There is a good reason to do so, too: Zara makes and offers shoppers about 20,000 different items per year, about triple what stores like Gap do. "At Gap, everything is the same;" said one Zara customer. "Buying from Zara, you'll never end up looking like someone else."

Rule number three: *Bombarding[4] shoppers with ads is a must.* Traditionally, stores like Gap and H&M spend an average of 4 percent of their total sales on ads. Zara takes a different approach. It devotes just 0.3 percent of its sales to ads. The high traffic[5] in its stores reduces the need for advertising in the media, so most of Zara's **marketing** serves as a reminder for shoppers to visit the stores.

Rule number four: *Outsource for cheaper production.* Stores like Gap and H&M do not own any production facilities. They pay other companies to make their products, sometimes in places far away from their headquarters. However, outsourcing production (mostly to Asia) requires a long lead time[6]—usually several months. In contrast, Zara once again deviated from the norm. By concentrating more than half of its production in-house—in Arteixo, Spain, and nearby, in Portugal and Morocco—Zara has

developed a super-responsive supply chain. This means it can design, produce, and deliver a new item of clothing to its stores in a mere 15 *days*, a pace that is unheard of in the industry. The best speed most of its **rivals** can achieve is two months. Also, outsourcing may not necessarily be "low cost." Errors in trend prediction can easily lead to unsold inventory,[7] forcing their retail stores to offer steep discounts. The industry average is to offer 40 percent discounts across all merchandise. In contrast, Zara's ability to design

[7]An **inventory** is a supply or stock of something—the number of items that a store has for sale.

---

[4]If you **bombard** someone with something, you make them face a great deal of it.

[5]When a place has **high traffic**, it is crowded and has many people coming and going.

[6]In the production process, the **lead time** is the period of time between the decision to make a product and the completion of actual production.

and make new clothes quickly means shorter lead times and an ever-changing inventory. So it sells more at full price, and—when it discounts—averages only 15 percent.

Rule number five: *Strive for efficiency through large batches.* By producing products in large quantities, as is the industry norm, companies can benefit from economies of scale.[8] Zara, however, intentionally deals in small batches. Because of

F

the greater flexibility and speed this approach affords, Zara does not worry about missing the boat when it comes to trends. When new trends emerge, Zara can react quickly. Also, it runs its supply chain like clockwork with a fast but predictable rhythm: Every store places orders on Tuesday/Wednesday and Friday/Saturday. Trucks and cargo flights run on established schedules—like a bus service. From Spain, shipments reach most European stores in 24 hours, U.S. stores in 48 hours, and Asian stores in 72 hours. And it is not only store staff who know exactly when

[8]**Economies of scale** refers to the proportionate savings in costs gained when the level of production increases.

Zara staff at the company's headquarters in Arteixo, Spain. Zara is able to design, make, and deliver new products to its stores in just over two weeks.

shipments will arrive, but regular customers too. This motivates them to check out the new merchandise more frequently, especially on the shipment arrival days, known by Zara fans as "Z days."

Certainly, Zara has no shortage of **competitors**. But few have successfully copied its fast fashion and flexible business model. "I would love to organize our business like Inditex [Zara's parent]," noted an **executive** from Gap, "but I would have to knock my company down and rebuild it from scratch." This does not mean Gap and other rivals are not trying to copy Zara. The question is how long it takes for Zara's rivals to out-Zara Zara.

G

Adapted from **Global Business** *4th Edition, by Mike W. Peng, © Cengage Learning 2015*

Mike W. Peng is the Jindal Chair of Global Business Strategy at the University of Texas at Dallas. A National Science Foundation (NSF) CAREER Award winner, Professor Peng is a fellow with the Academy of International Business and listed among Thomson Reuters' The World's Most Influential Scientific Minds.

ZARA: BIRTH OF A BRAND

In 1963, in the unremarkable seaside town of La Coruña, Spain, 27-year-old Amancio Ortega Gaona started a business making bathrobes. By 1975, Ortega had saved enough money from this business to open a clothing store in town. He named his store Zorba, after the movie *Zorba the Greek*. However, he soon learned that there was a bar in town called Zorba just a couple of blocks away. The bar owner thought that it might be confusing to have two businesses in town with the same name, so Ortega agreed to change the name of his store. The problem was that he had already made the letter molds for the store's sign. Rather than having new molds made, Ortega used some of the letters he already had molds for, and came up with a new name: Zara.

UNDERSTANDING THE READING

A Choose the statement that best summarizes the writer's main idea.

UNDERSTANDING
MAIN IDEAS

    a. Zara is successful because it follows established norms of the fashion industry.

    b. Zara has achieved success because it is run differently from other clothing companies.

    c. Zara owes its success to closely following the practices of other clothing companies.

B According to the passage, how does Zara operate its business? Check (✓) all that apply.

UNDERSTANDING
SUPPORTING IDEAS

    ☐ a. It manufactures small numbers of items at a time, so it can get them into stores quickly.

    ☐ b. It spends a lot of money on advertising.

    ☐ c. The company headquarters are based in a major city.

    ☐ d. Most Zara items are made in Spain or in nearby countries.

    ☐ e. It creates a certain cachet by charging high prices for clothing.

    ☐ f. It intentionally runs out of styles and replaces them with new ones.

> **CRITICAL THINKING** Some words are commonly grouped together to make **multiword units or phrases**. In these phrases, words often have different meanings than they do when they're used individually. It's important to learn these words as units and to use context to help you understand what they mean.

C Find and underline the following multiword phrases in the reading passage. Then circle the best meaning for each phrase.

CRITICAL THINKING:
UNDERSTANDING
MULTIWORD UNITS

    1. Something that **serves as a reminder** _____.

        a. distracts people from doing that thing

        b. helps people remember to do that thing

    2. Someone who has **deviated from the norm** has _____.

        a. followed well-established ways of doing things

        b. done something different from what was expected

    3. If you **miss the boat**, you _____.

        a. do not understand a new idea correctly

        b. are too late to take advantage of an opportunity

    4. If something operates **like clockwork**, it _____.

        a. works on a regular schedule

        b. has very complex working parts

    5. If you rebuild something **from scratch**, you build it _____.

        a. again, from the beginning

        b. in its old building, with some changes

D Complete the missing bars in the charts using information from the reading passage.

1. **Inditex Sales:**
   2001 vs. Today

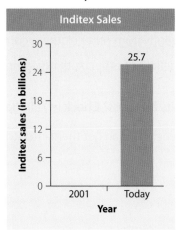

2. **Average Store Visits per Year:**
   Zara vs. Average London Stores

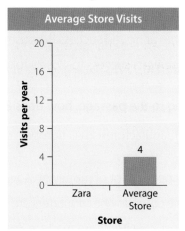

3. **No. of Items Made per Year:**
   Zara vs. Gap

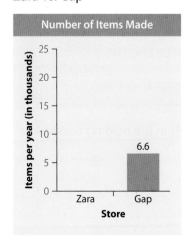

4. **Spending on Advertising:**
   Zara vs. Gap / H&M

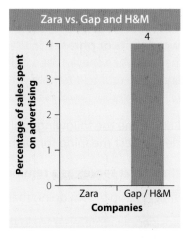

5. **Days from Design to in Store:**
   Zara vs. Competitors

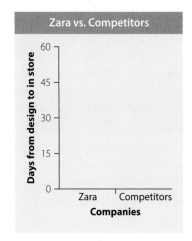

6. **Discounts on Unsold Inventory:**
   Zara vs. Industry Average

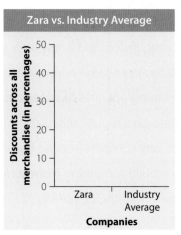

DEVELOPING READING SKILLS

A Look back at paragraphs C, D, E, and F in the reading passage. Find and underline all the initial phrases.

B Answer the questions. Use information from initial phrases you identified in **A**.

UNDERSTANDING
SENTENCES WITH
INITIAL PHRASES

1. Why are customers motivated to visit Zara stores more frequently than other stores?

    a. because items in Zara stores are only available for a relatively short time

    b. because Zara will regularly offer huge discounts on many of its products

2. How has Zara developed a super-responsive supply chain?

    a. by making most of its clothing in or near its headquarters

    b. by having factories in many different countries around the world

3. How do most fashion companies take advantage of economies of scale?

    a. by selling their items in huge stores

    b. by producing products in large batches

4. Why is Zara not worried about missing the boat when it comes to trends?

    a. because its designers are extremely good at predicting future fashion trends

    b. because it can keep up with trends by designing and making new products quickly

◀ **Boxes of ready-to-wear garments are prepared at Zara's headquarters in Arteixo, Spain.**

Italian fashion designer
Brunello Cucinelli

BEHIND THE BRAND

BEFORE VIEWING

DISCUSSION **A** What famous fashion designers do you know? What are they known for? Discuss with a partner.

_____

_____

LEARNING ABOUT THE TOPIC **B** Read the information. Then answer the questions.

Brunello Cucinelli is a luxury Italian fashion brand that sells high-end menswear and womenswear in countries around the world. The company—best known for its cashmere sweaters—had humble beginnings. Founder Brunello Cucinelli first started out dying cashmere in a small workshop. After some success, he founded the company in 1978, and since then, the brand has gone from strength to strength. Nowadays, Cucinelli is a highly influential figure in the fashion industry, and in the last ten years, the company has quadrupled in size.

1. What kinds of fashion products does the company Brunello Cucinelli make?

   _____

2. What factors do you think make a fashion brand successful?

   _____

   _____

C The words in **bold** below are used in the video. Match the correct form of each word to its definition.

> Versace, Gucci, and Armani are three of the most famous **high-end** fashion brands.
>
> In many parts of the world, working conditions are improving thanks to **enlightened** business owners recognizing the importance of workers' rights.
>
> The rise of big businesses has led to fewer and fewer people being able to make a living as self-employed **artisans**.
>
> Calvin Klein founded his **eponymous** fashion brand in New York in 1968.

1. _____ (adj) named after a particular person

2. _____ (adj) expensive and luxurious

3. _____ (adj) having modern, well-informed opinions

4. _____ (n) someone who works with their hands in a skilled profession

WHILE VIEWING

A ▶ Watch the video. According to the video, which two of the following have contributed to fashion brand Brunello Cucinelli's success?

☐ a. its ethical employment practices   ☐ c. its investment in foreign talent

☐ b. its location in a traditional Italian village   ☐ d. its use of modern technology

B ▶ Watch the video again. Note answers to the questions below. Then discuss with a partner.

1. How does Brunello Cucinelli ensure that its staff don't work too much?

   _____

   _____

2. In what ways has founder Brunello Cucinelli helped the local village?

   _____

   _____

AFTER VIEWING

A What does Cucinelli mean when he says, "I don't think it's time wasted watching a bird in the sky when you're sewing a button"? Discuss with a partner.

B In what ways are Zara and Brunello Cucinelli similar? In what ways are they different? Note your ideas below. Then discuss with a partner.

_____

_____

Writing

EXPLORING WRITTEN ENGLISH

VOCABULARY FOR WRITING | **A** The following words and phrases can be useful when writing a comparative essay. Some are used to show similarities, and some are used to show differences. Put each word in the correct category.

although	both	conversely	equally
have in common	however	in contrast (to)	in the same way (that)
instead (of)	likewise	on the contrary	on the other hand
similarly	the same is true for	whereas	unlike

Similarities	Differences

LANGUAGE FOR WRITING Using Sentences with Initial Phrases

You can use initial phrases (prepositional, time, and verbal phrases) to avoid short, choppy sentences. Using initial phrases is also a way to vary your sentence style and to show the relationship between ideas. Remember to use a comma to separate the initial phrase from the main clause.

To avoid short, choppy sentences:

> *Samsung first started business in 1938. It was originally a trading company.*

> **Founded in 1938,** *Samsung was originally a trading company.* (verbal phrase)

To vary sentence style and/or show the relationship between ideas:

> *Ortega changed his store's name to Zara when he discovered that the name Zorba was already being used.*

> **When he discovered that the name Zorba was already being used,** *Ortega changed his store's name to Zara.* (time phrase)

> *Sergey Brin developed a search engine that would become Google in a friend's garage.*

> **In a friend's garage,** *Sergey Brin developed a search engine that would become Google.* (prepositional phrase)

B Rewrite each sentence to include an initial phrase.

1. H&M only sold women's clothing when it opened for business in 1947.

   When _____

2. Karl-Johan Persson became H&M's CEO in 2009.

   _____

3. BRS distributed shoes for a Japanese shoe maker until the spring of 1971.

   _____

4. The company's name was changed to Nike when BRS's relationship with the Japanese shoe maker ended.

   _____

   _____

WRITING SKILL Organizing a Comparative Essay

There are two main ways to organize a comparative essay: the **block method** and the **point-by-point method**.

With the **block method**, you discuss all the points of comparison about one subject and then discuss those same points about the other subject. The outline looks like this:

Introduction + Thesis statement
Body paragraph 1: Subject A
      Point 1
      Point 2
      Point 3
Body paragraph 2: Subject B
      Point 1
      Point 2
      Point 3
Conclusion

With the **point-by-point method**, you discuss each subject in terms of the points of comparison you've chosen. If there are three points of comparison, the outline looks like this:

Introduction + Thesis statement
Body paragraph 1: Point 1
      Subject A
      Subject B
Body paragraph 2: Point 2
      Subject A
      Subject B
Body paragraph 3: Point 3
      Subject A
      Subject B
Conclusion

C Look at the notes for a comparative essay on two companies. Use the notes to fill in the outline for a block comparative essay.

Notes

	Apple	Samsung
Early years	founded in Silicon Valley, United States, 1976, as tech company by S. Jobs, S. Wozniak, R. Wayne	founded in Taegu, Korea, 1938, as trading company, by Lee Byung-Chul
Marketing	direct advertising, not much social media, famous for TV ads	relies heavily on social media, celebrity endorsements, sponsorship of global events
Product development	long time to create new products, e.g. iPad	faster than Apple to assess consumer interest/marketability

OUTLINE

Organization method: _Block_

Notes for introduction: _Apple and Samsung are both highly successful tech companies_

_____

Thesis statement: _____

_____

Body paragraph 1:

Topic sentence: _____

Details: _____

_____

_____

Body paragraph 2:

Topic sentence: _____

Details: _____

_____

_____

Notes for conclusion: _____

_____

_____

WRITING TASK

GOAL You are going to write a comparative essay on the following topic:

Compare two companies in the same industry. Consider aspects such as their history, location, product types, and business practices.

BRAINSTORMING

A Choose an industry that you are interested in and two companies to compare. Complete the Venn diagram with at least three similarities and/or differences that you know about between the two companies. Research additional information.

Industry: _____

Company 1: _____   **Company 2:** _____

PLANNING

B Follow the steps to make notes for your essay.

Step 1 Look at your brainstorming notes. Identify the three points of comparison that you want to write about. Summarize them in the thesis statement in the outline. Note some ideas for an introduction.

Step 2 Choose an organization method for your essay. Depending on your organizational method, complete the outline.

Step 3 Write a topic sentence for each body paragraph and note some examples or details that illustrate your comparison.

Step 4 Note some ideas for a conclusion.

OUTLINE

Organization method (block or point-by-point): _____

Notes for introduction: _____

_____

Thesis statement: _____

_____

Body paragraph 1:

Topic sentence: _____

_____

Details: _____

_____

_____

Body paragraph 2:

Topic sentence: _____

_____

Details: _____

_____

_____

Body paragraph 3 (for point-by-point method):

Topic sentence: _____

_____

Details: _____

_____

_____

Notes for conclusion: _____

_____

FIRST DRAFT **C** Use the information in your outline to write a first draft of your essay.

REVISING PRACTICE

The draft on the opposite page is a model of the essay you are writing. Follow the steps to create a better second draft.

1. Add the sentences or phrases (a–c) in the correct spaces.

   a. In contrast to Apple's direct marketing strategies,
   b. Apple Inc. is one of the largest information technology companies in the world.
   c. For example, its 2014 "Your Verse" campaign highlighted different ways people use their iPads (Beltrone, 2014).

2. Now fix the following problems (a–c) with the essay.

   a. Fix a problem with an initial phrase in paragraph B.
   b. Fix a problem with an initial phrase in paragraph C.
   c. Fix a problem with a comparison word in paragraph C.

A

From phones to tablets to TVs, Apple and Samsung products are household names around the world. In fact, both companies seem to dominate the mobile phone industry. However, while the two companies have certain features in common, they differ in terms of history, marketing styles, and the way they develop their products.

B

_____ Founded in 1976, in the heart of Silicon Valley Apple originally focused on the development and marketing of personal computers. Its founders were Steve Jobs, Steve Wozniak, and Ronald Wayne, and its early products included the Apple I, the Lisa, and the Macintosh. Today, Apple is known around the world for its well-designed phones, tablets, and other tech devices. In terms of marketing, Apple relies primarily on direct advertising and does not use social media to promote its products as much as other tech companies do. In fact, Apple is famous for its distinctive television ads. _____ Regarding product development and release, Apple usually takes quite a long time to create new products. For example, the company spent eight years developing the iPad. This reflects a key aspect of Apple's corporate culture: a determination to never release anything to the market unless it's perfect (Kaslikowski, 2013).

C

While Samsung, like Apple, is a technology company today, Samsung started out as a trading company in Taegu, Korea. Founded, in 1938 by Lee Byung-Chul, Samsung began as a grocery store, "trading and exporting goods produced in and around the city, like dried Korean fish and vegetables, as well as its own noodles" (Burris, 2017). Today, as a large conglomerate owning multiple companies, Samsung is one of the largest businesses in Korea. _____ Samsung relies heavily on social media as an avenue for advertising. The company also promotes its product with celebrity endorsements; participation in, and sponsorship of, global events; and discounts. Finally, likewise Apple spends a long time on product development, Samsung releases products in less time with the goal of assessing consumer interest and marketability. When a product is judged to be popular with consumers, then it is refined and improved.

D

Although both Apple and Samsung are leaders in the mobile phone market, their histories and strategies are distinctive. Over the years, the competitive nature of the technology industry has challenged the two companies to make each new phone more innovative than the last. Due to this, and the fact that Apple and Samsung are in intense competition with each other, it is likely the two companies will continue to create groundbreaking products far into the future.

References

Beltrone, Gabriel. (2014, Aug. 12). Apple's powerful "your verse" campaign rolls on, from Beijing and through Detroit. AdWeek. Retrieved from http://www.adweek.com/creativity/apples-powerful-your-verse-campaign-rolls-beijing-and-through-detroit-159442/.

Burris, Matthew. (2017, Sept. 7). The History of Samsung (1938-Present): Who Founded Samsung, When Samsung Was Created, and Other Facts. Lifewire. Retrieved from https://www.lifewire.com/history-of-samsung-818809.

Kaslikowski, Adam. (2013, Sept. 5). The difference between Samsung and Apple. Lucky Robot. Retrieved from http://luckyrobot.com/difference-between-samsung-and-apple/.

D Now use the questions below to revise your essay.

☐ Does your introduction have an interesting hook?

☐ Does your thesis state the main points of the essay?

☐ Did you use the block method or the point-by-point method to organize your essay?

☐ Do your body paragraphs include enough details to fully explain your ideas?

☐ Did you use initial phrases correctly?

☐ Does your concluding paragraph have a summary statement and a final thought?

EDITING PRACTICE

Read the information in the box. Then find and correct one mistake with initial phrases in each sentence (1–3).

In sentences with initial phrases, remember to:
- use a comma to separate the initial phrase from the main clause
- use a prepositional, time, or verbal phrase as the initial phase

1. In 1975 Steve Wozniak, and Steve Jobs built the first Apple computer.

2. It was founded in 1949, Adidas is now one of the world's leading sports brands.

3. Offering innovative tech products Samsung is one of the most successful businesses in Korea.

FINAL DRAFT **E** Follow the steps to write a final draft.

1. Check your revised draft for mistakes with referring to sources.

2. Now use the checklist on page 248 to write a final draft. Make any other necessary changes.

UNIT REVIEW

Answer the following questions.

1. What are two ways in which Zara differs from other clothing companies?

_____

_____

2. What are two ways in which Brunello Cucinelli is different from Zara?

_____

_____

3. What are two ways to organize a comparative essay?

_____

_____

4. Do you remember the meanings of these words? Check (✔) the ones you know. Look back at the unit and review the ones you don't know.

☐ apparel   ☐ merchandise

☐ brand   ☐ outsource

☐ competitive   ☐ profit

☐ competitor   ☐ retail

☐ executive   ☐ rival

☐ found AWL   ☐ shortage

☐ headquarters   ☐ supply chain

☐ marketing

WORKING TOGETHER 5

A four-man bobsleigh team prepares for its first run at the 2017 BMW IBSF World Cup in Innsbruck, Austria.

ACADEMIC SKILLS

READING Understanding complex sentences
WRITING Writing a summary essay
GRAMMAR Avoiding plagiarism (I) — Paraphrasing

THINK AND DISCUSS

1 In what situations do people work together in groups to make decisions or solve problems?
2 What are some advantages of working together in large groups? What are some of the disadvantages?

A **Look at the information on these pages and answer the questions.**

1. How is the photo an example of collaboration?
2. In what ways did primitive people collaborate?
3. What are some modern examples of collaboration? What purposes do they serve?

B **Match the correct form of the words in blue to their definitions.**

_____ (v) to succeed in doing something

_____ (adv) as a group

_____ (adj) difficult to understand; not simple

COLLABORATION

People collaborate when they work together to accomplish a task. Collaboration among early humans helped to ensure their survival. For example, early humans used teamwork in order to find food and raise children. In the modern world, collaboration is a key feature in organizational settings such as businesses—most organizational behavior experts agree, for example, that collaboration increases productivity. When people work together, they can use each other's knowledge to advance new ideas and solve complex problems.

In recent years, collaboration has been greatly enhanced by the Internet. In the past, people had to be in the same place in order to work together. Today, online collaboration allows people to accomplish a range of tasks collectively at any time and from any location. Crowdsourcing, which uses a network of a large number of people to help solve a problem, is increasing our scientific knowledge. Data collected from a crowdsourcing website called Cerberus, for example, is helping astronomers analyze satellite images of Mars.

What makes humans want to collaborate? James K. Rilling, an anthropologist at Emory University, looked at brain activity while participants were engaged in cooperative activities. His study showed that the desire to cooperate with others may be innate in humans. Researchers are also looking into ways to enhance human collaboration. Studies of the ways in which animal and insect groups—such as ants—collaborate may help us figure out ways to work together even more efficiently.

Contestants work together to construct a human tower during the 26th Tarragona Competition in Tarragona, Spain.

Reading

PREPARING TO READ

BUILDING VOCABULARY **A** The words in **blue** below are used in the reading passage. Match the correct word to its definition.

Insects may help us improve the way we deal with dangerous situations. Scientists around the world are studying insect behavior to create tiny robots that have many of the same **capabilities** as insects. Insects, for example, can fly in and land **precisely** on a tiny surface, and then flap their wings to fly off with amazing speed. One application for these tiny insectlike machines is in **defense**—robots will be able to scout battlefields and record images as they hover over dangerous areas. Engineers are also building ornithopters—aircraft that get all of their thrust and most of their lift from flapping wings. The flight mechanism of an ornithopter is essentially a **simulation** of the way that an insect flaps its wings to take off and fly. These **emergent** technologies offer several advantages. One benefit is that operators can **manipulate** the devices from a distance. As a result, they can stay out of harm's way while they perform dangerous missions in **unpredictable** environments, such as war zones.

1. _____ (n) action taken to protect against attack; also, the organization of a country's armies and weapons

2. _____ (v) to control, manage, or use carefully

3. _____ (n) a model; imitation of behaviors or processes

4. _____ (n) skills or qualities

5. _____ (adj) not able to be known in advance

6. _____ (adj) coming into existence

7. _____ (adv) accurately and exactly

BUILDING VOCABULARY **B** Complete the definitions with the words in the box. Use a dictionary to help you.

complementary	coordinate	declare	relevant	realistically

1. If people _____ something, they formally announce it.

2. Something that is _____ to a situation is important or significant.

3. To _____ with others is to work together efficiently.

4. When people show things _____, they show them in a way that is accurate and true to life.

5. _____ things are different from each other, but they make a good combination.

C Note answers to the questions below. Then discuss with a partner.

USING VOCABULARY

1. What are some **capabilities** of groups versus individuals?

_____

_____

2. Think of a group that you belong to. Are the skills of the group members **complementary**? Give examples.

_____

_____

3. Do you like to **coordinate** with others on projects? Why or why not?

_____

_____

D Note answers to the questions below. Then discuss in a small group.

BRAINSTORMING

1. What are some examples of group behavior among animals?

_____

_____

2. For what kinds of jobs is collaboration very important?

_____

_____

E Look at the photos and captions in the reading passage. Read the first and last paragraphs (A and V). Note answers to the questions below. Then discuss with a partner. Check your predictions as you read the rest of the passage.

PREVIEWING

1. What animals might the passage discuss?

_____

_____

2. What aspects of their behavior might the passage discuss?

_____

_____

3. What human activities or inventions might the passage discuss?

_____

_____

4. What do you think is the main purpose of the article?

_____

_____

THE SMART SWARM

by Peter Miller

Monarch butterflies
in flight in Michoacan,
Mexico

> The study of swarms is providing insights that can help humans manage complex systems, from online search engines to military robots.

1.5

How do the simple actions of individuals add up to the **complex** behavior of a group? How do hundreds of honeybees make a critical decision about their hive if many of them disagree? What

A enables a school of herring to **coordinate** its movements so **precisely** it can change direction in a flash—like a single, silvery organism? The answer has to do with a remarkable phenomenon I call *the smart swarm*.

A smart swarm is a group of individuals who respond to one another and to their environment in ways that give them the power, as a group, to cope with uncertainty, complexity, and change. Take birds, for example. There's a small park

B near the White House in Washington, D.C., where I like to watch flocks of pigeons swirl over the traffic and trees. Sooner or later, the birds come to rest on ledges of buildings surrounding the park. Then something disrupts them, and they're off again in synchronized flight.

The birds don't have a leader. No pigeon is telling the others what to do. Instead, they're each paying close attention to the pigeons next

C to them, each bird following simple rules as they wheel across the sky. These rules add up to a kind of swarm intelligence—one that has to do with precisely coordinating movement.

Craig Reynolds, a computer graphics researcher, was curious about what these rules might be. So, in 1986, he created a deceptively

simple steering program called boids. In this simulation, generic birdlike objects, or boids, were each given three instructions: (1) avoid crowding nearby boids, (2) fly in the average direction of

D nearby boids, and (3) stay close to nearby boids. The result, when set in motion on a computer screen, was a convincing **simulation** of flocking,[1] including lifelike and **unpredictable** movements.

At the time, Reynolds was looking for ways to depict animals **realistically** in TV shows and movies. (*Batman Returns* in 1992 was the first movie to use his approach, portraying a swarm of

E bats and an army of penguins.) Today he works at Sony doing research for games, such as an algorithm[2] that simulates in real time as many as 15,000 interacting birds, fish, or people.

By demonstrating the power of self-organizing models to mimic swarm behavior, Reynolds was also blazing the trail for robotics engineers. A team of robots that could coordinate its actions like a flock of birds could offer significant

F advantages over a solitary robot. Spread out over a large area, a group could function as a powerful mobile sensor net, gathering information about what's out there. If the group encountered something unexpected, it could adjust and respond quickly, even if the robots in the group

[1]When animals **flock**, they congregate and do things as a large group.
[2]An **algorithm** is a process to be followed in performing a calculation, especially by a computer.

Safety in numbers: A school of sardines acts as a single entity to defend against attack by an Atlantic sailfish.

weren't very sophisticated—just as ants are able to come up with various options by trial and error. If one member of the group were to break down, others could take its place. And, most important, control of the group could be decentralized, not dependent on a leader.

"In biology, if you look at groups with large numbers, there are very few examples where you have a central agent," says Vijay Kumar, a professor of mechanical engineering at the University of Pennsylvania. "Everything is very distributed: They don't all talk to each other. They act on local information. And they're all anonymous. I don't care who moves the chair, as long as somebody moves the chair. To go from one robot to multiple robots, you need all three of those ideas."

In the near future, Kumar hopes to put a networked team of robotic vehicles in the field. One purpose might be as first responders. "Let's say there's a 911 call," he says. "The fire alarm goes off. You don't want humans to respond. You want machines to respond, to tell you what's happening. Before you send firemen into a burning building, why not send in a group of robots?"

Taking this idea one step further, computer scientist Marco Dorigo's group in Brussels is leading a European effort to create a "swarmanoid," a group of cooperating robots with **complementary** abilities: "foot-bots" to transport things on the ground, "hand-bots" to climb walls and **manipulate** objects, and "eye-bots" to fly around, providing information to the other units.

The military is eager to acquire similar **capabilities.** On January 20, 2004, researchers released a swarm of 66 pint-size robots into an empty office building at Fort A. P. Hill, a training center near Fredericksburg, Virginia. The mission: Find targets hidden in the building.

Zipping down the main hallway, the foot-long (30 cm) red robots pivoted this way and that on their three wheels, resembling a group of large insects. Eight sonars[3] on each unit helped them avoid collisions with walls and other robots. As they spread out, entering one room after another, each robot searched for objects of interest with a small camera. When one robot encountered another, it used wireless network gear to exchange information. ("Hey, I've already explored that part of the building. Look somewhere else.")

In the back of one room, a robot spotted something suspicious: a pink ball in an open closet (the swarm had been trained to look for anything pink). The robot froze, sending an image to its human supervisor. Soon, several more robots arrived to form a perimeter around the pink intruder. Within half an hour, the mission had been **accomplished**—all six of the hidden objects had been found. The research team conducting the experiment **declared** the run a success. Then they started a new test.

[3]**Sonar** is equipment that can detect the position of objects using sound waves.

The demonstration was part of the Centibots project, an investigation to see if as many as a hundred robots could collaborate on a mission. If they could, teams of robots might someday be sent into a hostile village to flush out terrorists or locate prisoners; into an earthquake-damaged building to find victims; onto chemical-spill sites to examine hazardous waste; or along borders to watch for intruders. Military agencies such as DARPA (**Defense** Advanced Research Projects Agency) have funded a number of robotics programs using collaborative flocks of helicopters and fixed-wing aircraft, schools of torpedo-shaped underwater gliders, and herds of unmanned ground vehicles. But, at the time, this was the largest swarm of robots ever tested.

"When we started Centibots, we were all thinking, this is a crazy idea, it's impossible to do," says Régis Vincent, a researcher at SRI International in Menlo Park, California. "Now we're looking to see if we can do it with a thousand robots."

Swarm-bots work together using swarm theory.

In nature, of course, animals travel in even larger numbers. That's because, as members of a big group, whether it's a flock, school, or herd, individuals increase their chances of detecting predators, finding food, locating a mate, or following a migration route. For these animals, coordinating their movements with one another can be a matter of life or death.

"It's much harder for a predator to avoid being spotted by a thousand fish than it is to avoid being spotted by one," says Daniel Grünbaum, a biologist at the University of Washington. "News that a predator is approaching spreads quickly through a school because fish sense from their neighbors that something's going on."

When a predator strikes a school of fish, the group is capable of scattering in patterns that make it almost impossible to track any individual. It might explode in a flash, create a kind of moving bubble around the predator, or fracture into multiple blobs,[4] before coming back together and swimming away.

That's the wonderful appeal of swarm intelligence. Whether we're talking about ants, bees, pigeons, or caribou, the ingredients of smart group behavior—decentralized control, response to local cues, simple rules of thumb— add up to a shrewd strategy to cope with complexity.

[4]A **blob** is an indistinct or a shapeless form or object.

A huge herd of wildebeest surge across the flooded Mara River in Serengeti National Park, Tanzania.

"We don't even know yet what else we can do with this," says Eric Bonabeau, a complexity theorist and the chief scientist at Icosystem Corporation in Cambridge, Massachusetts. "We're not used to solving decentralized problems in a decentralized way. We can't control an **emergent** phenomenon like traffic by putting stop signs and lights everywhere. But the idea of shaping traffic as a self-organizing system, that's very exciting."

The Internet is already using a form of swarm intelligence. Consider the way Google uses group smarts to find what you're looking for. When you type in a search query, Google surveys billions of Web pages on its index servers[5] to identify the most **relevant** ones. It then ranks them by the number of pages that link to them, counting links as votes (the most popular sites get weighted[6] votes since they're more likely to be reliable). The pages that receive the most votes are listed first in the search results. In this way, Google says, it "uses the collective intelligence of the Web to determine a page's importance."

Wikipedia, a free collaborative encyclopedia, has also proved to be a big success, with millions of articles in more than 200 languages about everything under the sun, each of which can be contributed by anyone or edited by anyone. "It's now possible for huge numbers of people to think together in ways we never imagined a few decades ago," says Thomas Malone of MIT's new Center for Collective Intelligence. "No single person knows everything that's needed to deal with problems we face as a society, such as health care or climate change, but **collectively** we know far more than we've been able to tap so far."

Such thoughts underline an important truth about collective intelligence: Crowds tend to be wise only if individual members act responsibly and make their own decisions. A group won't be smart if its members imitate one another, slavishly follow fads, or wait for someone to tell them what to do. When a group is being intelligent, whether it's made up of ants or attorneys, it relies on its members to do their own part. For those of us who sometimes wonder if it's really worth recycling that extra bottle to lighten our impact on the planet, the bottom line is that our actions matter, even if we don't see how.

[5] A **server** is a part of a computer network that does a particular task such as maintaining an index of files.
[6] If something is **weighted**, it is given more value according to how important it is.

Adapted from "Swarm Theory," by Peter Miller: National Geographic Magazine July 2007

 Peter Miller has worked as a reporter for *Life* magazine and as a senior editor at *National Geographic*. He is the author of the best-selling book *The Smart Swarm: How to Work Efficiently, Communicate Effectively, and Make Better Decisions Using the Secrets of Flocks, Schools, and Colonies.*

UNDERSTANDING THE READING

UNDERSTANDING
MAIN IDEAS

A Note answers to the questions below. Write the paragraph letter(s) in which you find the answers.

1. What is a "smart swarm"? Explain it in your own words.

_____

_____ Paragraph _____

2. How does being part of a large group help animals?

_____

_____ Paragraph _____

3. What are the three key aspects of swarm intelligence?

_____

_____ Paragraph _____

4. How are search engines and online encyclopedias examples of collaboration?

_____

_____ Paragraph _____

UNDERSTANDING
PURPOSE

B Match each section of the reading to its main purpose. Write the paragraph letters.

B–C	D–N	O–Q	R	T–U	V

1. _____ to give examples of human activities and organizations that use swarm intelligence

2. _____ to summarize the three key ingredients of swarm intelligence

3. _____ to connect the topic with our everyday decisions and actions

4. _____ to show the purpose of swarm behavior for animals

5. _____ to give an example of swarm intelligence that most people are familiar with

6. _____ to describe technology applications that mimic swarm behavior

CRITICAL THINKING:
GUESSING MEANING
FROM CONTEXT

C Find and underline the following expressions in the reading passage. Use the context to match each expression with its definition.

1. _____ **add up to** (paragraph A)
2. _____ **set in motion** (paragraph D)
3. _____ **blazing the trail** (paragraph F)
4. _____ **by trial and error** (paragraph F)
5. _____ **flush out** (paragraph M)
6. _____ **a matter of life or death** (paragraph O)
7. _____ **the bottom line** (paragraph V)

a. to force people or animals to leave a place where they are hiding

b. the essential idea

c. to start; to initiate an action

d. to equal

e. something extremely important

f. doing something for the first time as an example for others

g. trying out different methods

D Complete the concept map with information from paragraphs B–N.

Swarm Intelligence

Example in the Animal World

- Flocks of [1]_____ are an example of swarm intelligence.
- **Characteristics:**
  (1) There's no [2]_____.
  (2) They watch and follow [3]_____.

Human Applications

Entertainment

- Used to create rules for computer graphics e.g., boids.
- **Rules:** (1) avoid crowding, (2) [4]_____,
  (3) [5]_____

Robot Teams

- **Advantages:** Robot teams respond more effectively than individual robots. If one breaks down, another can [6]_____.
- **Rules:** Everything is distributed; they use [7]_____; they're anonymous.
- **Examples:** [8]_____ for moving things; [9]_____ to climb walls and manipulate things; [10]_____ to fly around and collect [11]_____.
- **Military uses:** Centibots could locate terrorists or [12]_____; help people in disasters, such as [13]_____; find and analyze dangerous [14]_____ after a chemical spill.

> **CRITICAL THINKING** Writers often quote experts to support their main ideas. It's important to **evaluate** the source of each quote. When you read a quote, ask yourself: What are the credentials of the person being quoted? What is his or her background or affiliation? How is his or her experience or expertise relevant to the topic? Then ask yourself how the quotes support the writer's main ideas.

CRITICAL THINKING:
EVALUATING SOURCES

E Find the following quotes in the reading. Note the paragraph where you find each one.

1. _____ "In biology, … you need all three of those ideas."

2. _____ "It's much harder for a predator … to avoid being spotted by one ….

   News that a predator is approaching spreads quickly … that something's going on."

3. _____ "It's now possible … in ways we never imagined a few decades ago ….

   No single person … we know far more than we've been able to tap so far."

Now discuss answers to the questions below with a partner.

1. What are the credentials of the people being quoted? How is their experience or expertise relevant to the topic?

2. What main ideas do the quotes support? Match each quote (1–3) with one of the following ideas.

   a. _____ Swarm behavior is a survival strategy.

   b. _____ Modern technology has facilitated swarm intelligence among humans.

   c. _____ Decentralization is a key aspect of swarm intelligence.

CRITICAL THINKING:
ANALYZING AND
APPLYING

F Look again at paragraph V. Note answers to the questions below. Then discuss with a partner.

1. According to the author, for crowd intelligence to work, how should the individuals behave?

   _____

   _____

2. What example of an everyday activity does the author give to illustrate this point?

   _____

   _____

3. What "smart swarms" are you a part of? Make a list.

   _____

   _____

DEVELOPING READING SKILLS

READING SKILL Understanding Complex Sentences

It's important for overall reading comprehension to be able to understand complex sentences. One way to do this is to break down complex sentences into smaller parts. Follow these steps:

1. Identify the main clause and any dependent clauses in the sentence.

main clause	dependent clause	main clause

A team of robots that could coordinate its actions like a flock of birds could offer significant advantages over a solitary robot.

2. Identify the subject, verb, and object in the main clause.

subject	verb	object

A team of robots … could offer significant advantages over a solitary robot.

3. Look back at the dependent clauses for any extra information to help you understand the full sentence.

A Use the steps above to break down the following complex sentences. Then answer the questions.

UNDERSTANDING COMPLEX SENTENCES

1. Taking this idea one step further, computer scientist Marco Dorigo's group in Brussels is leading a European effort to create a "swarmanoid," a group of cooperating robots with complementary abilities.

   a. What is Dorigo's group doing? _____

   b. What is a swarmanoid? _____

2. The result, when set in motion on a computer screen, was a convincing simulation of flocking, including lifelike and unpredictable movements.

   a. What was the result? _____

   b. What did the simulation include? _____

3. Zipping down the main hallway, the foot-long (30 cm) red robots pivoted this way and that on their three wheels, resembling a group of large insects.

   a. What was zipping down the main hallway? _____

   b. What did they look like? _____

B Scan paragraphs K, M, U, and V to find more examples of complex sentences. When you find them, underline the subjects and circle the main verbs.

APPLYING

Fire ants form a floating raft on the surface of water.

ANT TEAMWORK

BEFORE VIEWING

DISCUSSION **A** What types of group behavior have you seen ants display? Discuss with a partner.

_____

_____

LEARNING ABOUT THE TOPIC **B** Read the information. Then answer the questions.

Ants are known to be amazing collaborators—they work together to build homes, find food, and fight off their enemies. But perhaps one of the most astounding examples of ant teamwork is the ingenious way that fire ants are able to cope with flooding. If their home is flooded, fire ants will join themselves together, gripping tight with their jaws and legs, to form a pizza-like shape that can float on water like a raft. Some rafts can last up to three weeks, and it is thought that some of the bigger structures may have more than 100,000 ants. But if you see one, stay well clear. Fire ants have a painful sting and are thought to be even more aggressive than usual when in a raft formation.

1. Why do fire ants create rafts? How do they do it?

_____

2. How is this behavior an example of swarm intelligence?

_____

C Read these extracts from the video. Match the correct form of each **bold** word to its definition.

VOCABULARY IN CONTEXT

> "By identifying individuals, Nigel can tell who collects information, how they communicate it, and how a **consensus** is reached."
>
> "The ants begin **inspecting** their two options. Every time an individual enters or exits the potential nests, a laser beam records its passing."
>
> "They do a very special form of **recruitment** called tandem running. That's when one ant literally leads just a single other nest mate."

1. _____ (n) the process of getting individuals to join an organization, a group, or an activity

2. _____ (n) an agreement made by all members of a group

3. _____ (v) to look carefully at something to make a judgment about it

WHILE VIEWING

A ▶ Watch the video. Complete the sentences below.

UNDERSTANDING MAIN IDEAS

a. The purpose of the experiment is to _____.

b. In the experiment, the ants need to _____.

c. It takes the ants around _____ to make a successful choice.

B ▶ Watch the video again. Note answers to the question below.

UNDERSTANDING A PROCESS

1. Why were microchips attached to the ants?

   _____

2. How does an individual ant report its findings?

   _____

3. What is "tandem running"?

   _____

AFTER VIEWING

A Dr. Franks says that "tandem-running qualifies as teaching." How do you think scientists decide if an action in the animal world qualifies as teaching? Discuss your ideas with a partner.

REACTING TO THE VIDEO

B Imagine the employees in a company have to agree on a new office space. What would their process be? How would it compare with the ants' process? Discuss your ideas in a small group.

CRITICAL THINKING: SYNTHESIZING

Writing

EXPLORING WRITTEN ENGLISH

LANGUAGE FOR WRITING Avoiding Plagiarism (I)—Paraphrasing

When you write a summary, it's important to paraphrase; that is, to use your own words. One method is to use synonyms for words that are in the original text.

~~Crowds~~ tend to be ~~wise~~ only if ~~individual~~ members ~~act responsibly~~ and make their own ~~decisions~~.

| | | | | |
| Groups | intelligent | single | behave appropriately | choices |

If you don't know a synonym for a word, you can use a thesaurus. However, it's important to make sure the synonym you choose matches the word in the context of your sentence. For example, *knowledgeable*, and *informed* are both synonyms for *wise*, but only *intelligent* works well in the context of the sentence above.

In addition to using synonyms, you can also change sentence structure and use different parts of speech. For example:

Only when single members behave appropriately and make their own choices, do groups tend to be intelligent.

A Choose the best synonym for each underlined word.

1. If one member of the group were to <u>break down</u>, others could take its place.

   a. explain   b. stop working   c. destroy

2. The robot <u>froze</u>, sending an image to its human supervisor.

   a. stopped   b. suspended   c. solidified

3. The research team <u>conducting</u> the experiment declared the run a success.

   a. behaving   b. passing through   c. performing

APPLYING **B** Find a synonym for one other word or phrase in each of the sentences in exercise **A**. Then rewrite each sentence, changing the sentence structure and using different parts of speech when possible.

1. _____

   _____

2. _____

   _____

3. _____

   _____

WRITING SKILL Writing a Summary

When you write a summary, you report—in your own words—only the most important information from a passage in the same order that it is given in the original. A summary is shorter than the original passage. Follow these steps to summarize successfully.

1. Read the passage once. As you read, underline only the most important information. Then, without looking at it, write notes about the passage.

2. Reread the passage, comparing your notes against it to check your understanding. Correct any incorrect notes.

3. Use your notes to write a summary. Remember that the introductory statement in a summary is not quite the same as the thesis statement in a regular essay. The introductory statement is more like a restatement of the original author's main idea.

4. Compare your summary with the original. Make sure that your summary expresses the same meaning as the original.

5. Check your sentence structures and word choices. If your summary is very similar to the original, change your sentence structures and replace some content words (e.g., key nouns or noun phrases) with synonyms.

C Read the summaries of paragraph B of "The Smart Swarm." Answer the questions about the summaries below. With a partner, decide which summary is more successful. Why do you think so?

EVALUATING SUMMARIES

A According to Peter Miller, smart swarms are groups of individuals who react to their surroundings and each other and work together in order to make collective decisions. He explains that a group of birds is one example of a smart swarm. They fly to a location in a group, then fly away again in a coordinated manner.

B According to Peter Miller, a smart swarm is a group of people who work together as a group to deal with complex, uncertain things as well as change. He gives birds as an example of this. He watches flocks of pigeons in a park in Washington, D.C., and notices the way that birds move together as a group. They fly over cars and trees together and land at the same time on the ledges of buildings around the park. Then something disturbs them, and they take off again in a synchronized manner.

	A	B
1. Does the summary express the same meaning as the original?		
2. Does the summary include only important information from the original?		
3. Are the word choices different from those in the original?		
4. Are the sentence structures different from the structures in the original?		
5. Is the summary shorter than the original?		

WRITING TASK

GOAL You are going to write a summary essay on the following topic:

Write a summary of "The Smart Swarm."

BRAINSTORMING **A** Without looking back at the reading passage in this unit, write down the main ideas and details that you can remember. Share your ideas with a partner.

Author's main idea; what is one example of smart swarms?	
How can understanding smart swarms affect technology?	
How does swarm intelligence help animals?	
How do humans use swarm intelligence?	
What do individuals in human "smart swarms" have to do?	

TAKING NOTES **B** Look again at the reading passage in this unit. Compare the information with your notes from exercise **A** to check your understanding. Make any necessary corrections or additions.

VOCABULARY FOR WRITING **C** The words below can be useful when writing a summary. You can use these verbs to introduce an author's idea.

analyzes	argues	believes	calls for	claims
demands	discusses	disputes	examines	explains
explores	focuses on	mentions	provides	questions
recommends	reports	suggests	urges	wonders

Circle the correct word to complete the sentences below. Use a dictionary to help.

1. The writer **suggests** / **urges** us all to take immediate action on this critical issue.

2. Kolbert **discusses** / **calls for** the causes of deforestation in great depth.

3. The author **argues** / **disputes** some of the ideas put forward by other historians.

4. There has been decades of concern for tigers, but Alexander **mentions** / **questions** whether any progress has been made at all.

5. The writer **claims** / **provides** plentiful evidence to support her views on the topic.

D Follow the steps to make notes for your essay.

Step 1 Complete the introductory statement in the outline.

Step 2 Write the main questions that the author answers. Use these to organize the main points of your summary.

Step 3 For each body paragraph, write two or three examples or details that support your topic sentence.

Step 4 As a conclusion, write down Peter Miller's ideas for what he believes individuals in human "smart swarms" need to do.

OUTLINE

Introduction:

In "The Smart Swarm," author Peter Miller _____

_____

Body paragraph 1: What is a smart swarm?

Topic sentence: _____

_____

Details: _____

_____

_____

Body paragraph 2: _____?

Topic sentence: _____

_____

Details: _____

_____

_____

Body paragraph 3: _____?

Topic sentence: _____

Details: _____

_____

_____

Notes for conclusion: _____

_____

E Use the information in your outline to write a first draft of your essay.

REVISING PRACTICE

The draft below is a model of a summary essay. It summarizes the article "A Cry for the Tiger" from Unit 2. Follow the steps to create a better second draft.

Fix the following problems (1–3) with the essay.

1. Which two body paragraphs are in the wrong order?

2. Delete an unimportant detail in paragraph C.

3. Choose the best final sentence for the conclusion.

    a. According to the author, animal conservationists hope to work together to double the number of wild tigers in India within the next few years.

    b. The author calls on tiger conservationists to work extremely hard and to remain determined in order to save the tiger from extinction.

    c. The author believes that we need to act quickly because tiger populations are declining fast due to poaching and attacks by villagers.

A

In the article "A Cry for the Tiger," author Caroline Alexander argues that the beautiful and regal tiger is worth protecting, and that we need to find effective ways to keep it from disappearing.

B

According to Alexander, the tiger faces several threats. First, tigers are losing habitat because of quickly growing human populations. Second, this rapid population growth leads to poaching. Third, tiger parts are valuable in the black market. Finally, one of the least-discussed threats is the fact that strategies to protect tigers have been ineffective. In fact, experts estimated that there were about 8,000 tigers in the wild in the early 1980s. Now, decades later, there are fewer than 4,000.

C

Alexander reports that the countries that have wild tigers want to protect the animals, but it's difficult to find an effective solution. Right now, there are many tiger-conservation programs, and a lot of money is spent on tiger protection. For example, the Save the Tiger Fund gave more than $17 million in grants for tiger protection between 1995 and 2009. However, each program focuses on different strategies. Alexander argues that we need to spend our money and energy on four specific issues in order to protect tigers in the long run: core breeding populations, tiger reserves, wildlife corridors, and safety from poaching and killing. She believes that we have to prioritize these four issues, especially the protection of a core breeding population, and not spend money on things like eco-development and social programs.

D

Alexander explains that India is home to about 50 percent of the wild tiger population, and about one-third of these tigers live outside tiger reserves. In order for these tigers to survive in the wild, we need to ensure there are protected corridors of land between the safe areas. This way, the tigers outside of reserves can move freely without being killed by humans. Also, these corridors will allow tigers to mate and reproduce with tigers that live in different areas, resulting in greater genetic diversity. These corridors are necessary, but Alexander wonders if they are possible. Future infrastructure projects may make the creation of the corridors very difficult.

E

Is it possible not only to protect the remaining tigers but also to increase the wild tiger population? According to Alexander, most authorities believe that it is possible. But it won't be an easy fight. _____

F Now use the questions below to revise your essay.   REVISED DRAFT

- ☐ Have you paraphrased the language the author uses?
- ☐ Does your summary contain an introductory statement?
- ☐ Have you included any unnecessary details?
- ☐ Are your paragraphs in the correct order?
- ☐ Does your summary include the author's conclusion?

There are estimated to be fewer than 600 Siberian tigers left in the wild.

EDITING PRACTICE

Read the information below.

When you use synonyms, remember to make sure your synonym:
- has the same meaning as the original word.
- fits in the context of the sentence.

Find and correct one mistake with the underlined synonyms in each of the paraphrases below.

1. Original: What enables a <u>school</u> of herring to coordinate its movements so <u>precisely</u> it can change direction <u>in a flash</u> … ?

   Paraphrase: What enables a <u>group</u> of herring to coordinate its movements so <u>accurately</u> it can change direction <u>continuously</u> … ?

2. Original: <u>Within</u> five years, Kumar hopes to put a <u>networked</u> team of robotic vehicles <u>in the field</u>.

   Paraphrase: <u>In less than</u> five years, Kumar hopes to put a <u>connected</u> team of robotic vehicles <u>on the pitch</u>.

3. Original: When a predator <u>strikes</u> a school of fish, the group is capable of <u>scattering</u> in patterns that make it almost impossible to <u>track</u> any individual.

   Paraphrase: When a predator <u>attacks</u> a school of fish, the group is capable of <u>throwing</u> in patterns that make it almost impossible to <u>follow</u> any individual.

FINAL DRAFT   **G**   Follow the steps to write a final draft.

1. Check your revised draft for mistakes with paraphrasing.

2. Now use the checklist on page 248 to write a final draft. Make any other necessary changes.

UNIT REVIEW

Answer the following questions.

1. What are two examples of how humans can use swarm behavior?

   _____

   _____

2. What are two ways that ants collaborate?

   _____

   _____

3. Why is it important to paraphrase?

   _____

   _____

4. Do you remember the meanings of these words? Check (✓) the ones you know. Look back at the unit and review the ones you don't know.

   ☐ accomplish   ☐ emergent AWL
   ☐ capability AWL   ☐ manipulate AWL
   ☐ collectively   ☐ precisely AWL
   ☐ complementary AWL   ☐ realistically
   ☐ complex AWL   ☐ relevant AWL
   ☐ coordinate AWL   ☐ simulation
   ☐ declare   ☐ unpredictable AWL
   ☐ defense

LANGUAGE AND CULTURE 6

Students study Chinese calligraphy at a high school in Oxford, England.

ACADEMIC SKILLS

READING Understanding verbal phrases
WRITING Writing an opinion essay
GRAMMAR Adding information with verbal phrases
CRITICAL THINKING Inferring an author's attitude

THINK AND DISCUSS

1 What are some benefits of being able to use a second or foreign language?
2 What do you think is the most difficult thing about learning a new language?

A Look at the information on these pages and answer the questions.

1. Who is the most translated author in the world?

2. Who is the most translated author whose original language was not English?

3. Have you read a book by any of the authors on the list?

B Match the correct form of the words in blue to their definitions.

_____ (adj) large in amount or degree

_____ (v) to make someone very interested

_____ (adj) many; several

Danielle Steel
3,628

Charles Perrault
1,401

Stephen King
3,357

WRITERS OF THE WORLD

Jules Verne
4,751
Jules Verne's (1828–1905) most famous works include *Journey to the Center of the Earth*, *Twenty Thousand Leagues Under the Sea*, and *Around the World in Eighty Days*.

Oscar Wilde
1,788

The names on this page are some of the most translated authors in the world. The works of each writer on the list have been translated into **multiple** languages and have **captivated** generation after generation of readers from around the globe. Number one on the list is Agatha Christie, who produced a **substantial** number of works during an incredibly successful career.

Astrid Lindgren
2,271

Franz Kafka
1,494

Barbara Cartland
3,652

KEY

Size of last name corresponds to the number of translations (listed below name).

Number of translations refers to the total number of each author's translated publications.

Color indicates language of original publication.

■ English   ■ German   ■ French

■ Russian   ■ Danish

■ Swedish   ■ Spanish

Charles Dickens
2,112

Alexandre Dumas
2,540

Nora Roberts
2,597

Rudyard Kipling
1,424

Anton Chekhov
1,477

Hans Christian
Andersen
3,520

Hans Christian Andersen (1805–1875) is best known for his fairy tales such as *The Little Mermaid*, and *The Ugly Duckling*. One collection of his stories, *Andersen's Fairy Tales*, has been translated into over 150 languages.

Robert Louis
Stevenson
2,041

Hermann
Hesse
1,523

Mary Higgins
Clark
1,485

René
Goscinny
2,234

Roald
Dahl
1,398

Rudolf
Steiner
1,869

William
Shakespeare
4,296

J.R.R.
Tolkien
1,459

Isaac
Asimov
2,159

Mark
Twain
2,431

Fyodor
Dostoevsky
2,342

Agatha
Christie
7,236

Agatha Christie (1890–1976) is the world's most translated author. During a long career, Christie wrote 73 novels, 16 plays, and also published a large number of short story collections. Her work has been translated into more than 100 different languages.

Edgar Allan
Poe
1,437

Georges
Simenon
2,315

Grimm
Brothers
2,977

Jack
London
2,182

Honoré de
Balzac
1,590

Ernest
Hemingway
1,570

Johann Wolfgang von
Goethe
1,399

Arthur Conan
Doyle
2,496

Leo
Tolstoy
2,178

Enid
Blyton
3,924

Gabriel
García Márquez
1,396

Source: UNESCO Translationum

Reading

PREPARING TO READ

A The words in blue below are used in the reading passage. Complete the definitions.

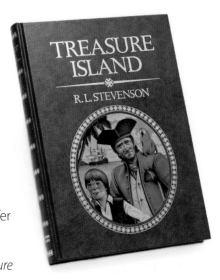

I can't **definitively** say which Robert Louis Stevenson book is my favorite. He wrote so many great stories.

As a child, I had an **irresistible** desire to pick up a book and start reading.

Reading *Treasure Island* again made me feel really **nostalgic** about my childhood.

In *Treasure Island*, a main character named Jim Hawkins discovers a **cryptic** treasure map.

I don't enjoy books with complicated plots. I prefer something a little more **straightforward**.

Long John Silver is an **integral** character in *Treasure Island*.

1. If something (e.g., a message) is _____, it contains a hidden meaning or is difficult to understand.

2. If you describe something as "_____," you approve of it because it is easy to do or understand.

3. If you do something _____, it is done in a way that provides a firm conclusion.

4. When you feel _____, you think about the past in a positive way.

5. If you describe something as "_____," you mean that it is so good or attractive that you cannot stop yourself from liking it or wanting it.

6. Something that is a(n) _____ part of something is an essential part of that thing.

B Complete the sentences with the words in the box. Use a dictionary to help you.

excluded	simultaneously	on the contrary
monotonous	evidently	metaphor

1. You use "_____" when you have just said or implied that something is not true and you are going to say that the opposite is true.

2. Something that is _____ is very boring because it has a regular, repeated pattern that never changes.

3. If two events occur _____, they happen at the same time.

4. If someone is _____ from a place or an activity, that person is prevented from entering it or joining it.

5. If something is _____ true, there is proof that it is true.

6. A(n) _____ is a way of describing something by referring to another thing with similar characteristics.

C Note answers to the questions below. Then discuss with a partner.

1. What are some of the benefits of speaking **multiple** languages?

_____

_____

2. Is it a good idea to learn two languages **simultaneously**? Why or why not?

_____

_____

D Discuss your answers to this question in small groups: What are some different ways to learn new words or phrases in a foreign language? Note your ideas below.

_____studying song lyrics_____

_____

_____

E Read the first and last paragraphs of the reading passage on the following pages. What kind of reading is this? Circle your answer and check your prediction as you read the rest of the passage.

a. a book review
b. a personal essay
c. a short fiction story

THE SECRET LANGUAGE

by Daisy Zamora

"I was 14 years old when I went to the States for the first time—the same age as my grandmother Ilse when she watched New Orleans fade into the distance from the deck of a steamship."

> Language can be a barrier—but also a window through which we experience new visions of the world.

🎧 2.1

The first words I heard in English were from my grandmother Ilse Gamez, who I remember as a magical presence in my childhood. Everything about her seemed legendary to me. Among the stories she used to tell, my favorites were about her life in New Orleans, where she and her family arrived from Europe and where she spent her childhood until she was 14, when they set sail again, bound for Nicaragua, fulfilling her parents' wish to return definitively to their country of origin. Her stories of New Orleans were filled with references and names in English (frequently also in French), and those mysterious words, so different from the ones I heard in everyday speech, produced in me an irresistible fascination. They sounded like strange music, an exotic melody coming from faraway fantastic places where life had an agitation,[1] a rhythm, an acceleration[2] unknown and unheard of in the peaceful world I shared with my parents, sisters, and brothers. We were all part of an enormous family that included grandparents, great-aunts, great-uncles, uncles, aunts, and first cousins, as well as a second and third level of blood relatives, followed immediately by all the other people in the category of relatives included in the family universe and its state of perpetual expansion.

The English I heard from my grandmother Ilse had nothing to do with the English I was taught in kindergarten through songs teaching us to count from one to ten, or the language that appeared in the English textbooks we studied in the second and third grade of primary school: "See Dick. See Jane. See Spot. See Puff. See Spot run. See Puff jump." For me, that English lacked charm, instead sounding like the noise of my shoes crunching in the gravel of the schoolyard during recess. But that other English, the one my grandmother and her sisters spoke, possessed multiple and varied registers[3] that always amazed me. Sometimes it sounded like the trill of a bird, light and crystalline, and at other times flowed in dense, thick amber[4] like honey. It would rise in high notes with the lonely, nostalgic sound of a flute, or swirl in a whirlpool like the frenzied crowds I imagined rushing around the streets of a big metropolis . . .

Before long, my ears began to discern another way of speaking the language. It was not the cryptic and fantastic English full of attractions and mystery that I loved to listen to, nor the tiresome, repetitious one that sounded like a cart struggling over cobbled streets. No, this other English expressed things in a different way that was not enigmatic[5] and seductive, nor dumb and monotonous, but dramatic and direct: whatever the characters said, happened simultaneously. That is to say, a word was an act; words and action occurred at the same time. An activity was named at the very moment it took place. For example, a character that was evidently crying would say: "I'm crying." Another one, obviously hiding something, would declare: "I'll hide this!"

[1] If someone is in a state of **agitation**, he or she is very worried or upset.
[2] An **acceleration** is an increase in speed.
[3] **Register** refers to the range of musical sounds that a voice or a musical instrument can make.
[4] **Amber** is a hard yellowish substance that is often used in jewelry.
[5] Someone or something that is **enigmatic** is mysterious and difficult to understand.

It was the English I started to learn from cartoons on television, where the characters expressed thoughts, emotions, and feelings in a **straightforward** way: "Out! Help! Stop it! Don't go away! I'll be back! Let's go!" I learned phrases and words that communicated necessity in a fast, precise manner. The language of cartoons also introduced me to **metaphors**. The first time I heard characters in a downpour shouting their heads off with the phrase "The sky is falling, the sky is falling!" I believed it was the proper way to say in English, "It's a downpour," or "It's raining very hard."

I had no choice but to learn yet another kind of English from cowboy movies, because my cousins constantly used it in their games. Also, in a mechanical way, I learned by heart the English names for all the plays in baseball, the most popular sport in Nicaragua.

Gradually, the English that was so dull to me in the first grades of school expanded and deepened, with readings transforming it into a beautiful language that kept growing inside, becoming more and more a part of my consciousness, invading my thoughts and appearing in my dreams. Understanding the language and speaking it in a natural way became **integral** to my being, my way of appreciating literature, especially poetry, and enjoying the lyrics of my favorite songs, which I was able to repeat perfectly.

Literature classes were my favorite. To act as a character in any of Shakespeare's plays, or to read an O. Henry short story out loud to my classmates, or a chapter of Robert Louis Stevenson's *Treasure Island,* or a sonnet[6] by Elizabeth Barrett Browning, brightened my day. At the school library, I discovered, among other authors, Walt Whitman, Emily Dickinson, and Edna St. Vincent Millay, then Carl Sandburg and William Carlos Williams. Further along, I encountered William Blake, the sisters Brontë, Jane Austen, and Ernest Hemingway. Years later, while at university, I read the Americans William Faulkner, Ezra Pound, and Gertrude Stein, and the Irish authors William Butler Yeats and James Joyce.

[6] A **sonnet** is a special type of poem with 14 lines and regular rhymes.

Along with my intense reading, I also became a music lover and put together a rather **substantial** collection of Frank Sinatra and Beatles records—my favorites, although my interests included many other groups and singers in English. From that deep relationship with the language, I wound up with what I considered a broad and complex knowledge of English, the sounds of which **captivated** me in the first years of life.

But my true encounter with living English (that is, the one spoken in everyday life) happened in the United States, where I went to spend my school vacations in Middletown, Connecticut. My first impression of the country was completely idyllic. My aunt and uncle's house, where I would stay for three months, was a beautiful and comfortable three-story building, an old New England manor with a gorgeous garden out back, an orchard, a stable with horses, and a pond full of trout. A dense wood of birch and a variety of pine and spruce trees, crisscrossed by narrow paths dotted with wildflowers, went around the edge of that peaceful pond in a landscape that seemed like it was lifted from a fairy tale. Those vacations are part of the happy memories of my life because I also had the unforgettable experience of going to New York City for the first time and visiting the 1964 World's Fair. However, what is most deeply imprinted in my memory of that first visit to the United States is the shock I received from the language I had believed I understood and spoke correctly.

Almost immediately, I realized that my English, that is, the English through which I expressed myself, sounded strange to everybody. My cousins, not to mention their friends, listened to me with surprise or mocking looks. In turn, their English was almost unintelligible to me because they spoke, of course, in teenage slang. When one of my cousins couldn't stand it anymore, she told me that I was a weirdo, that I spoke like a philosopher, some sort of Socrates or something, and asked me to make an effort to try to talk like normal people so I could make some friends. She didn't have a clue about the extreme anguish I was going through trying to understand what was being

The 1964 New York World's Fair was a showcase of mid-20th-century American culture.

said around me, trying to decipher everything I misunderstood, assuming one thing for another. Desolate, I thought about the abundant literature I had read up to then, and the songs I had worked so hard to memorize. It was all worthless for learning to speak practical English that would help me establish bonds with boys and girls my own age. **On the contrary**, the vocabulary I learned from books, especially from the poetry that taught me to love the language, had no place in the everyday speech of my contemporaries.

L

To be accepted by everybody, I started paying extreme attention to how I expressed myself and to the words I chose. I anxiously searched for ways to adapt my way of speaking, imitating what I heard from others, so I wouldn't be **excluded** from their conversations or activities. I understood that if I didn't do that, I would be left on the fringes of the main current, the mainstream where all U.S. teenagers lived, with space only for themselves. The barrier was not easy to cross, and when I couldn't do it, my consolation was to take

K

refuge in the library of the house, where I read, during that first vacation, an English translation of Fyodor Dostoevsky's *Crime and Punishment*.

I was 14 years old when I went to the States for the first time—the same age as my grandmother Ilse when she watched New Orleans fade into the distance from the deck of a steamship—and ever since then I've understood what it means to live in direct contact with a language through the people who speak it, through their culture, and through their vision of the world.

Adapted from "The Secret Language" by Daisy Zamora, reprinted with permission of the National Geographic Society from the book How I Learned English.

Daisy Zamora is one of Latin America's leading contemporary poets. She has been named Writer of the Year by the National Association of Artists in Nicaragua.

UNDERSTANDING THE READING

A In the reading passage, Zamora describes the different ways she experienced English. Match the correct paragraph letter(s) to each method (1–6).

A–B	B	C–E	F–G	H	I–J

1. ____ by reading literature

2. ____ by encountering native speakers in the United States (her cousins)

3. ____ as a child, from her family (grandmother)

4. ____ from TV and movies

5. ____ from her school

6. ____ by listening to music

B How does Zamora describe the English she was exposed to? Match the sentence halves.

1. Her grandmother's English ____   a. was impossible to understand.

2. The English in primary school ____   b. contained mysterious words.

3. The English in cartoons ____   c. communicated in a fast, precise manner.

4. The English of literature ____   d. lacked charm.

5. The English of her cousins ____   e. brightened her day.

> **CRITICAL THINKING**   An author's use of language can help us understand his or her **attitude** toward, or feelings about, a subject. For example, in personal essays or narratives, writers often use figurative or sensory language to convey their feelings now or in the past. When Zamora describes her grandmother as "a magical presence in my childhood," we can infer that she had—and probably still has—a warm and loving feeling toward her grandmother, even though she doesn't state that explicitly.

C Note answers to the questions (1–4) . Then discuss with a partner.

1. What adjectives does Zamora use to describe her grandmother's English? What does she compare it to? What can we tell about her feelings about this language?

_____

_____

_____

2. What does Zamora tell us about the English she learned at school? What two sounds does she compare it to? What can we infer about her feelings about this type of language?

_____

_____

_____

3. What adjectives and phrases does Zamora use to describe her childhood vacation home in Connecticut? What does she compare the landscape to? What can we infer about her feelings toward that place today?

_____

_____

_____

4. How does Zamora describe her experience of speaking with teenagers in the United States? Who does Zamora's cousin compare her to? What can we infer about how Zamora felt at that time?

_____

_____

_____

D Find and underline the following phrases in the reading passage. Use the context to help you identify the meaning of each phrase. Then match each phrase with its definition.

CRITICAL THINKING: GUESSING MEANING FROM CONTEXT

1. _____ Paragraph A: **unheard of**
2. _____ Paragraph A: **perpetual**
3. _____ Paragraph B: **gravel**
4. _____ Paragraph D: **precise**
5. _____ Paragraph J: **not to mention**
6. _____ Paragraph J: **had no place**
7. _____ Paragraph J: **bonds**
8. _____ Paragraph K: **on the fringes of the main current**

a. connections

b. small stones used to make outdoor surfaces

c. left out or excluded from the most popular group

d. never ending

e. exact

f. nonexistent

g. plus; in addition

h. didn't belong

E In the reading passage, author Daisy Zamora uses a range of formal and informal expressions. Find the following informal words and expressions in the reading passage. Study their contexts. Then match each one with the more formal equivalent, one that you would use in academic writing. Use a dictionary to help you.

Informal phrases

1. __C__ shout your head off

2. ____ dumb

3. ____ had nothing to do with

4. ____ didn't have a clue

5. ____ weirdo

6. ____ wound up with

Formal equivalent

a. a strange person

b. unintelligent

c. shout very loudly

d. eventually had

e. knew nothing

f. was not related to

F The sentences (1–6) all contain an informal word or phrase in **bold**. Replace each one with a more formal equivalent from the box below.

acceptable	a large number of	currently
highly	it is widely accepted	received

1. Author Stephen King has written **lots of** horror novels.

2. H. G. Wells's *War of the Worlds* had a **very** significant impact on science fiction writing.

3. **Everyone knows** that Shakespeare was one of the greatest writers in history.

4. **Nowadays**, J. K. Rowling is one of the most famous authors in the world.

5. In 2017, George Saunders **got** the Man Booker Prize for his novel *Lincoln in the Bardo*.

6. In many literature examinations, a score of around 60 percent is considered **OK**.

G Read the following extracts from the reading passage in Unit 5. Some of the formal expressions from the original passage have been replaced with informal equivalents (in **bold**). What do you think the original phrases were? Look back at the reading passage to check your ideas.

1. Today [Craig Reynolds] works at Sony doing research for games, **like** an algorithm that simulates … interacting birds, fish, or people. (Paragraph E)

   _____

2. The military **really wants** to acquire similar capabilities. (Paragraph J)

   _____

3. The Internet is already using a form of swarm intelligence. **Think about** the way Google uses group smarts to find what you're looking for. (Paragraph T)

   _____

DEVELOPING READING SKILLS

READING SKILL Understanding Verbal Phrases

Verbals are forms of verbs that are used as other parts of speech.
The three kinds of verbals are:

- participles (words formed from verbs and used as adjectives, usually ending in **-ing** or **-ed**)

  Speaking slowly, *she gave me directions to the train station.* =
  She spoke slowly. She gave me directions to the train station.

- gerunds (**-ing** verbs used as nouns)

  Reading literature *gave Zamora a deeper understanding of English.* =
  Zamora read literature. It gave her a deeper understanding of English.

- infinitives (base forms of verbs starting with **to**)

  To learn Japanese quickly, *I didn't allow myself to speak English for a month.* =
  I wanted to learn Japanese quickly. I didn't allow myself to speak English for a month.

A verbal phrase is a phrase that begins with a verbal. Writers often use verbal phrases to vary their sentence patterns and to combine short sentences. Verbal phrases are sometimes separated from the rest of the sentence with commas.

A Underline the verbal phrases in the following sentences.

1. I had a whole conversation in Spanish, surprised that I was able to communicate at all.
2. Learning Hungarian was the most difficult thing I did when I was an undergraduate.
3. To get familiar with Japanese pronunciation, I watched a lot of Japanese TV shows.
4. Being unable to communicate with her teenage cousins, Zamora decided to improve her way of speaking.
5. Determined to sound like a native speaker, I took an online conversation class.

IDENTIFYING VERBAL
PHRASES

B Underline the verbal phrases in these excerpts (some have more than one). Note answers to the questions and share your ideas with a partner.

ANALYZING

Example: For me, that English lacked charm, instead <u>sounding like the noise of my shoes crunching in the gravel of the schoolyard during recess</u>.

What does the verbal phrase describe? _____ *the type of English* _____

1. The first time I heard characters in a downpour shouting their heads off with the phrase "The sky is falling, the sky is falling!"

   Who does the verbal phrase describe? _____

2. Understanding the language and speaking it in a natural way became integral to my being …

   What is the main verb in this sentence? Does the verbal phrase function as the subject or the object of the sentence?

   _____

3. To be accepted by everybody, I started paying extreme attention to how I expressed myself and to the words I chose.

   What does the verbal phrase do: ask a question, give a reason, or describe a thing?

   _____

Video

CULTURE SHOCK

Two Kenyan men experienced an eye-opening tour of the United States for the show *Warrior Road Trip*.

BEFORE VIEWING

LEARNING ABOUT THE TOPIC

A You are going to watch a clip from a TV series called *Warrior Road Trip*. Read about the show. Then answer the question.

Warrior Road Trip is a TV travel series where two Kenyan men visit the United States for the first time. The stars of the show are Boniface Kandari Parsulan (Boni) and Loyapan Lemarti (Lemarti). Boni is a Maasai warrior from southern Kenya, and Lemarti is a Samburu warrior from northern Kenya. Both the Maasai and Samburu people have retained their traditional way of life. The two groups live in simple villages and rely on raising cattle for their food needs. During their visit, Boni and Lemarti learn about American culture and notice the stark differences between their traditional lifestyles and the lives of people in the United States.

What cultural differences do you think Boni and Lemarti noticed on their trip to the United States? Discuss with a partner and list your ideas.

_____

_____

_____

VOCABULARY IN CONTEXT

B The informal words and phrases in **bold** below are used in the video. Match the correct form of each word or phrase to its definition.

"We're walking through the … park. It's a lot of people sitting around eating, drinking, **chilling**."

"You know, people eat a lot here, people **graze like cows**, man."

"After [a] long flight from Africa, we wanted to get out and **stretch our legs** …"

"René said, 'Hey, let's **grab something** to eat, guys.'"

1. _____ (v) to eat snacks throughout the day in place of full meals

2. _____ (v) to walk around after sitting for a long period of time

3. _____ (v) to get; to pick up quickly

4. _____ (v) to relax

WHILE VIEWING

UNDERSTANDING MAIN IDEAS

A ▶ Watch the video. How many of the things on your list in Before Viewing A were mentioned? What else did Boni and Lemarti find surprising?

_____

_____

_____

UNDERSTANDING DETAILS

B ▶ Watch the video again. Answer the questions.

1. What new words and phrases did Boni and Lemarti pick up from their guide?

_____

_____

2. Why does Lemarti compare an ATM with a goat?

_____

_____

AFTER VIEWING

REACTING TO THE VIDEO

A Note answers to the questions below. Then discuss with a partner.

1. What insights do you have into Boni and Lemarti's culture after seeing their reactions to New York?

_____

_____

2. How were Boni and Lemarti's experiences similar to those of Daisy Zamora?

_____

_____

3. What do you think would surprise Boni and Lemarti about your hometown?

_____

_____

Writing

EXPLORING WRITTEN ENGLISH

VOCABULARY FOR WRITING

A You can use phrases such as *I think*, *I believe*, and *In my opinion* to introduce your opinion. However, varying your phrases can add interest to your writing. Some of the phrases below can introduce personal opinions, and some can introduce general opinions. Write each phrase in the correct column in the chart.

As far as I'm concerned,	It is thought that	Some people say that
In my experience,	. . . is generally considered to be . . .	Speaking for myself,
It is accepted that	Personally, I think	Most would agree that

Personal Opinion	Opinions of People in General

LANGUAGE FOR WRITING Adding Information with Verbal Phrases

You can use a present or past participle verbal phrase to add extra information to a sentence, or to combine two sentences that have the same subject. Look at the examples below.

> Jack apologized to his sister. He was feeling terrible about what he'd done.
> Jack apologized to his sister, feeling terrible about what he'd done.
> present participle

> *Carrie* was published in 1973. It was Stephen King's first novel.
> Published in 1973, *Carrie* was Stephen King's first novel.
> past participle

Verbal phrases can be used at the start, middle, or end of sentences.

> Jack apologized to his sister, feeling terrible about what he'd done.
> Jack, feeling terrible about what he'd done, apologized to his sister.
> Feeling terrible about what he'd done, Jack apologized to his sister.

B Circle the correct word to complete each sentence.

1. He studied hard for his English test, **memorized** / **memorizing** each piece of vocabulary.
2. **Felt** / **Feeling** a little unwell, he decided to take the day off work.
3. He stopped talking, **interrupted** / **interrupting** by the noise in the other room.
4. **Excited** / **Exciting** to see her, the young boy ran quickly to his mother.

C Combine the following pairs of sentences using a verbal phrase.

1. Many students rely solely on online self-study language programs. They are missing out on opportunities to interact with others.

   _____

2. Some language learners tend to drop out in their second year. They are defeated by increasingly complex grammar.

   _____

3. Many language students are able to learn quickly. They are motivated by their teachers' positive feedback.

   _____

4. I picked up Chinese really quickly. I was surprised by the simplicity of the grammar.

   _____

A class of young students in England take lessons in Mandarin.

The first paragraph of an essay—the introductory paragraph—includes the thesis statement and general information about the essay topic. To grab the reader's attention, you can start with a surprising statement, an interesting question, a quotation, or a brief story.

The last, or concluding, paragraph of an essay should give the reader a sense of completeness. The conclusion usually includes a restatement of the thesis, a summary of the main supporting points made in the paper, and/or a final thought about the topic. The final thought can take the form of a provocative question or statement.

ANALYZING **D** Identify the features (a–e) in the following introduction and conclusion. Write the correct letter next to each feature. Share your answers with a partner.

a. summary of the main supporting points

b. interesting quotation/introduction to topic

c. restatement of thesis

d. thesis statement

e. final thought

Essay topic:
The ability to communicate with someone who speaks a different language is the main benefit of learning a second language. To what extent do you agree with this statement?

Introduction:
Nelson Mandela once said, "If you talk to a man in a language he understands, that goes to his head. If you talk to him in his own language, that goes to his heart." In other words, you can only truly communicate with another person if you speak that person's language. While the ability to communicate with someone who speaks a different language is a great benefit of language learning, I believe that studying a second language can improve our lives in other ways.

Conclusion:
There are, therefore, benefits of language learning that are just as important as gaining the ability to communicate with someone who speaks another language. Studying a second language can improve our reading skills and listening skills in our own language. Having better reading and listening skills can make us better students. Studies show that language learning can also improve our memories and our problem-solving skills. These abilities can help us in school, at work, and in life in general. Moreover, scientists have recently discovered that studying a second language can actually change the brain's shape. These changes can help us become better thinkers. However, motivations for language learning vary from person to person. As such, the relevant importance of each benefit stated in this thesis can only really be determined by the individual language learner.

WRITING TASK

> **GOAL** In this lesson, you are going to write an opinion essay on the following topic:
>
> What is the most effective way to learn a second/foreign language?

A Consider the methods of learning a second/foreign language listed below. How effective is each one? Discuss the pros and cons of each method with a partner.

BRAINSTORMING

attending a language school

reading books

watching TV/movies

traveling/living overseas

self-studying online

taking part in a language exchange

B Decide which of the methods you discussed in activity **A** is the most effective. Follow the steps to make notes for your essay.

PLANNING

Step 1 Make notes for your introduction in the outline.

Step 2 Write your thesis statement.

Step 3 For each topic sentence, write one reason why the method is effective.

Step 4 For each body paragraph, note examples or details that support your topic sentence. Include examples of personal experiences where possible.

Step 5 Make notes for your conclusion.

OUTLINE

Introduction: _____

_____

_____

_____

Thesis statement: _____

_____

_____

_____

Body paragraph 1:

Topic sentence: _____

_____

Details: _____

_____

_____

Body paragraph 2:

Topic sentence: _____

Details: _____

_____

_____

Body paragraph 3:

Topic sentence: _____

Details: _____

_____

_____

Conclusion: _____

_____

Restatement of thesis: _____

Final thought: _____

FIRST DRAFT **C** Use the information in your outline to write a first draft of your essay.

REVISING PRACTICE

The following draft is a model of a similar essay to the one you are writing. It is on the following topic:

Reading books aloud to young children is a vital step in developing a child's reading skills. To what extent do you agree with this statement?

Follow the steps to create a better second draft.

1. Write the sentences (a–c) in the correct spaces.

    a. Therefore, understanding the value of reading at a very young age can only benefit children in the future.

    b. Finally, reading skills are developed further when children are challenged.

    c. Author Emilie Buchwald once said, "Children are made readers on the laps of their parents." I agree with her statement.

2. Now fix the following problems (a–c) with the essay.

    a. Fix an error with a verbal phrase in paragraph B.

    b. Fix an error with a verbal phrase in paragraph D.

    c. Delete an unrelated idea in paragraph C.

A

_____C_____ I think that some children very easily begin reading on their own as a result of having been read to by their parents. However, I also believe that it is not always that straightforward, and that the choice of book or story by the parent is a highly important factor. For reading aloud to be truly beneficial to children, the chosen stories must be interesting, relatable, and pose a challenge.

B

When books are interesting, children understand that reading can be exciting and, as a result, they pay attention. Exciting by the events in a story, children have a purpose for listening as someone reads to them—they need to find out what happens next. That purpose can increase reading comprehension. When children begin reading on their own and are given books that they will enjoy, they have a purpose for reading, which will motivate them to try to understand what they're reading.

C

Even books without exciting stories can be interesting if children can connect the books to their own lives. Very young children often struggle to deal with the abstract concepts featured, for example, in fantasy novels. Fantasy novels are much more popular with teenagers. Stories dealing with familiar, everyday experiences and featuring relatable characters are often much easier for children to appreciate. Such stories also give children something to discuss after a book is finished, and also often teach them practical knowledge that they can apply to their own lives.

D

_____b_____ To increase vocabulary, children need to encounter words that they don't know. Confused or puzzled by unfamiliar words, children will push themselves to learn because the words are relevant to the story. When parents or teachers realize that they have just read an unfamiliar word, they should resist explaining the definition right away. By rereading the surrounding sentences slowly, children can be encouraged to use context to guess the meaning of the word, teaches them an important skill they can use throughout their reading lives.

E

When children are encouraged to see books and stories as tools that can excite them and teach them, they are motivated to read. This motivation goes a long way to creating strong readers. Reading aloud interesting, relatable, and challenging stories to children can help build in them a strong desire to read and an understanding of what words have to offer. With the rise of the Internet and social media, reading skills are more important than ever before. _____A_____

D   Now use the questions below to revise your essay.   REVISED DRAFT

☐ Does your introduction provide relevant background information on the topic?
☐ Does your thesis state the main points of the essay?
☐ Do your body paragraphs include enough details to fully explain your ideas?
☐ Did you use verbal phrases correctly?
☐ Do all your sentences relate to the main idea?
☐ Does your concluding paragraph have a summary statement and a final thought?

EDITING PRACTICE

Read the information below. Then find and correct one mistake with verbal phrases in each sentence (1–5). Then write the letter for the type of mistake you find.

When you use verbal phrases, remember:

- verbal phrases modify nouns, pronouns, or whole clauses.
- to separate a verbal phrase from a clause with a comma.
- you don't need a comma if an infinitive verbal phrase comes at the end of a sentence.

Types of mistakes:

a. no noun, pronoun, or clause after the verbal phrase

b. unnecessary comma

c. missing comma

1. _____ Taking classes every night,ᵃ learned a lot quickly.

2. _b_ You can take private lessons, to learn a new language.

3. _c_ Living in a bilingual household I learned Spanish easily.

4. _____ To improve your pronunciation you have to practice.

5. _a_ Watching TV in English, learned a lot of natural language.

FINAL DRAFT **E** Follow the steps to write a final draft.

1. Check your revised draft for mistakes with verbal phrases.

2. Now use the checklist on page 248 to write a final draft. Make any other necessary changes.

UNIT REVIEW

Answer the following questions.

1. What are two things that helped Daisy Zamora increase her understanding of English?

_____

_____

2. What are two things you should include when writing a conclusion to an essay?

_____

_____

3. Write a sentence using a verbal phrase.

_____

_____

4. Do you remember the meanings of these words? Check (✔) the ones you know. Look back at the unit and review the ones you don't know.

☐ captivated
☐ cryptic
☐ definitively AWL
☐ evidently AWL
☐ excluded AWL
☐ integral AWL
☐ irresistible
☐ metaphor

☐ monotonous
☐ multiple
☐ nostalgic
☐ on the contrary AWL
☐ simultaneously
☐ straightforward AWL
☐ substantial

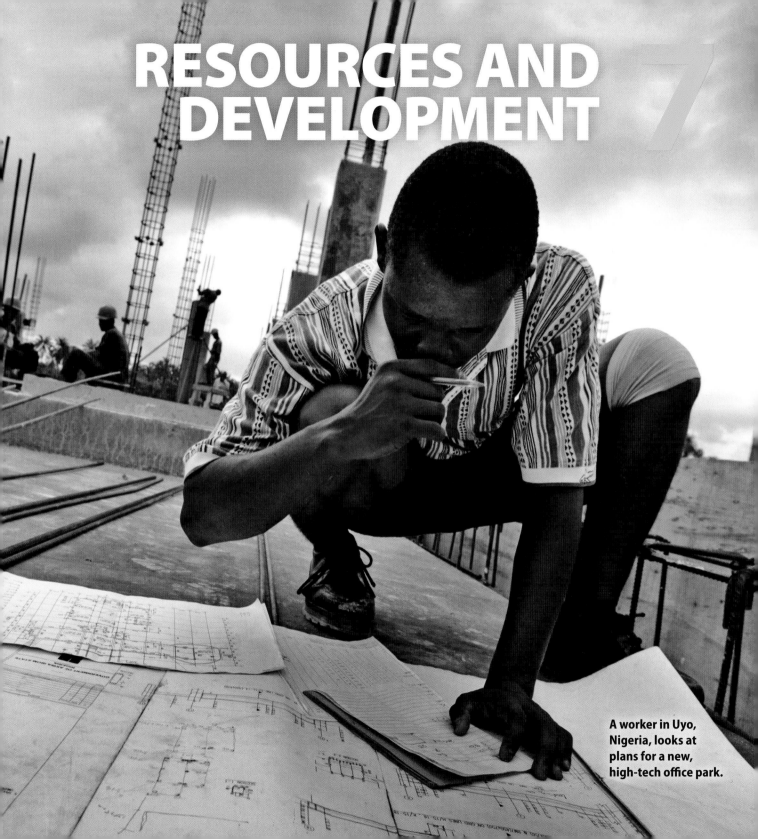

RESOURCES AND DEVELOPMENT

7

A worker in Uyo, Nigeria, looks at plans for a new, high-tech office park.

A Look at the information on these pages. Then answer the questions.

1. What regions have the highest concentrations of low-income people? What regions have the highest concentrations of high-income people?

2. How are developing and developed countries different?

B Match the words in blue to their definitions.

_____ (n) plants like wheat that are grown for food

_____ (n) animals that are kept on a farm

_____ (adj) relating to business and money

○ City with population of 10 million or more

0 mi   1000
0 km   1000

MAP DATA: OAK RIDGE NATIONAL LABORATORY
LANDSCAN 2009 (POPULATION DENSITY)

GLOBAL DEVELOPMENT

Where and How We Live

The map shows population density; the brightest points are the highest densities. Each region is colored according to its average annual gross national income per capita (GNI), using categories established by the World Bank.

LOW INCOME LEVEL
$995 or less a year

100   1,000   10,000
People per square mile

LOWER MIDDLE
$996 to $3,945

100   1,000   10,000
People per square mile

UPPER MIDDLE
$3,946 to $12,195

100   1,000   10,000
People per square mile

HIGH
$12,196 or more

100   1,000   10,000
People per square mile

Defining Development

In economics, development is often used to refer to a change from a traditional economy to one based on technology. A traditional economy usually centers on individual survival. Families and small communities often make their own clothing, housing, and household goods. They also typically raise their own **livestock** and grow their own **crops**. The economies of most developing countries rely heavily on agriculture. Developing countries also rely on raw materials, which can be traded to developed countries for finished goods. These raw materials include oil, coal, and timber.

Developed countries have economies that are more diverse. Their economies rely on many different people and organizations performing specialized tasks. Agriculture and raw materials represent only part of the economy of a developed country. Other sectors include manufacturing, banking and finance, and services such as hairdressing and plumbing.

Reading

PREPARING TO READ

BUILDING
VOCABULARY

A The words in blue below are used in the reading passage. Match the correct form of each word to its definition.

For people in developing nations, solar-powered devices can offer many **distinct** advantages. The availability of low-cost solar lamps, for example, means longer working hours and better security at night. One organization in Uganda—Solar Sister—is using solar power to turn local women into entrepreneurs. Solar Sister participants sell solar-powered products such as lamps and phone chargers. The women can start with only basic business skills, because Solar Sister provides training. In addition, women can start a business with no initial financial **investment**, because Solar Sister provides products for them to sell when they begin. The women can then repay these costs once their businesses start to **prosper**. A successful entrepreneur can make up to $540 in **annual** income. One success story is a Ugandan woman named Grace. **Revenue** from her new business tripled the family income, **thereby** allowing her children to start school.

1. _____ (adj) yearly

2. _____ (adj) clear and definite

3. _____ (n) the use of money for income or profit

4. _____ (n) money that a company earns

5. _____ (v) to do well and be successful

6. _____ (adv) by this means

BUILDING
VOCABULARY

B Complete the sentences with the words in the box. Use a dictionary to help you.

associate	denied	evolutionary	minority	orientation	tensions

1. The _____ of a thing is its position relative to something else.

2. If you _____ one thing with another thing, you make a connection between the two things.

3. If you are _____ something, you cannot do it or have it.

4. "_____" describes a process of gradual change and development.

5. _____ are feelings that occur where there is a possibility of violence or conflict.

6. A _____ is a smaller number or part of things in a larger group.

USING
VOCABULARY

C Discuss the questions below with a partner.

1. What is the minimum **annual** income that people in your country need to live well?

2. What do people usually **associate** your country or region with?

DEVELOPING READING SKILLS

READING SKILL Annotating a Text

Annotating—marking up—a text while you read it helps you to stay focused on what you are reading. It also helps you to remember and find important information later. Here are some ways to annotate a text with an example paragraph below.

- Highlight the most important ideas—use one color for main ideas and another for supporting information.
- Circle new vocabulary to check later.
- Underline parts you don't understand and put a question mark in the margin so you can reread them later.
- Break the text into sections by subtopic and label each section.

For people in developing nations, solar-powered devices can offer several distinct advantages. The availability of low-cost solar lamps, for example, means longer working hours and better security at night. One organization in Uganda—Solar Sister—is using solar power to turn local women into solar entrepreneurs. Solar Sister participants sell solar-powered products such as lamps and phone chargers. The women can start with only basic business skills, because Solar Sister provides training. In addition, women can start a business with no initial financial investment, because Solar Sister provides products for them to sell when they begin. **?**

In the paragraph above, a reader has highlighted the main idea in blue and the supporting ideas in yellow. An unfamiliar word, *entrepreneur*, is circled to look up later. A question mark indicates that the student wants to find out more about the last sentence.

A Read paragraphs A and B of the reading passage on the next spread. Follow the tips in the box above to annotate the paragraph.

ANNOTATING

B Work with a partner. Compare your annotations. Are there any other ways you could annotate these paragraphs? Note your ideas.

DISCUSSION

_____

_____

_____

C Read the whole passage. Continue to annotate as you read.

ANNOTATING

THE SHAPE OF AFRICA

by Jared Diamond

> The hope for Africa's future lies with its abundant human and natural resources.

🎧 2.2

Ask someone to tell you quickly what they associate with Africa and the answers you'll get will probably range from "cradle of humankind" and "big animals" to "poverty" and "tribalism." How did one continent come to embody such extremes?

Geography and history go a long way toward providing the explanations. Geographically, Africa resembles a bulging sandwich. The sole continent to span both the north and south temperate zones,[1] it has a thick tropical core lying between one thin temperate zone in the north and another in the south. That simple geographic reality explains a great deal about Africa today.

As to its human history, this is the place where—some seven million years ago—the evolutionary lines of apes and protohumans[2] diverged. It remained the only continent our ancestors inhabited until around two million years ago, when *Homo erectus* expanded out of Africa into Europe and Asia. Over the next 1.5 million years, the populations of those three continents followed such different evolutionary courses that they became distinct species. Europe's became the Neandertals, Asia's remained *Homo erectus*, but Africa's evolved into our own species, *Homo sapiens*. Sometime between 100,000 and 50,000 years ago, our African ancestors underwent some further profound change. Whether it was the development of complex speech or something else, such as a change in brain wiring, we aren't sure. Whatever it was, it transformed those early *Homo sapiens* into what paleoanthropologists[3] call "behaviorally modern" *Homo sapiens*. Those people, probably with brains similar to our own, expanded again into Europe and Asia. Once there, they exterminated or replaced or interbred with Neandertals and Asia's hominins[4] and became the dominant human species throughout the world.

In effect, Africans enjoyed not just one but three huge head starts over humans on other continents. That makes Africa's economic struggles today, compared with the successes of other continents, particularly puzzling. It's the opposite of what one would expect from the runner first off the block. Here again, geography and history give us answers.

It turns out that the rules of the competitive race among the world's humans changed radically about 10,000 years ago, with the

[1] **Temperate zones** are areas between the tropics and the polar circle.
[2] A **protohuman** is an early human ancestor.

[3] **Paleoanthropologists** are scientists who study human fossils.
[4] **Hominins** are the early forms of humans that descended from primates.

Botswana's San people, or Bushmen, are some of the world's last surviving hunter-gatherers.

origins of agriculture. The domestication of wild plants and animals meant our ancestors could grow their own food instead of having to hunt or gather it in the wild. That allowed people to settle in permanent villages, to increase their populations, and to feed specialists—inventors, soldiers, and kings—who did not produce food. With domestication came other advances, including the first metal tools, writing, and state societies.

The problem is that only a tiny **minority** of wild plants and animals lend themselves to domestication, and those few are concentrated in about half a dozen parts of the world. As every schoolchild learns, the world's earliest and most productive farming arose in the Fertile Crescent of southwestern Asia, where wheat, barley, sheep, cattle, and goats were domesticated. While those plants and animals spread east and west in Eurasia, in Africa they were stopped by the continent's north-south **orientation**. **Crops** and **livestock** tend to spread much more slowly from north to south than from east to west because different latitudes require adaptation to different climates, seasonalities, day lengths, and diseases. Africa's own native plant species— sorghum, oil palm, coffee, millets, and yams— weren't domesticated until thousands of years after Asia and Europe had agriculture. And Africa's geography kept oil palm, yams, and other crops of equatorial Africa from spreading into southern Africa's temperate zone. While South Africa today boasts[5] the continent's richest agricultural lands, the crops grown there are mostly northern temperate crops, such as wheat and grapes, brought directly on ships by European colonists. Those same crops never succeeded in spreading south through the thick tropical core of Africa.

[5]To **boast** is to possess a feature that is a source of pride.

The domesticated sheep and cattle of Fertile Crescent origins took about 5,000 years to spread from the Mediterranean down to the southern tip of Africa. The continent's own native animals—with the exception of guinea fowl and possibly donkeys and one breed of cattle—proved impossible to domesticate. History might have turned out differently if African armies, fed by barnyard-giraffe meat and backed by waves of cavalry[6] mounted on huge rhinos, had swept into Europe to overrun its mutton-fed soldiers mounted on puny horses. That this didn't happen was no fault of the Africans; it was because of the kinds of wild animals available to them.

Ironically, the long human presence in Africa is probably the reason the continent's species of big animals survive today. African animals co-evolved with humans for millions of years, as human hunting prowess gradually progressed from the basic skills of our early ancestors. That gave the animals time to learn a healthy fear of man and, with it, a healthy avoidance of human hunters. In contrast, North and South America and Australia were settled by humans only within the last tens of thousands of years. To the misfortune of the big animals of those continents, the first humans they encountered were already fully modern people, with modern brains and hunting skills. Most of those animals—woolly mammoths, saber-toothed cats, and, in Australia, marsupials[7] as big as rhinoceroses—disappeared soon after humans arrived. Entire species may have been exterminated before they had time to learn to beware of hunters.

Unfortunately, the long human presence in Africa also encouraged something else to thrive—diseases. The continent has a well-deserved reputation for having spawned some of our nastiest ones: malaria, yellow fever, East African sleeping sickness, and AIDS. These and many other human illnesses arose when microbes causing disease in animals crossed species lines to evolve into a human disease. For a microbe already adapted to one species, to adapt to another can be difficult and require a lot of evolutionary time. Much more time has been available in Africa, cradle of humankind, than

[6]A **cavalry** is a group of soldiers who ride horses.

[7]**Marsupials** are animals such as kangaroos. Female marsupials carry their babies in pouches on their bellies.

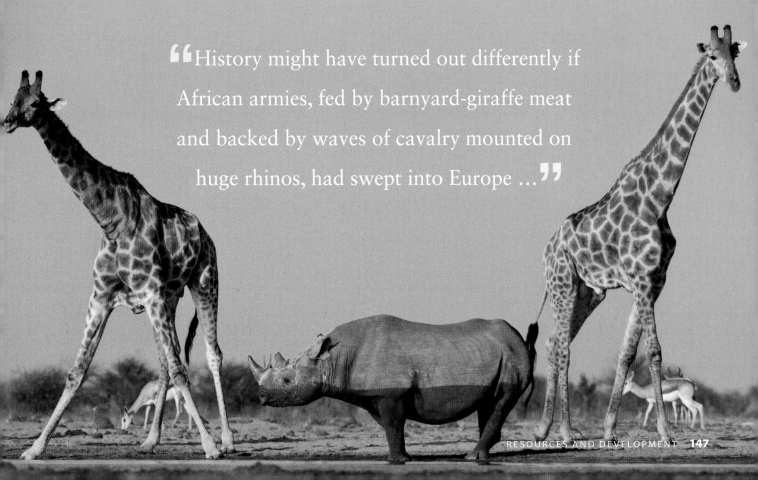

" History might have turned out differently if African armies, fed by barnyard-giraffe meat and backed by waves of cavalry mounted on huge rhinos, had swept into Europe … "

in any other part of the planet. That's half the answer to Africa's disease burden; the other half is that the animal species most closely related to humans—those whose microbes required the least adaptation to jump species—are the African great apes and monkeys.

Africa continues to be shaped in other ways by its long history and its geography. Of mainland Africa's ten richest countries—the only ones with **annual** per capita gross domestic products over $3,300—eight lie partly or entirely within its temperate zones: Egypt, Libya, Tunisia, and Algeria in the north; and Angola, South Africa, Botswana, and Namibia in the south. Gabon and Equatorial Guinea are Africa's only tropical countries to make the list. In addition, nearly a third of the countries of mainland Africa (15 out of 47) are landlocked, and the only African river navigable[8] from the ocean for long distances inland is the Nile. Since waterways provide the cheapest way to transport cumbersome[9] goods, geography again thwarts Africa's progress.

All these factors can lead to the question: "Is the continent, or at least its big tropical core, doomed eternally to wars, poverty, and devastating diseases?" I'd answer, "Absolutely not." On my own visits to Africa, I've been struck by how harmoniously ethnic groups live together in many countries—far better than they do in many other parts of the globe. **Tensions** arise in

[8]A **navigable** river is wide enough for a boat to travel along safely.
[9]If something is **cumbersome**, it is large and heavy and therefore difficult to carry or handle.

A busy bakery in Kinshasa, Democratic Republic of the Congo

Africa, as they do elsewhere, when people see no other way out of poverty except to fight their neighbors for dwindling resources. But many areas of Africa have an abundance of resources: The rivers of central Africa are great generators of hydroelectric power; the big animals are a major source of ecotourism revenue in eastern and southern Africa; and the forests in the wetter regions, if managed and logged sustainably, would be renewable and lucrative[10] sources of income.

As for Africa's health problems, they can be greatly alleviated with the right planning and funding. Within the past half century, several formerly poor countries in Asia recognized that tropical diseases were a major drain on their

[10]A **lucrative** activity, job, or business is very profitable.

economies. By investing in public health measures, they have successfully curbed those diseases, and the increased health of their people has led to far healthier economies. Within Africa itself, some international mining and oil companies have been funding successful public health programs throughout their concession areas[11] because they realized that protecting the health of their workers was an excellent business investment for them.

What's the best case for Africa's future? If the continent can overcome its health problems and the corruption that plagues many of its governments and institutions, then it could take advantage of today's globalized, technological world in much the same way that China and India are now doing. Technology could give Africa the connections that its geography, particularly its rivers, long denied it. Nearly half of all African countries are English speaking—an advantage in trade relations—and an educated, English-speaking workforce could well attract service jobs to many African countries.

If Africa is to head into a bright future, outside investment will continue to be needed, at least for a time. The cost of perpetual aid to or military intervention in Africa is thousands of times more expensive than solving health problems and supporting local development, thereby heading off[12] conflicts. Not only Africans but the rest of us will be healthier and safer if Africa's nations increasingly take their places as peaceful and prospering members of the world community.

[11]A **concession area** is a place where someone is given the right to sell a product or run a business.
[12]If you **head off** an event, you keep it from happening.

Adapted from "The Shape of Africa," by Jared Diamond: National Geographic Magazine, September 2005

Jared Diamond is an American ecologist, geographer, and anthropologist. His book, *Guns, Germs, and Steel: The Fates of Human Societies* won the Pulitzer Prize.

UNDERSTANDING THE READING

UNDERSTANDING MAIN IDEAS

A Write the correct paragraph letter (B, C, D, E, F, G, H) next to each main idea.

1. _____ The co-evolution of animals and humans affected the survival of some species in Africa.

2. _____ Humans have been in Africa for a very long time.

3. _____ Africa's geographical orientation affected the spread of agriculture on the continent.

4. _____ It's a mystery why the long human history of Africa hasn't been an advantage.

5. _____ Africa's geographic location explains the extremes that exist on the continent.

6. _____ The development of agriculture impacts a culture.

7. _____ Animal domestication took a long time to spread across Africa.

UNDERSTANDING MAIN IDEAS

B Complete the main idea statements for paragraphs I, J, and K. Then write the main ideas of paragraphs L, M, and N. Use the paraphrasing strategies you learned in Unit 4.

1. Paragraph I: The long human presence in Africa led to _____

_____

2. Paragraph J: The richest countries in Africa lie in _____

_____

3. Paragraph K: Africa has hope because of _____

_____

4. Paragraph L: _____

_____

5. Paragraph M: _____

_____

6. Paragraph N: _____

_____

CRITICAL THINKING: UNDERSTANDING CHRONOLOGY

C Look again at paragraph C. Put the events (a–f) in the correct order in the time line.

a. "Behaviorally modern" *Homo sapiens* appears in Africa.

b. *Homo erectus* evolves into three distinct species: Neandertals in Europe, *Homo erectus* in Asia, *Homo sapiens* in Africa.

c. Apes and protohumans split.

d. *Homo erectus* moves to Europe and Asia.

e. *Homo sapiens* becomes dominant species as other early forms of humans die out

f. *Homo sapiens* moves into Europe and Asia.

D Find and underline the following words and phrases in the reading passage. Use the context to help you identify the meaning of each word or phrase. Match each word or phrase with its definition.

CRITICAL THINKING: GUESSING MEANING FROM CONTEXT

1. ____ Paragraph B: **go a long way toward**
2. ____ Paragraph D: **head starts**
3. ____ Paragraph F: **lend themselves to**
4. ____ Paragraph I: **spawned**
5. ____ Paragraph J: **landlocked**
6. ____ Paragraph K: **struck**
7. ____ Paragraph L: **a (major) drain on**
8. ____ Paragraph M: **plagues**

a. a heavy use of something such as resources

b. caused to happen

c. surrounded by other countries and not having access to bodies of water

d. contribute greatly to

e. advantages in a competition

f. continually causes problems

g. surprised or greatly affected

h. are suitable for, or adapt easily to

E Note answers to the questions below. Then discuss with a partner.

UNDERSTANDING DETAILS

1. What are the "head starts" that Diamond refers to in paragraph D?

_____

2. What are some effects of the development of agriculture?

_____

_____

3. What blocked the spread of agriculture in Africa?

_____

_____

4. Why did many animal species survive in Africa, unlike other places such as Australia?

_____

_____

5. Why is the proximity to great apes and monkeys a problem in Africa?

_____

_____

6. What two geographical conditions affect the wealth of Africa?

_____

_____

7. How does Diamond describe the potential of Africa's resources?

_____

_____

8. What actions may give Africa a better future?

_____

_____

CRITICAL THINKING:
ANALYZING POINT
OF VIEW

F Read the statements below. How strongly do you think the author of the reading passage would agree or disagree with each one? Use the scale below and rate each statement from 1 to 5. Note down any key words or phrases in the passage that helped you understand the author's point of view. Discuss your ideas with a partner.

1 = strongly disagrees
2 = disagrees
3 = neither agrees or disagrees
4 = agrees
5 = strongly agrees

1. Large species of animals remain in Africa today because humans have lived there for so long. (paragraph H)

    1   **2**   **3**   **4**   **5**

    key words/phrases:

    _____

2. Africa is "doomed eternally to wars, poverty, and devastating diseases." (paragraph K)

    1   **2**   **3**   **4**   **5**

    key words/phrases:

    _____

3. In Africa, many ethnic groups live together happily. (paragraph K)

    1   **2**   **3**   **4**   **5**

    key words/phrases:

    _____

4. Many areas of Africa have adequate natural resources. (paragraph K)

    1   **2**   **3**   **4**   **5**

    key words/phrases:

    _____

5. Africa will have a bright future. (paragraph N)

    1   **2**   **3**   **4**   **5**

    key words/phrases:

    _____

International sales of Penja pepper have been a major boost for Cameroon's economy.

Terre Exotique
Poivre Blanc

HONEY AND PEPPER

BEFORE VIEWING

A What products do you know that come from specific regions of the world? Work with a partner and make a list.

DISCUSSION

B Read the information. Then answer the questions.

LEARNING ABOUT THE TOPIC

Many products are associated with a specific region of the world, such as Greece's feta cheese or England's Cumberland sausage. In order to protect these products from lower quality imitations, many products now have a Geographical Indication (G.I.) label. The label is awarded to products that have qualities which are unique to the location in which they are produced. A Cumberland sausage with a G.I. label, for example, assures the consumer that the product was produced in Cumbria, United Kingdom, and has a meat content of at least 80 percent.

1. What is the purpose of a Geographical Indication (G.I.) label?

_____

2. What products in your country might have a G.I. label? What is unique about them?

_____

C The words in **bold** below are used in the video. Match the correct form of each word to its definition.

> Coffee from Mokha, Yemen, has a unique chocolate-like **aroma**.
>
> In the future, climate change may negatively affect farmers' **yields** of certain crops such as wheat.
>
> Intellectual property refers to the **notion** that an idea, invention, or creation, can legally belong to a person.

1. _____ (n) the amount of crops harvested by a farmer
2. _____ (n) a smell, usually a pleasant one
3. _____ (n) a belief or concept

WHILE VIEWING

A ▶ Watch the video. What is it mainly about?

a. products in Africa that hope to receive a G.I. label in the future

b. the problems of getting a G.I. label for a product in Africa

c. two successful African products that have received a G.I. label

B ▶ Watch the video again. Complete the Venn diagram. Write the letters a–e.

a. It is made in Cameroon.

b. Its unique properties come from the volcanic soil in the area.

c. Its unique properties come from the flowers which grow in the area.

d. Its price has risen recently.

e. It is popular with chefs in Europe.

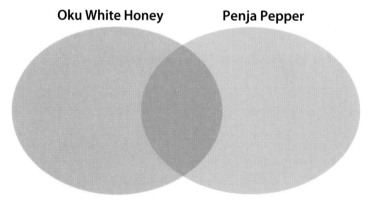

Oku White Honey   **Penja Pepper**

AFTER VIEWING

A Why do you think obtaining a G.I. label often leads to a rise in the price of a product? Note your ideas below. Then discuss with a partner.

_____

_____

_____

Writing

EXPLORING WRITTEN ENGLISH

A The following words and expressions can be useful when writing about geography and history. Find them in this unit's reading passage, and use the context to guess their meanings. Then match each word to its definition.

VOCABULARY FOR WRITING

span (paragraph B)	**tropical** (paragraph B)	**undergo** (paragraph C)
concentrated (paragraph F)	**temperate** (paragraph F)	**latitudes** (paragraph F)
native (paragraph G)	**mainland** (paragraph J)	**shape** (paragraph J)

1. _____ (adj) naturally originating from a particular place

2. _____ (v) to experience; suffer from

3. _____ (v) to extend over a large area

4. _____ (v) to influence and change

5. _____ (adj) located in one place; not spread out

6. _____ (adj) having a climate that is never extremely hot or extremely cold

7. _____ (adj) located in the regions near the Earth's Equator

8. _____ (n) the distances that places lie from the Earth's Equator

9. _____ (adj) describing the greater part of a country or continent, excluding its islands

B Read the sentence below, which refers to an argument made by Jared Diamond in this unit's reading passage. Then answer the questions.

NOTICING

As Jared Diamond **says**, "Unfortunately, the long human presence in Africa also encouraged something else to thrive—diseases."

1. Which two words from the box below can be used to replace the word *say*? Why are the other words not as suitable?

feels	informs	suggests	states	tells

2. What other words do you know that could replace the word *say*? Note some ideas below. Then compare your answers with a partner.

   _____

   _____

   _____

When you use other people's ideas in your writing, you either quote them directly or you paraphrase them. Try to paraphrase as much as possible, but use direct quotations when the original words are particularly effective. Use the following words and phrases to refer to sources.

> **According to Diamond**, *"The long human presence in Africa is probably the reason the continent's species of big animals survive today."*
>
> **As Diamond says**, *"The long human presence in Africa is probably the reason the continent's species of big animals survive today."*
>
> **Diamond says that** *"the long human presence in Africa is probably the reason the continent's species of big animals survive today."*
>
> **Diamond says that** *the fact that humans have been in Africa for a very long time probably explains why many large animal species still exist on the continent.*

It's common to use *that* after reporting verbs in academic writing. Note that when you use *that* in a quote, it must fit grammatically into the sentence.

Vary your style by using different reporting verbs, such as the following: *says, states, claims, believes, explains, points out, suggests, reports, concludes, argues.*

Choose a reporting verb that matches the meaning you intend. For example, if you are reporting on research, you might say, "X <u>concludes</u> that." If you are reporting on a persuasive idea, you might say, "X <u>argues</u> that." If you are reporting on an opinion, you might say, "X <u>thinks/believes/feels</u> that."

C Use information from the reading passage to answer the questions below.

1. Write a quote from the author, Jared Diamond, that answers this question: What may have happened to the large animals that disappeared in Australia and North and South America? (paragraph H)

   _____

   _____

2. Write a quote that expresses Diamond's opinion on how people get along with each other in Africa. (paragraph K)

   _____

   _____

3. Write the main idea of paragraph L using a reporting verb.

   _____

   _____

4. Write the main idea of paragraph M using a reporting verb.

   _____

   _____

When researching information online, you may need to choose and evaluate sources quickly and efficiently. You will also need to note the most relevant information. Use these tips to make your research and note-taking more effective.

Researching

- Limit search results by using precise key words within quotation marks.

- Scan the URLs in your search results to quickly eliminate sites that seem irrelevant.

- Avoid encyclopedia sites as your main source, if possible. You will write a better essay if you use original sources. However, encyclopedia sites may be a good place to find original sources—check the References at the end of each article.

- When you go to a source site, preview the content: Read the title and the subheads, look at the pictures, and read the captions. As you preview, ask yourself: Is the site trustworthy? Is the information accurate? Is it current?

Note-taking

- Avoid plagiarism by having index cards handy or a note-taking document open while you are doing online research. When you find information that is useful, write the ideas in your own words. Never cut and paste text from websites! When paraphrasing an idea, be careful not to change the original meaning.

- In your notes, include all correct source information: the correct names of people and the publications you will refer to in your essay.

- For ideas that you will quote directly, write the source of the quotation and the exact words that you will quote.

- Label your notes with a *P* for information that you have paraphrased and a *Q* for information you have quoted.

D Work with a partner. Look at the following research questions and discuss your answers to these questions: What key words should you use for an online search? What types of websites would give you the best information?

CRITICAL THINKING: RESEARCHING

1. What are some ways to improve agricultural production in Africa?

2. What languages are spoken in Africa?

3. What are some examples of how outside aid has helped Africa?

E Compare the following notes on an original text. Which is the better version? Why? Share your answer with a partner.

CRITICAL THINKING: NOTE-TAKING

The impacts of slavery on Africa are widespread and diverse. Computerized calculations have projected that if there had been no slave trade, the population of Africa would have been 50 million instead of 25 million in 1850.

Source: education.nationalgeographic.com

a. Slavery has had a huge impact on Africa. There would have been 50 million inhabitants in Africa instead of only 25 million in 1850 if there had been no slave trade.

b. Slavery had several damaging effects on Africa; for example, it reduced the population by 50 percent in the 19th century.

APPLYING   **F**   **Research a country that interests you. Take notes on the following points.**

1. Find background information on the country or region. What is it like today?

    _____

    _____

    _____

2. Find out about the geography of the country or region. How does its geography affect its current situation? Find out where it is located, what its climate is like, what its main resources are, and so on.

    _____

    _____

    _____

    _____

3. Find out about the history of the country or region. What are three key events that have shaped the country's current situation?

    _____

    _____

    _____

    _____

Singapore's geographical location on a key shipping route between Europe and Asia has led to it having one of the busiest harbors in the world.

WRITING TASK

GOAL In this lesson, you are going to write an essay on the following topic:

Choose a country or region and explain how it has been affected by its history and geography.

PLANNING

A Use your research notes to plan your essay. Follow the steps.

Step 1 Choose three aspects of the geography and history of the country or region that you want to discuss. Write a thesis statement in the outline.

Step 2 Write a topic sentence for each of your body paragraphs. Remember to reflect your key concepts in your topic sentences.

Step 3 For each body paragraph, write two to three examples or details that explain the ideas in your topic sentences.

Step 4 Note some ideas for an introduction and a conclusion for your essay.

OUTLINE

Thesis statement: (three aspects of the country's/region's geography/history that affect the way it is today)

_____

_____

_____

Body paragraph 1: one aspect of its geography/history

Topic sentence: _____

_____

Explanation and examples: _____

_____

_____

Body paragraph 2: another aspect of its geography/history

Topic sentence: _____

_____

Explanation and examples: _____

_____

_____

Body paragraph 3: third aspect of its geography/history

Topic sentence: _____

_____

Explanation and examples: _____

_____

_____

Ideas for introduction and conclusion: _____

_____

FIRST DRAFT **B** Use the information in your outline to write a first draft of your essay.

REVISING PRACTICE

The draft below is a model of the essay you are writing. Follow the steps to create a better second draft.

1. Add the sentences (a–c) in the correct spaces.
   a. As with many countries, Singapore has been shaped by its geography and history.
   b. Its geographical location, lack of natural resources, and recent immigration history have all played a part in shaping this small island nation.
   c. Today, the Port of Singapore is one of the busiest in the world.

2. Now fix the following problems (a–c) with the essay.
   a. Fix a problem with referring to a source in paragraph C.
   b. Fix a problem with referring to a source in paragraph D.
   c. Fix a problem with a verbal phrase in paragraph C.

A

Singapore is a collection of small islands in Southeast Asia. The majority of the population is concentrated on the mainland, a diamond-shaped island 30 miles (49 km) wide and 15.5 miles (25 km) long. Singapore boasts the world's largest concentration of millionaires, is culturally diverse, and frequently ranks in the top 10 in work-and personal-life satisfaction surveys. What makes Singapore the place that it is today?

_____

B

Thanks to its geography, trade is one of the most important aspects of Singapore's economy. The country lies to the south of Malaysia, from which it is separated by a narrow body of water called the Johor Strait. Its southern coast is on the Singapore Strait, which separates it from Indonesia. Its advantageous location made it a key stopping-off point for ships traveling from Asia to Europe. As a result, Singapore became an important center for international trade. This made it even easier for ships to come and go. _____ This has helped Singapore to become the 14th largest exporter and the 15th largest importer in the world.

C

The lack of natural resources, especially fresh water, has also shaped Singapore. Has a rain forest climate, Singapore receives over 90 inches of rainfall a year. However, because it has little land to retain the water, the supply of fresh drinking water for Singapore's residents is very limited. As a result, Singapore must import water from nearby countries. In addition, the country has built water recycling and desalination plants. Water-recycling plants transform wastewater into drinking water, and desalination plants make use of the abundant seawater that surrounds the island. According to the Public Utilities Board (PUB) current and planned plants will meet up to 55 percent of the demand for fresh water by 2060.

D

Singapore's recent history of immigration goes a long way toward explaining its rich cultural diversity. For many years, the government of Singapore had liberal immigration policies. The country needed foreign workers partly due to its low birthrate: there are only 1.20 births per woman, which is below the replacement rate of 2.1. By 2010, almost 43 percent of the population was made up of people born outside of Singapore. Although there has been some opposition to these liberal immigration policies in recent history, many experts believe that immigration is necessary to maintain a strong workforce and to offset an aging population. In a *Forbes* magazine interview, investor and Singapore resident Jim Rogers argued that if Singapore cannot get enough labor through immigration, inflation may result, with an overall detrimental effect on the country's economy. "Every country in history that has a backlash against foreigners is going to go into decline."

E

_____ Since gaining its independence from Malaysia in 1965, the tiny city-state has gone from a poor trading port to one of the wealthiest states in the world. And it shows: High-rise condos and skyscrapers dominate the landscape, and shoppers peruse the latest designer goods in its many upscale malls and boutiques. Although Singapore is a small country with a declining birthrate and few natural resources, its advantageous location in the heart of Southeast Asia will continue to make it attractive to immigrants, tourists, and investors alike.

C   **Now use the questions below to revise your essay.**   REVISED DRAFT

☐   Does your introduction provide relevant background information on the topic?

☐   Does your thesis state the main points of the essay?

☐   Do your body paragraphs include enough details to fully explain your ideas?

☐   Did you refer to sources correctly?

☐   Do all your sentences relate to the main idea?

☐   Does your concluding paragraph have a summary statement and a final thought?

EDITING PRACTICE

Read the information below. Then find and correct one mistake with quotes or paraphrases in each sentence (1–4).

When you refer to sources, remember:

- to use quotation marks and a comma to separate a person's exact words from the rest of the sentence.

- In American English, commas and periods should go inside the end quotation marks. For example:

    Correct: *"With time running out," says Alexander, "tough priorities must be set."*

    Incorrect: *"With time running out", says Alexander, "tough priorities must be set".*

- to use a comma after the phrase that includes *According to.*

- to make sure that sentences referring to sources are grammatical. For example, do not use *that* with "As X says ~~that~~ …"

1. "To photograph", says Susan Sontag, "is to confer importance."

2. According to Griffiths photography has influenced our notion of what is beautiful.

3. Diamond asks, What's the best case for Africa's future?"

4. As Kolbert says that, "Probably the most obvious way humans are altering the planet is by building cities."

FINAL DRAFT **D** **Follow the steps to write a final draft.**

1. Check your revised draft for mistakes with referring to sources.

2. Now use the checklist on page 248 to write a final draft. Make any other necessary changes.

UNIT REVIEW

Answer the following questions.

1. What are some characteristics of traditional economies?

_____

_____

2. What are two things that could help Africa achieve a bright future?

_____

_____

3. What are two ways to refer to a source in a text?

_____

_____

4. Do you remember the meanings of these words? Check (✔) the ones you know. Look back at the unit and review the ones you don't know.

☐ annual AWL	☐ livestock
☐ associate	☐ minority
☐ crops	☐ orientation AWL
☐ deny AWL	☐ prosper
☐ distinct AWL	☐ revenue AWL
☐ economic AWL	☐ tensions AWL
☐ evolutionary AWL	☐ thereby AWL
☐ investment AWL	

LIVING LONGER

8

Studies show that regular physical activity can increase a person's life expectancy by several years.

ACADEMIC SKILLS

READING Asking questions as you read
WRITING Writing an argumentative essay
GRAMMAR Explaining the significance of evidence
CRITICAL THINKING Interpreting visual data

THINK AND DISCUSS

1 What daily habits can contribute to good health?
2 How do you think a person's genes can affect their health?

A Look at the information on these pages and answer the questions.

1. Which animal has the longest life span?
2. Which mammal has the longest life span?
3. Why do you think these animals have such amazing longevity?

B Match the correct form of the words in blue to their definitions.

_____ (n) the period of time for which something lives

_____ (n) the ability to live for a long time

_____ (prep) past a particular point or stage

LIFE SPANS

In the animal kingdom, life expectancy varies from just a few hours to over 200 years.

Cat
15 years

Dog
13 years

Bengal tiger
10 years

Lion
20 years

Burmese python
22 years

Grizzly bear
25 years

Giant tortoise
120 years

Human (female)
72 years

Great white shark
70 years

Bowhead whale
200 years

Bowhead whales have amazing longevity and are thought to have the longest life span of any mammal. Scientists believe the animals are able to live beyond 200 years of age.

Quahog clam
225 years

The world's longest living animal is the quahog clam, with an estimated life span of around 225 years. In 2006, scientists discovered a quahog that was thought to be an incredible 507 years old.

Mayfly Hours–1 week

Some species of adult mayflies have a life span of just a few hours. After maturing into adulthood, mayflies have roughly three hours to find a partner and reproduce before they die.

Mosquito
2 weeks– 6 months

Dragonfly
4 months

Red fox
4 years

Cottontail rabbit
3 years

Common octopus
1–2 years

Golden eagle
30 years

Ostrich
35 years

Rhinoceros
40 years

Human (male)
68 years

American lobster
50 years

Chimpanzee
45 years

Immortal jellyfish
Forever?

While it seems nobody really knows how long these animals live in the wild, theoretically, the "immortal jellyfish" (*Turritopsis dohrnii*) could live forever. This amazing species has the ability to "age backwards" from an adult stage to an immature stage over and over again.

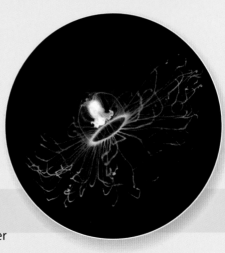

Reading

PREPARING TO READ

A The words and phrases in **blue** below are used in the reading passage. Use the context to guess the meaning of each word or phrase and complete the sentences.

When people want to lose weight, they often skip meals and try to eat smaller amounts of food. They're usually hungry as a result, but it seems like the logical thing to do. Eating and losing weight seem to be two **contradictory** ideas. However, studies show that eating when you're hungry can actually help you lose weight, and, **conversely**, skipping meals can make you gain weight. Why? We have **mechanisms** in our bodies that let us know when we're hungry and when we're full. "Overhunger" can interfere with those mechanisms, and research shows that when people skip a meal and let themselves be overly hungry, they tend to eat more than they need to at their next meal.

The **implication** of this research isn't that you can eat anything you want when you're hungry and still lose 10 pounds; you also need to embrace certain dietary **restrictions**. For example, maintain a low intake of fats and simple carbohydrates such as white bread and pastries. Instead, eat lean proteins and plenty of fruits and vegetables. It's also important to be aware of what you eat. Write down everything you eat—and when you eat it—in a food diary. That way, you can easily **reconstruct** your food intake. Doing so can help you **gain insight** into what is making you gain weight or what is keeping you from losing weight.

1. If two or more facts, ideas, or statements are _____, they state or imply that opposite things are true.

2. You say "_____" to indicate that the situation you are about to describe is the opposite or reverse of the one you have just described.

3. If you _____ into a complex situation or problem, you get an accurate and deep understanding of it.

4. The _____ of a statement, an event, or situation is what it suggests is the case.

5. If you _____ an event that happened in the past, you try to get a complete understanding of it by combining a lot of small pieces of information.

6. You can refer to things that limit what you can do as _____.

7. A(n) _____ is a process or system that enables something to take place.

B Complete the sentences with the words in the box. Use a dictionary to help you.

| intact | outcome | outnumbers | ratio | undermine |

1. A(n) _____ is an end result.

2. If you _____ something, you make it less strong or secure.

3. If one group _____ another, the first group has more people or things than the second group.

4. Something that is _____ is complete and has not been damaged or changed.

5. A(n) _____ is a relationship between two things in numbers or amounts.

C Discuss these questions with a partner.

1. What are some common dietary **restrictions** that people have?

2. What are some possible benefits of **longevity**? Some disadvantages?

3. What do you think is the **ratio** of vegetarians to nonvegetarians in your country?

D Note answers to the questions below. Then discuss your ideas with a partner.

1. What are some factors that can affect a person's life expectancy?

_____

2. What do you think are the most important factors that influence life expectancy?

_____

E Skim the reading passage. Which of your ideas in **D** above are mentioned? What other factors that can affect a person's life expectancy are mentioned?

◀ **Centenarian Masa Narita eats a self-made lunch in Osaka, Japan.**

DEVELOPING READING SKILLS

READING SKILL Asking Questions as You Read

Asking yourself questions as you read can give you a deeper understanding of the information in the text. It can also help you make inferences about the writer's intent. Engaging with a text by asking questions is almost like having a conversation with the writer.

As you read, predict answers to your questions. For example, after reading paragraph A of the reading you might ask, "Why are Passarino and Berardelli going to Molochio?" You might predict that they are going there to learn about the culture, to talk to a centenarian, or to learn what it's like to be a centenarian. After reading paragraph B, you learn that the two men are going to talk with centenarian Salvatore Caruso. Then you might ask, "Why do they want to talk to Caruso?"

ANALYZING **A** As you read the passage, complete the chart. After you read each section (e.g., A–D, E–H), complete the corresponding row in the chart.

Paragraphs	Information That You Learned or That Surprised You	Questions That You Have About the Information
A–D		
E–H		
I–L		
M–P		
Q–S		

BEYOND 100

by Stephen S. Hall

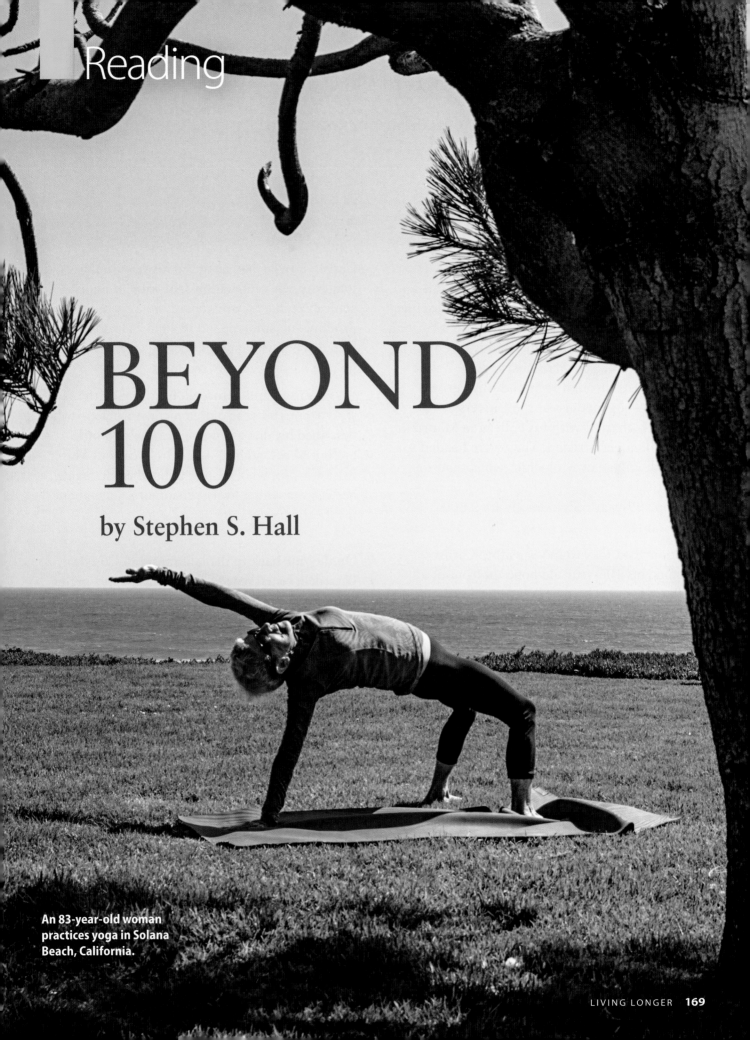

An 83-year-old woman practices yoga in Solana Beach, California.

> Our genes harbor many secrets to a long and healthy life. And now scientists are beginning to uncover them.

On a crisp January morning, with snow topping the distant Aspromonte mountains and oranges ripening on the nearby trees, Giuseppe Passarino guided his silver minivan up a curving mountain road into the hinterlands of Calabria, mainland Italy's southernmost region. As the road climbed through fruit and olive groves, Passarino—a geneticist at the University of Calabria—chatted with his colleague Maurizio Berardelli, a geriatrician. They were headed for the small village of Molochio, which had the distinction of numbering four centenarians—and four 99-year-olds—among its 2,000 inhabitants.

Soon after, they found Salvatore Caruso warming his 106-year-old bones in front of a roaring fire in his home on the outskirts of the town. Known in local dialect as "U' Raggiuneri, the Accountant," Caruso was calmly reading an article about the end of the world in an Italian version of a supermarket tabloid.[1] A framed copy of his birth record, dated November 2, 1905, stood on the fireplace mantle.

Caruso told the researchers he was in good health, and his memory seemed prodigiously intact. He recalled the death of his father in 1913, when Salvatore was a schoolboy; how his mother and brother had nearly died during the great influenza pandemic of 1918–19; how he'd been dismissed from his army unit in 1925 after accidentally falling and breaking his leg in two places. When Berardelli leaned forward and asked Caruso how he had achieved his remarkable **longevity,** the centenarian said with an impish smile, "*No Bacco, no tabacco, no Venere*—No drinking, no smoking, no women." He added that he'd eaten mostly figs and beans while growing up and hardly ever any red meat.

Passarino and Berardelli heard much the same story from 103-year-old Domenico Romeo—who described his diet as "*poco, ma tutto*—a little bit, but of everything"—and 104-year-old Maria Rosa Caruso, who, despite failing health, regaled[2] her visitors with a lively version of a song about the local patron saint.[3]

On the ride back to the laboratory in Cosenza, Berardelli remarked, "They often say they prefer to eat only fruits and vegetables."

"They preferred fruit and vegetables," Passarino said drily, "because that's all they had."

Although eating sparingly may have been less a choice than an involuntary circumstance of poverty in places like early 20th-century Calabria, decades of research have suggested that a severely restricted diet is connected to a long **life span.** Lately, however, this theory has fallen on hard scientific times. Several recent studies have **undermined** the link between longevity and caloric **restriction.**

In any case, Passarino was more interested in the centenarians themselves than in what they had eaten during their lifetimes. In a field historically

---

[1]A **tabloid** is a newspaper that has small pages, short articles, and a lot of photographs. Tabloids are usually considered to be less serious than other newspapers.

[2]If you **regale** people with songs or stories, you entertain them.

[3]The **patron saint** of a place, an activity, or a group of people is believed to give them special help and protection.

Salvatore Caruso aged 106

marred[4] by exaggerated claims, scientists studying longevity have begun using powerful genomic technologies, basic molecular research, and—most importantly—data on small, genetically isolated communities of people to gain increased insight into the maladies of old age. In regions around the world, studies are turning up molecules and chemical pathways that may ultimately help everyone reach an advanced age in good, or even vibrant, health.

In Calabria, the hunt for hidden molecules and mechanisms that confer longevity on people like Salvatore Caruso begins in places like the *Ufficio Anagrafe Stato Civile* (Civil Registry Office) in the medieval village of Luzzi. The office windows here offer stunning views of snow-covered

mountains to the north, but to a population geneticist the truly breathtaking sights are hidden inside the tall file cabinets ringing the room, and on shelf after shelf of precious ledgers numbered by year—starting in 1866. Despite its well-earned reputation for chaos and disorganization, the Italian government—shortly after the unification of the country in 1861—ordered local officials to record the birth, marriage, and death of every citizen in each *comune*, or township.

Since 1994, scientists at the University of Calabria have combed through these records in every one of Calabria's 409 *comuni* to compile an extraordinary survey. Coupling family histories with simple physiological[5] measurements of frailty and the latest genomic technologies, they set out to address fundamental questions about longevity.

---

[4]If something is **marred**, it is spoiled or damaged.

[5]**Physiology** is the study of how bodies function.

How much of it is determined by genetics? How much by the environment? And how do these factors interact to promote longevity—or, **conversely**, to hasten the aging process? To answer all those questions, scientists must start with rock-solid demographic[6] data.

"Here is the book from 1905," explained Marco Giordano, one of Giuseppe Passarino's young colleagues, opening a tall green ledger. He pointed to a record, in careful cursive, of the birth of Francesco D'Amato on March 3, 1905. "He died in 2007," Giordano noted, describing D'Amato as the central figure of an extensive genealogical tree. "We can **reconstruct** the pedigrees[7] of families from these records."

Cross-checking the ledger entries against meticulously detailed registry cards (pink for women, white for men) going back to the 19th century, Giordano—along with researchers Alberto Montesanto and Cinzia Martino—has reconstructed extensive family trees of 202 nonagenarians and centenarians in Calabria. The records document not only siblings of people who lived to 100, but also the spouses of siblings, which has allowed Passarino's group to do a kind of historical experiment on longevity. "We compared the ages of D'Amato's brothers and sisters to the ages of their spouses," Giordano explained. "So they had the same environment. They ate the same food. They used the same medicines. They came from the same culture. But they did not have the same genes." In a 2011 paper, the Calabrian researchers reported a surprising conclusion: Although the parents and siblings of people who lived to at least 90 also lived longer than the general population—a finding in line with earlier research—the genetic factors involved seemed to benefit males more than females.

The Calabrian results on gender offer yet another hint that the genetic twists and turns that confer longevity may be unusually complex. Major European studies had previously reported that women are much likelier to live to 100, **outnumbering** male centenarians by a **ratio** of four or five to one, with the **implication** that some of the reasons are genetic. But by teasing out details from family trees, the Calabrian researchers discovered an intriguing paradox:

[6]**Demographic** information is information about people in a particular society or age group.
[7]Someone's **pedigree** is his or her background or ancestors.

Aged 82, Madonna Buder became the oldest woman ever to finish an Ironman Triathlon.

The genetic component of longevity appears to be stronger in males—but women may take better advantage of external factors such as diet and medical care than men do.

In the dimly lit, chilly hallway outside Passarino's university office stand several freezers full of tubes containing centenarian blood. The DNA from this blood and other tissue samples has revealed additional information about the Calabrian group. For example, people who live into their 90s and **beyond** tend to possess a particular version, or allele, of a gene important to taste and digestion. This allele not only gives people a taste for bitter foods like broccoli and field greens, which are typically rich in compounds that promote cellular health, but also allows cells in the intestine to extract nutrients more efficiently from food as it's being digested.

Passarino has also found in his centenarians a revved-up[8] version of a gene for what is called an uncoupling protein. The protein plays a central role in metabolism—the way a person consumes energy and regulates body heat—which in turn affects the rate of aging.

"We have dissected five or six pathways that most influence longevity," says Passarino. "Most of them involve the response to stress, the metabolism of nutrients, or metabolism in general—the storage and use of energy." His group is currently examining how environmental influences—everything from childhood diet to how long a person attends school— might modify the activity of genes in a way that either promotes or curtails longevity.

Around the world, studies are being done to determine the causes of longevity and health in old age. If nothing else, the plethora of new studies indicates that longevity researchers are pushing the scientific conversation to a new level. In October 2011, the Archon Genomics X Prize launched a race among research teams to sequence the DNA of a hundred centenarians (dubbing the contest "100 over 100").

[8]If something is **revved up**, it is more active than usual.
[9]A **cautionary tale** is one that is intended to give a warning to people.

But genes alone are unlikely to explain all the secrets of longevity, and experts see a cautionary tale[9] in recent results concerning caloric restriction. Experiments on 41 different genetic models of mice, for example, have shown that restricting food intake produces **outcomes** that are wildly **contradictory**. About half the mouse species lived longer, but just as many lived less time on a restricted diet than they would have on a normal diet. And last August, a long-running National Institute on Aging experiment on primates concluded that monkeys kept on a restricted-calorie diet for 25 years showed no longevity advantage. Passarino made the point while driving back to his laboratory after visiting the centenarians in Molochio. "It's not that there are good genes and bad genes," he said. "It's certain genes at certain times. And in the end, genes probably account for only 25 percent of longevity. It's the environment, too, but that doesn't explain all of it either. And don't forget chance."

Which brought to mind Salvatore Caruso of Molochio, 107 years old and still going strong. Because he broke his leg 88 years ago, he was unfit to serve in the Italian Army when his entire unit was recalled during World War II. "They were all sent to the Russian front," he said, "and not a single one of them came back." It's another reminder that although molecules and mechanisms yet unfathomed[10] may someday lead to drugs that help us reach a ripe and healthy old age, a little luck doesn't hurt either.

[10]If something is **unfathomed**, it is not understood or explained, usually because it is very strange or complicated.

Adapted from "On Beyond 100," by Stephen S. Hall: National Geographic Magazine, May 2013

Award-winning writer Stephen S. Hall has written extensively about science and society for nearly 30 years. His work has appeared in numerous publications including the New York Times Magazine.

United States $7,290

THE COST OF CARE

The United States spends more on medical care per person than any country, yet life expectancy is shorter than in most other developed nations and many developing ones. Lack of health insurance is a factor in life span and contributes to an estimated 45,000 deaths a year. Why the high cost? The United States has a fee-for-service system that pays medical providers piecemeal for appointments, surgery, and the like. That can lead to unneeded treatment that doesn't reliably improve a patient's health. Says Gerard Anderson, a professor at Johns Hopkins Bloomberg School of Public Health who studies health insurance worldwide, "More care does not necessarily mean better care."

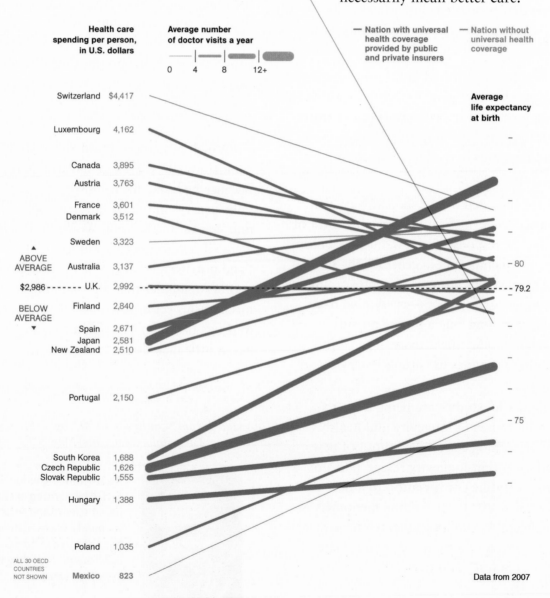

	Health care spending per person, in U.S. dollars
Switzerland	$4,417
Luxembourg	4,162
Canada	3,895
Austria	3,763
France	3,601
Denmark	3,512
Sweden	3,323
Australia	3,137
U.K.	2,992
Finland	2,840
Spain	2,671
Japan	2,581
New Zealand	2,510
Portugal	2,150
South Korea	1,688
Czech Republic	1,626
Slovak Republic	1,555
Hungary	1,388
Poland	1,035
Mexico	823

Average number of doctor visits a year
0   4   8   12+

Nation with universal health coverage provided by public and private insurers

Nation without universal health coverage

Average life expectancy at birth

ABOVE AVERAGE ▲
$2,986 - - - - - -
BELOW AVERAGE ▼

— 80
- - - 79.2
— 75

ALL 30 OECD COUNTRIES NOT SHOWN

Data from 2007

UNDERSTANDING THE READING

A Note answers to the questions below. Then discuss with a partner.

UNDERSTANDING
MAIN IDEAS

1. Why is Calabria a good place to study longevity?

   _____

   _____

2. What are some of the main points scientists have learned about longevity?

   _____

   _____

   _____

   _____

B Work with a partner. Find information in the reading passage to answer these questions.

UNDERSTANDING
DETAILS

1. Why did the researchers compare centenarians with their spouses and siblings?

   _____

   _____

2. What tools did the researchers use to make family trees of people in Calabria?

   _____

   _____

3. What are two ways that genetics can contribute to longevity?

   _____

   _____

4. What evidence shows that caloric restriction may not lead to longevity?

   _____

   _____

An 89-year-old fisherman from Okinawa Island, Japan, shows off his muscles.

C Complete the chart with information about how three factors affect the lives of each individual or group. If the information is not included in the reading, leave the space blank.

	Genetics	External Factors	Chance
Salvatore Caruso			
Men, in general			
Women, in general			

D Find and underline the following words in the reading passage. Use the context to help you match each word with its definition.

1. ___ Paragraph C: **prodigiously**

2. ___ Paragraph C: **impish**

3. ___ Paragraph G: **sparingly**

4. ___ Paragraph I: **breathtaking**

5. ___ Paragraph I: **chaos**

6. ___ Paragraph L: **meticulously**

7. ___ Paragraph L: **nonagenarians**

8. ___ Paragraph M: **paradox**

a. a state of complete disorder and confusion

b. largely, impressively

c. disrespectful or naughty in a playful way

d. infrequently or in small quantities

e. very carefully, with great attention to detail

f. extremely beautiful or amazing

g. a situation that involves two things that seem to contradict each other

h. people who are between 90 and 99 years old

CRITICAL THINKING When you **interpret visual data**, it's important to consider the implications of the information given. To determine the implications, pay attention to the relationships among the sets of data. Ask yourself if there is any correlation (link) between two sets of data. Is the correlation strong or weak? What conclusions can you draw from the entire data set?

E Look at the infographic about healthcare at the end of the reading passage and note answers to the questions below.

INTERPRETING VISUAL DATA

1. Which country spends the most per person on health care? The least?

   Most: _____   Least: _____

2. Which countries in the chart do not have universal health care?

   _____

3. Which countries have the highest number of annual doctor visits? The lowest?

   Highest: _____

   Lowest: _____

4. Which country in the chart has the longest life expectancy? The shortest?

   Longest: _____   Shortest: _____

F Look again at the infographic and answer the questions below.

INTERPRETING VISUAL DATA

1. Which sentence best summarizes the correlation between **life expectancy** and **healthcare spending**?

   a. In general, the countries with the lowest life expectancy also have the lowest level of healthcare spending.

   b. The countries with the highest healthcare spending have a lower than average life expectancy.

2. Which sentence best summarizes the correlation between **healthcare spending** and the **average number of doctor visits per year**?

   a. In general, the reason for higher than average healthcare spending in most countries is the higher number of doctor visits per year.

   b. High levels of healthcare spending do not seem to be the result of a higher number of doctor visits per year.

3. Which sentence best summarizes the correlation between **life expectancy** and the **average number of doctor visits per year**?

   a. There is no clear link between life expectancy and the average number of doctor visits per year.

   b. There is a strong correlation between life expectancy and the average number of doctor visits per year.

G Would you like to live to be a centenarian? Why or why not? Note your answer below. Then discuss with a partner.

PERSONALIZING

_____

_____

Video

Mist descends from the mountains around Bama village, Guangxi Province, China

LONGEVITY VILLAGE

BEFORE VIEWING

LEARNING ABOUT THE TOPIC

A Look at the information. Then answer the questions.

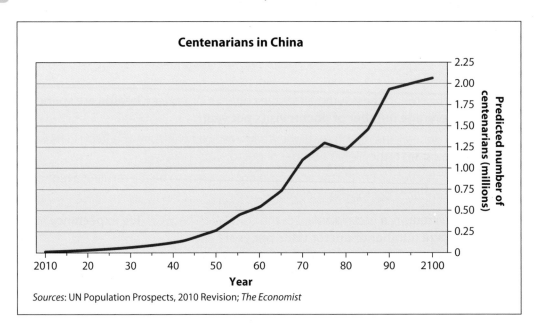

Centenarians in China

Year

Sources: UN Population Prospects, 2010 Revision; *The Economist*

1. Around which year is the number of centenarians in China expected to reach one million?

2. Why do you think the number of centenarians in China is rising?

3. Do you think a rising number of centenarians could cause any problems for a country?

B The words in **bold** below are used in the video. Match the correct form of each word to its definition.

It is a **paradox** experienced by many developing countries—wealth brings better food, which should bring better health, but wealth also brings fast food, which creates problems like diabetes and heart disease.

Today, more people are able to visit remote areas of the world. This **influx** of tourists is likely to bring changes to these places.

Some think there is a **hereditary** factor to longevity; that is, people live long because their ancestors did.

1. _____ (adj) determined by genetics; passed from parent to child

2. _____ (n) an idea that contradicts itself

3. _____ (n) the arrival of a large number of people or things

WHILE VIEWING

A ▶ Watch the video. What changes occurring in Bama County are mentioned?

a. ☐ There has been an increase in tourism.

c. ☐ Climate change is causing severe weather.

b. ☐ It's improving economically.

d. ☐ People are starting to eat junk food.

B ▶ Watch the video again. Why do people in Bama live so long? List four reasons.

_____

_____

_____

_____

AFTER VIEWING

A Do you think the benefits of tourism in Bama outweigh the disadvantages? Why or why not? Note your ideas below. Then discuss with a partner.

_____

_____

B Compare the centenarians of Calabria with the centenarians in Bama. What do they have in common? Note your ideas and discuss with a partner.

_____

_____

_____

Writing

EXPLORING WRITTEN ENGLISH

WRITING SKILL Planning an Argumentative Research Paper

In an essay, the writer usually presents his or her views about a topic and may or may not refer to sources. A research paper is different because it must include information from outside sources, such as journals, books, and websites.

An argumentative research paper involves expressing an opinion on a topic and then using researched examples and evidence to support the thesis. There are several steps involved in planning an argumentative research paper.

Choose a topic: The topic for your essay may be given to you (e.g. in an exam). If you are free to choose your own topic, pick something you can research and that you can argue about. (In this unit's writing task, the topic is chosen for you.) Consider a possible thesis statement or question, but be flexible. You may change your mind after you do some research.

Brainstorm ideas: Note down any ideas that answer your question and/or areas of research that you will need to do.

Do research: Take notes on relevant information that supports your potential thesis. Remember also to keep note of the sources of any information you find. (Review Researching and Note-taking in Unit 7.)

Draft a thesis statement: Decide on your overall argument, or thesis statement. Remember that your thesis statement needs to present an opinion that you can support with evidence.

Make an outline: Ask: *What is the best way to convince my readers that my argument is valid? What idea do I want to share first? What do I want to share next? What evidence supports each idea?* Draft a basic outline of your paper. Then complete your outline with information from your notes.

CRITICAL THINKING: EVALUATING

A Check (✓) the three statements that would be most suitable as argumentative research topics. Share your reasons with a partner. Could the other three statements be rewritten to be more suitable?

☐ 1. Cigarette advertisements are no longer permitted in some countries.

☐ 2. Fast food advertisements on television are harmful.

☐ 3. There would be fewer auto accidents if the legal driving age were changed to 21.

☐ 4. The legal driving age is different all over the world.

☐ 5. Cigarette smoking around children should be made illegal.

☐ 6. In the past, tobacco was used medicinally.

B Check (✓) the three pieces of evidence that best support the following thesis: "Cigarette smoking around children should be made illegal."

CRITICAL THINKING: EVALUATING

☐ 1. Smoking is common in countries around the world.

☐ 2. Some cigarette advertisements target children.

☐ 3. According to James Garbarino of Cornell University, "More young children are killed by parental smoking than by all unintentional injuries combined."

☐ 4. A recent study shows that the children of smokers are more likely to become smokers than the children of parents who don't smoke.

☐ 5. A recent German study showed that teenagers who are exposed to tobacco ads are more likely to start smoking than teens who don't see these ads.

☐ 6. According to recent figures, the total number of smokers in the world is approaching one billion.

☐ 7. According to the World Health Organization, 600,000 nonsmokers die from secondhand smoke every year.

C What other evidence could you research that might support the thesis in activity **B**?

D The sentences below explain the significance of the research mentioned in this unit's reading passage. Complete the sentences with the words in the box. Look back at the reading passage to check your answers.

NOTICING

hint	implication	indicates	suggested	undermined

1. … decades of research have _____ that a severely restricted diet is connected to a long life span. (Paragraph G)

2. Several recent studies have _____ the link between longevity and caloric restriction. (Paragraph G)

3. The Calabrian results on gender offer yet another _____ that the genetic twists and turns that confer longevity may be unusually complex. (Paragraph M)

4. Major European studies had previously reported that women are much likelier to live to 100, … with the _____ that some of the reasons are genetic. (Paragraph M)

5. … the plethora of new studies _____ that longevity researchers are pushing the scientific conversation to a new level. (Paragraph Q)

As a writer, you have to show your readers why a piece of evidence is important. After you have provided a piece of evidence from your research, explain how that evidence supports your argument. You can introduce your explanation with the following phrases:

This research shows that …   *This supports/undermines the idea that …*

As this evidence shows, …   *This demonstrates/indicates that …*

The evidence suggests that …   *The implication of this is …*

For example: *A recent German study showed that teenagers who are exposed to tobacco ads are more likely to start smoking than teens who don't see these ads.* **This research shows that** *tobacco advertisements negatively affect teenagers, encouraging them to start smoking and potentially increasing their chances of having tobacco-related medical problems such as lung cancer and a stroke.*

APPLYING **E** Write an explanation for each piece of evidence that supports the following thesis statement: "Cigarette smoking around children should be made illegal."

1. According to James Garbarino of Cornell University, "More young children are killed by parental smoking than by all unintentional injuries combined."

   This demonstrates that _____

   _____

   _____

2. According to the World Health Organization, 600,000 nonsmokers die from secondhand smoke every year.

   _____

   _____

   _____

3. A recent study shows that the children of smokers are more likely to become smokers than the children of parents who don't smoke.

   _____

   _____

   _____

WRITING TASK

GOAL In this lesson you are going to write an argumentative essay on the following topic:

Governments should not invest so much in helping people live 100 years or longer. An aging population will cause problems for society.

To what extent do you agree?

A Explore the question above by completing the T-chart with your own ideas. Research the topic further and add to your notes.

BRAINSTORMING

Arguments that support this point of view	Arguments against this point of view
If most people live to 100, who will take care of all the elderly people?	Research into longevity may help us all be healthier.

B Follow the steps to make notes for your essay.

PLANNING

Step 1 Write notes about the background of your topic. For example, how quickly is the world population aging?

Step 2 Decide on your thesis statement and note it in the outline.

Step 3 Choose three arguments from your T-chart to support your thesis. It is often a good idea to present your strongest argument last.

Step 4 Write a topic sentence for each of your body paragraphs.

Step 5 For each body paragraph, write one or two pieces of evidence that support the ideas in your topic sentences. Include reasons why the evidence is significant.

Step 6 Note ideas for your conclusion.

OUTLINE

Introductory paragraph:

Give some background about the topic (e.g., how quickly is the world population aging?). What is your thesis statement?

_____

_____

_____

Body paragraph 1: What is one argument in support of your thesis?

Topic sentence: _____

_____

Explanation and examples: _____

_____

Body paragraph 2: What is a second argument in support of your thesis?

Topic sentence: _____

_____

Explanation and examples: _____

_____

Body paragraph 3: What is the strongest argument in support of your thesis?

Topic sentence: _____

_____

Explanation and examples: _____

_____

Concluding paragraph: Review your main points and your thesis statement.

_____

_____

FINAL DRAFT **C** Use the information in your outline to write a first draft of your essay.

REVISING PRACTICE

The draft on the opposite page is a model of an argumentative essay. Add the missing information (a–f) to create a better second draft.

a. According to WHO, while secondhand smoke can cause serious heart and lung diseases in adults, it can cause sudden death in infants (2013).

b. For that reason, new laws should be created that make it illegal to smoke around children.

c. Research shows that secondhand smoke

d. These statistics combined show that

e. Perhaps most importantly, it would protect those who can't protect themselves.

f. In addition to endangering children's health, exposure to smoking encourages children to smoke as teenagers and adults.

A

In the 1500s, when Europeans began using tobacco, people were not aware of the dangers of smoking. In fact, according to the article "Tobacco: From Miracle Cure to Toxin," doctors often prescribed tobacco as medicine, believing it could cure cancer and many other diseases (Wexler, 2006). But in the early 20th century, people began to suspect that tobacco was dangerous rather than helpful. These days, it is widely accepted that cigarette smoking is dangerous and can cause medical problems such as lung cancer and stroke. In some countries, tobacco companies are required to include health warnings on their cigarette packs. Right now, many people believe that secondhand smoke is dangerous, but not everyone agrees. Therefore, there are no laws protecting nonsmokers from secondhand smoke. As history has shown, we have been wrong about the safety of tobacco in the past and people suffered as a result. _____

B

_____ endangers nonsmokers' lives. The World Health Organization (WHO) states that 600,000 nonsmokers die from secondhand smoke every year. Approximately 28 percent of these people are children. According to the WHO's statistics, 40 percent of children have at least one smoking parent (2013). It's true that secondhand smoke is everywhere, and making smoking illegal around children won't protect them from all secondhand smoke. Nevertheless, as James Garbarino of Cornell University states, "More young children are killed by parental smoking than by all unintentional injuries combined" (Lang, 1998). If children were not forced to breathe their parents' secondhand smoke, their exposure to tobacco smoke would decrease dramatically. This demonstrates that enacting laws that prohibit people from smoking around children would have a positive impact on children's health and life expectancy.

C

Of course, secondhand smoke endangers everyone, not just children. However, laws should be enacted to protect children specifically because they can't protect themselves. If an adult doesn't want to be around secondhand smoke, he or she can just walk away. However, children don't always have that option. Children of smokers are especially in danger of suffering from secondhand smoke because smoking occurs in their homes every day. Secondhand smoke might be in every breath that they breathe. In addition, secondhand smoke affects infants differently than it does adults. _____

D

_____ According to an article in *Medical News Today*, a study showed that the children of smokers were "more than two times as likely to begin smoking cigarettes on a daily basis between the ages of 13 and 21 than were children whose parents didn't use tobacco" (Schwarz, 2005). This greatly increases the child's chances of an early death. WHO statistics show that tobacco use kills six million people a year (2013). _____ exposure to smoking is deadly for children, and lives would be saved if smoking around children were illegal.

E

Cigarette smoking is so popular that it will probably never completely disappear, even though people are aware of the dangers. However, there are things we can do in order to protect nonsmokers, especially children. Making it illegal to smoke around children would result in fewer children dying from secondhand smoke and fewer children becoming smokers. _____

One way to cite your sources is to include the last name of the author and the year in parentheses. If you introduce your information with the author's name, you include only the year in parentheses. This paper uses the APA (American Psychological Association) style.

You can use the background information in your opening paragraph to lead your reader to your thesis statement.

You can introduce opposing arguments in your research paper and then refute them.

Reference List

Lang, Susan S. (1998, Spring). Child protection expert says parental smoking is abuse. Human Ecology Forum, 26, 22. Retrieved from https://www.questia.com/library/journal/1G1-20979940/child-protection-expert-says-parental-smoking-is-abuse

Schwarz, Joel. (2005, September 28). Children whose parents smoked are twice as likely to begin smoking between ages 13 and 21 as offspring of nonsmokers. University of Washington. Retrieved from https://www.washington.edu/news/2005/09/28/children-whose-parents-smoked-are-twice-as-likely-to-begin-smoking-between-ages-13-and-21-as-offspring-of-nonsmokers/

Wexler, Thomas A. (2006, June 12). Tobacco: from miracle cure to toxin. YaleGlobal Online. Retrieved from https://yaleglobal.yale.edu/tobacco-miracle-cure-toxin

World Health Organization. (2013, July). Tobacco: fact sheet N° 339. Retrieved from www.who.int/mediacentre/factsheets/fs339/en/

REVISED DRAFT   **D**   **Now use the questions below to revise your essay.**

- ☐ Does your introduction give background on the topic?
- ☐ Does your thesis state the main points of the essay?
- ☐ Did you include and refute opposing viewpoints?
- ☐ Did you provide evidence in your body paragraphs?
- ☐ Did you use words and expressions for explaining the significance of evidence correctly?
- ☐ Does your concluding paragraph have a summary statement and a final thought?

FINAL DRAFT   **E**   **Follow the steps to write a final draft.**

1. Check your revised draft for mistakes with words and expressions for explaining the significance of evidence.

2. Now use the checklist on page 248 to write a final draft. Make any other necessary changes.

UNIT REVIEW

Answer the following questions.

1. What are two factors associated with human longevity?

   _____

   _____

2. What is one aspect of longevity you would like to know more about?

   _____

   _____

3. What are two phrases that you can use to explain the significance of evidence?

   _____

   _____

4. Do you remember the meanings of these words? Check (✔) the ones you know. Look back at the unit and review the ones you don't know.

   ☐ beyond   ☐ mechanisms AWL
   ☐ contradictory AWL   ☐ outcome AWL
   ☐ conversely AWL   ☐ outnumber
   ☐ gain insight AWL   ☐ ratio AWL
   ☐ implication AWL   ☐ reconstruct AWL
   ☐ intact   ☐ restriction AWL
   ☐ life span   ☐ undermine
   ☐ longevity

TRUTH AND DECEPTION

9

The Malaysian orchid mantis
deceives its prey with its
flower-like appearance.

ACADEMIC SKILLS

READING	Understanding a research summary
WRITING	Writing a research summary
GRAMMAR	Introducing results and describing data
CRITICAL THINKING	Evaluating research

THINK AND DISCUSS

1 Is it ever okay to lie? Why or why not?
2 How do you feel when you tell a lie? How do you feel when you find out someone has lied to you?

A Look at the information on these pages and answer the questions.

1. What kinds of lies are most common?

2. Why did the people or organizations listed below lie? In which categories of the chart would you put the lies they told?

Nixon: _____ Barnum: _____

White Sox: _____

B Match the words in blue to their definitions.

_____ (v) to hide the truth about a mistake or wrongdoing

_____ (v) to give false information or guide someone wrongly

_____ (n) lack of guilt, the state of having done nothing wrong

In 2016, behavioral scientist Timothy Levine conducted a survey to find out why people lie. He asked approximately 500 participants from five countries—including Guatemala, Egypt, and the United States—to describe a time that they lied or that someone lied to them. He found that there were four main categories of reasons that people **mislead** others: to protect oneself; to promote oneself; to impact others—that is, to protect them or to harm them; and for reasons that are not clear.

The infographic breaks down the four ▶ main categories into more specific reasons for lying, such as to **cover up** a mistake (to protect oneself) and to gain financial benefits (to promote oneself).

FAMOUS LIES

Richard Nixon

TIM MCDONAGH

In June 1972, five men broke into the Watergate building in Washington, D. C. to photograph documents and secretly record phone conversations in order to help President Richard Nixon win his reelection campaign. Nixon denied all involvement and asserted his **innocence**, declaring, "I am not a crook." But the White House cover-up failed, and Nixon resigned from office.

P. T. Barnum

TIM MCDONAGH

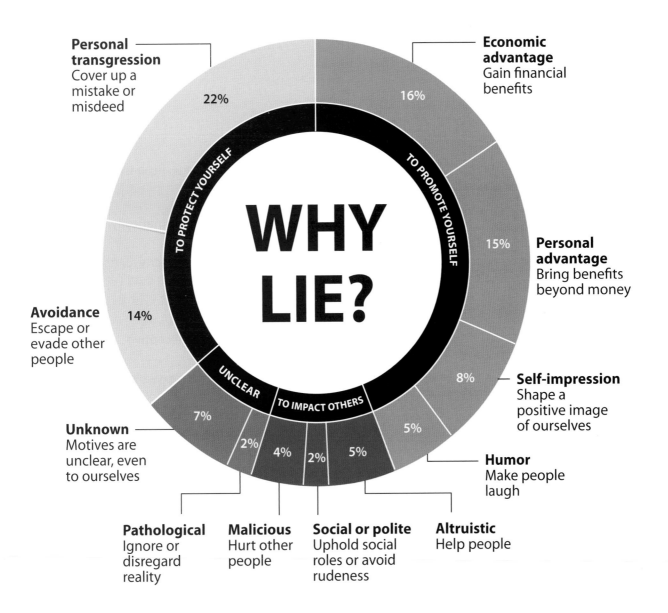

WHY LIE?

TO PROTECT YOURSELF

Personal transgression
Cover up a mistake or misdeed
22%

Avoidance
Escape or evade other people
14%

TO PROMOTE YOURSELF

Economic advantage
Gain financial benefits
16%

Personal advantage
Bring benefits beyond money
15%

Self-impression
Shape a positive image of ourselves
8%

Humor
Make people laugh
5%

UNCLEAR

Unknown
Motives are unclear, even to ourselves
7%

TO IMPACT OTHERS

Pathological
Ignore or disregard reality
2%

Malicious
Hurt other people
4%

Social or polite
Uphold social roles or avoid rudeness
2%

Altruistic
Help people
5%

P. T. Barnum, a showman and businessman from the United States, was famous for promoting and profiting from elaborate hoaxes. In 1835, for example, Barnum claimed that a woman in one of his shows was Joice Heth, George Washington's nursemaid, who would have been 161 years old. Crowds paid to see "the greatest natural and national curiosity in the world." After her death, however, an examination of the woman's body found her to be no more than 80 years old.

The 1919 Chicago White Sox

TIM MCDONAGH

Nearly a century ago, some members of the Chicago White Sox baseball team accepted a huge amount of money to deliberately lose the 1919 World Series. The eight players who took the bribe were caught and banned from the game for life.

Reading

PREPARING TO READ

BUILDING
VOCABULARY

A The words in blue below are used in the reading passage. Read the sentences. Then match the correct form of each word to its definition.

> A polygraph, or lie detector, is a machine designed to **automatically** recognize when a person is lying.
>
> According to a study in *Nature Neuroscience*, a person's **capacity** for dishonesty increases each time they lie; that is, as they lie more, they get better at it.
>
> The **emergence** of new social science data in the form of studies and surveys continually improves our understanding of human behavior.
>
> The harmless appearance of a box jellyfish is incredibly **deceptive**—its venom is among the most deadly in the world.
>
> Kang Lee, a **prominent** behavioral psychologist, has done extensive research into the development of lying in children.
>
> Frank Abagnale, Jr., was able to fly around the world for free by impersonating an airline pilot. When he was found to be an **impostor**, he was jailed for six months.

1. _____ (adj) giving an appearance or impression that is misleading or untrue

2. _____ (adj) important and well-known

3. _____ (n) a person who dishonestly pretends to be someone else

4. _____ (n) the process of something coming into existence

5. _____ (n) the amount that something is able to produce

6. _____ (adv) done without thinking

BUILDING
VOCABULARY

B Complete the definitions with the words in the box. Use a dictionary to help you.

deceitful	gullible	fundamental	prone to	systematically	thrive

1. If someone is _____, they behave in a dishonest way.

2. To _____ is to become successful or to grow and increase in strength.

3. If a person is _____ doing something, they do it often and will likely do it again.

4. If someone is _____, they can be easily tricked.

5. If you do something _____, you do it following a fixed method or plan.

6. A _____ part of something is a basic and essential aspect of it.

C Note answers to the questions below. Then discuss with a partner.

1. Are people in certain professions more **prone to** lying than others? Why or why not?

   _____

   _____

2. How can you tell if someone is being **deceitful**?

   _____

   _____

3. Do you think we become less **gullible** as we get older? Explain your answer.

   _____

   _____

D Work with a partner. Make a list of things that people often lie about. Note your ideas below.

   _____

   _____

   _____

E Skim the passage. How many of your ideas in **D** are mentioned?

Leonardo DiCaprio (center) plays Frank Abagnale, Jr., in the 2002 movie *Catch Me If You Can.*

WHY WE LIE

by Yudhijit Bhattacharjee

> Honesty may be the best policy, but scheming and dishonesty may be part of what makes us human.

🔊 2.4

The history of humankind is filled with skilled and practiced liars. Many are criminals who spin lies and weave **deceptive** tales to gain unjust rewards. Some are politicians who lie to gain power, or to cling to it. Sometimes people lie to boost their image, others lie to **cover up** bad behavior. Even the academic science community—a world largely devoted to the pursuit of truth—has been shown to contain a number of deceivers. But the lies of **impostors**, swindlers, and boasting politicians are just a sample of the untruths that have characterized human behavior for thousands of years.

Lying, it turns out, is something that most of us are very skilled at. We lie with ease, in ways big and small, to strangers, co-workers, friends, and loved ones. Our **capacity** for lying is as **fundamental** to us as our need to trust others. Being **deceitful** is part of our nature, so much so that we might say that to lie is human.

Our natural tendency to lie was first **systematically** documented by Bella DePaulo, a social psychologist at the University of California, Santa Barbara. Two decades ago, DePaulo and her colleagues asked 147 adults to note down every instance they lied or tried to **mislead** someone during one week. The researchers found that the subjects lied on average one or two times a day. Most of these untruths were harmless, intended to hide one's failings or to protect the feelings of others. Some lies were excuses—one person blamed their failure to take out the garbage on not knowing where it needed to go. Yet other lies—such as a claim of being a diplomat's son—were told to present a false image. While these were minor transgressions, DePaulo and other colleagues observed [in a later study] that most people have, at some point, told one or more "serious lies": hiding an affair from a husband or wife, for example, or making false claims on a college application.

That human beings should universally possess a talent for deceiving one another shouldn't surprise us. Researchers speculate that lying as a behavior arose not long after the **emergence** of language. The ability to manipulate others without using physical force may have helped us compete for resources—something similar to the evolution of deceptive strategies like camouflage[1] in the animal kingdom. "Lying is so easy compared to other ways of gaining power," notes ethicist[2] Sissela Bok of Harvard University, one of the most **prominent** thinkers on the subject. "It's much easier to lie in order to get somebody's money or wealth than to hit them over the head or rob a bank."

As dishonesty has come to be recognized as a fundamental human trait, social science researchers and neuroscientists have sought to understand the nature and roots of the behavior. How and when do we learn to lie? What are the psychological foundations of dishonesty? And why do we believe lies so easily?

[1]**Camouflage** is the way in which some animals are colored and shaped so that they cannot easily be seen in their surroundings.
[2]An **ethicist** is someone who studies questions about what is morally right and wrong.

Lying is something of a developmental milestone—like learning to walk and talk. Parents often find their children's lies troubling, as they signal the beginning of a loss of **innocence**. However, Kang Lee, a psychologist at the University of Toronto, sees the emergence of the behavior in toddlers as a reassuring sign that their cognitive growth is on track.

To study lying in children, Lee and his colleagues use a simple experiment. They ask kids to guess the identity of hidden toys, based only on an audio clue. For the first few toys, the clue is obvious—a bark for a dog, a meow for a cat—and the children answer easily. Then they play a sound that has nothing to do with the toy. "So you play Beethoven, but the toy's a car," Lee explains. The experimenter leaves the room pretending to take a phone call—a lie for the sake of science—and asks the child not to peek[3] at the toy. Returning, the experimenter asks the child for the answer, then follows up with the question: "Did you peek?"

Using hidden cameras, Lee and his researchers have discovered that the majority of children can't resist[4] peeking. The percentage of children who peek and then lie about it depends on their age. Among two-year-olds who peek, only about one third lie about it. Among three-year-olds, half lie. And by age eight, approximately 80 percent of the children tested claim they didn't peek.

Kids also get better at lying as they get older. When asked to guess the identity of the toy (that they have secretly looked at), three- and four-year-olds typically give the right answer straightaway—they don't realize that this reveals that they cheated. At seven or eight, kids learn to deliberately give a wrong answer at first, or they try to make their answer seem like a reasoned guess.

Five- and six-year-old kids fall in between. In one study, Lee used a Barney the dinosaur toy. One five-year-old girl denied that she had looked at the toy, which was hidden under a cloth. Then she told Lee she wanted to feel it before guessing. "So she puts her hand underneath the cloth, closes her eyes, and says, 'Ah, I know it's Barney,'" Lee recalls. "I ask, 'Why?' She says, 'Because it feels purple.'"

What drives this increase in lying sophistication[5] is the development of a child's ability to put himself or herself in someone else's shoes. Known as "theory of mind," this is the facility we acquire for understanding the beliefs, intentions, and knowledge of others. Also fundamental to lying is the brain's executive function: the abilities required for planning, making decisions, and self-control. This explains why the two-year-olds who lied and lied well in Lee's experiments performed better on tests of theory of mind and executive function than those who didn't.

[3]If you **peek** at something, you have a quick look at it, often secretly.
[4]If you **resist** doing something, you stop yourself from doing it even though you would like to.

[5]If something has a high level of **sophistication**, it is more advanced or complex than others.

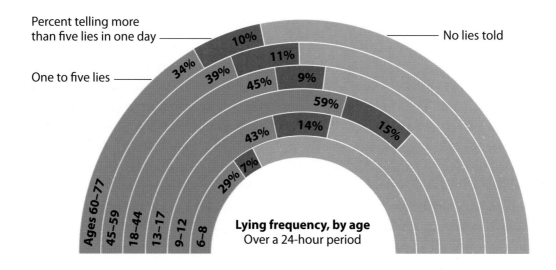

Percent telling more than five lies in one day — 10% — No lies told

One to five lies — 34% 39% 11%

45% 9%

59%

43% 14%

29% 7% 15%

Ages 60–77 / 45–59 / 18–44 / 13–17 / 9–12 / 6–8

Lying frequency, by age
Over a 24-hour period

As we grow older, much of the knowledge we use to navigate the world comes from what others tell us. Without the implicit[6] trust that we place in human communication, we would be paralyzed[7] as individuals and cease to have social relationships. "We get so much from believing, and there's relatively little harm when we occasionally get duped," says Tim Levine, a psychologist at the University of Alabama.

Being programmed to trust makes us naturally **gullible**. "If you say to someone, 'I am a pilot,' they are not sitting there thinking: 'Maybe he's not a pilot. Why would he say he's a pilot?' They don't think that way," says Frank Abagnale, Jr. Now a security consultant, Abagnale's cons[8] as a young man—including forging checks and pretending to be an airline pilot—inspired the 2002 movie *Catch Me If You Can*. "This is why scams work," he says. "When the phone rings and the caller ID says it's the Internal Revenue Service,[9] people **automatically** believe it is the IRS. They don't realize that someone could manipulate the caller ID."

Robert Feldman, a psychologist at the University of Massachusetts, calls that "the liar's advantage." "People are not expecting lies, people are not searching for lies," he says, "and a lot of the time, people want to hear what they are hearing." We put up little resistance[10] to the deceptions that please or comfort us—such as false praise or the promise of impossibly high investment returns. And when we deal with people who have wealth, power, and status, the lies appear to be even easier to swallow.

Researchers are now learning that we are **prone to** believe some lies even when they're clearly contradicted by evidence. These insights suggest that our skill at deceiving others—combined with our vulnerability[11] to being deceived—is especially consequential in the age of social media. Research has shown, for example, that we are especially prone to accepting lies that affirm our worldview. False news stories **thrive** on the Internet and in social media because of this vulnerability, and disproving them does not tend to lessen their power. This is because people assess the evidence presented to them through a framework of preexisting beliefs and prejudices, says George Lakoff, a cognitive linguist at the University of California, Berkeley. "If a fact comes in that doesn't fit into your frame, you'll either not notice it, or ignore it, or ridicule it, or be puzzled by it—or attack it if it's threatening."

What then might be the best way to impede the rapid advance of untruths into our collective lives? The answer isn't clear. Technology has opened up a new frontier for deceit, adding a 21st-century twist to the age-old conflict between our lying and trusting selves.

[11]**Vulnerability** is the state of being open to attack or damage.

Adapted from "Why We Lie," by Yudhijit Bhattacharjee, National Geographic Magazine June 2017.

[6]If someone has **implicit** trust in something, they trust absolutely, without any doubts.
[7]If you are **paralyzed**, you are unable to act or function properly.
[8]Short for confidence trick, a **con** is a trick in which someone deceives you, usually with the intention of gaining money or power.
[9]In the United States, the **Internal Revenue Service (IRS)** is the government authority that collects taxes.
[10]To **put up resistance** to something means to refuse to accept it and try to prevent it.

Yudhijit Bhattacharjee is an award-winning writer whose features and essays on science, espionage, cybercrime, and medicine have appeared in *The New Yorker, The New York Times Magazine, National Geographic, Wired*, and other magazines.

UNDERSTANDING THE READING

UNDERSTANDING
MAIN IDEAS

A Check (✓) the four topics that the writer covers in the reading passage.

a. ☐ the reasons that people lie

b. ☐ how often people lie

c. ☐ why people believe lies

d. ☐ cross-cultural differences in lying

e. ☐ the emotional effects of lying and being deceptive

f. ☐ the relationship between lying and cognitive development

IDENTIFYING
SUPPORTING IDEAS

B Complete the summaries below with details from the reading passage.

We are natural liars	We are naturally gullible
Psychologist Bella DePaulo asked 147 adults to write down every time they attempted to ¹_____ for a period of ²_____.	Tim Levine says that getting tricked occasionally isn't a problem because we get so much benefit from believing others.
It was discovered that people lied an average of ³_____ times a day, though most of these lies were ⁴_____.	According to Frank Abagnale, Jr., scams work because we are trained to ⁸_____ people in authority.
In a later study, DePaulo and other colleagues learned that most people have told ⁵_____ lies at some point in their lives.	Psychologist Robert Feldman says that we don't ⁹_____ lies; we want to believe what we hear, especially if it's ¹⁰_____.
Researchers think that humans began lying with the invention of ⁶_____ because it's easier to lie to get what we want than it is to use ⁷_____.	Research shows we tend to believe things that are clearly ¹¹_____. Cognitive linguist George Lakoff explains that we are more likely to believe lies when they fit into our preexisting ¹²_____.

IDENTIFYING
MEANING FROM
CONTEXT

C Find and underline the following words and phrases in the reading passage. Use the context to match each word or phrase to its definition.

> **unjust** (paragraph A)   **manipulate** (paragraph D)   **reassuring** (paragraph F)
> **on track** (paragraph F)   **get duped** (paragraph L)   **twist** (paragraph P)

1. _____ (adj) not fair

2. _____ (adj) making you feel less worried about something

3. _____ (v) to control or influence a person or situation, often unfairly

4. _____ (n) an unexpected and significant occurrence

5. _____ (v) to be tricked into believing something that is not true

6. _____ (adj) following a course likely to result in success

CRITICAL THINKING   Writers sometimes refer to scientific research and behavioral studies to support their main ideas. When you read information about an experiment or study, it's important to ask yourself questions to **evaluate the research** and identify any limitations. For example, you can ask:

- How did the researchers choose or gather the subjects?
- Were the subjects representative of the population studied in terms of age, gender, and so forth?
- Were the results reliable? Were they interpreted correctly?

D Work with a partner. Note answers to the questions below. Then discuss with a partner.

CRITICAL THINKING: EVALUATING RESEARCH

1. Do you think the people in DePaulo's study record their answers truthfully? Why or why not?

_____

_____

2. Which untruths do you think the participants were more likely to record?

_____

_____

3. Is there a better way to do the study? What might you have done differently?

_____

_____

E Look back at the quote from George Lakoff in the final sentence of paragraph O. What does he mean by "doesn't fit into your frame"? Discuss your ideas with a partner.

CRITICAL THINKING: INTERPRETING

F Think of a news story that you heard about that turned out to be false. Note answers to the questions below. Then discuss with a partner.

CRITICAL THINKING RELATING

1. What was the story about?

_____

_____

2. How could you tell the story was false?

_____

_____

3. What problems do you think misleading news stories like this could cause?

_____

_____

DEVELOPING READING SKILLS

READING SKILL Understanding a Research Summary

When writers refer to studies, they often summarize the main points of the research. These points usually include:

- the **purpose** of the study (the question that they want to answer)
- the **method** (how they set up and carried out the study)
- the **results** (what the study found)
- and the **conclusion** (the significance of the results—that is, how they answered the research question)

When reading a research summary, it's useful to highlight these points and identify them in the margins.

UNDERSTANDING A RESEARCH SUMMARY

A The sentences below summarize a piece of research known as "The Matrix Experiments." What does each sentence describe? Write **purpose**, **method**, **results**, or **conclusion**.

In the experiments, over 40,000 volunteers were given a five-minute test with 20 simple math problems. They were then asked to state how many questions they had answered correctly. _____

The Matrix Experiments were a series of studies designed to measure dishonesty in adults. _____

The results suggested that while lying is common, there are very few people who tell big lies. _____

On average, 70% of people lied about their test results. But only 20 out of the 40,000 claimed to have solved all 20 problems. _____

UNDERSTANDING A RESEARCH SUMMARY

B Reread paragraphs G–I of the reading passage. Highlight and label the parts that explain the **purpose**, **method**, and **results** of Kang Lee's study.

UNDERSTANDING A RESEARCH SUMMARY

C Write a concluding sentence to explain the significance of the results.

_____

_____

Video

LEARNING TO LIE

In 2015, psychologist Kang Lee analyzed the lying habits of young children.

BEFORE VIEWING

A In what situations might children tell lies? Discuss with a partner.

DISCUSSION

B Read about some more of psychologist Kang Lee's research. Then answer the questions.

LEARNING ABOUT THE TOPIC

What makes children good liars? For over 20 years, Kang Lee, a psychologist at the University of Toronto, has been studying how children lie. He has found that there are two key ingredients that make some children better liars than others. One is the ability to recognize that another person's knowledge of a situation may be less complete than your own. Known as "theory of mind," this ability allows a person to identify circumstances in which a lie might be believed. The second factor is self-control. In order to lie well, children have to be able to control their body language and their facial expressions. This is because, unless they are well controlled, a person's body and facial movements can often indicate that they are lying.

1. What are two skills children need in order to be good at telling lies?

   _____

   _____

2. Look back at the reading passage. Why does Kang Lee believe lying can be a good sign in children?

   _____

   _____

C The words in **bold** below are used in the video. Match the correct form of each word to its definition.

> In one of Lee's studies, a child peeked at a toy when he was told not to. Then he lied in order to cover up his **transgression**.
>
> We don't normally **condone** lying in children. In fact, many parents do not tolerate this behavior.
>
> Lee states that lying is a **milestone** in a child's life because when children start to do it, it's an indication that they are developing normally.

1. _____ (v) to approve of or allow something

2. _____ (n) the act of doing something wrong

3. _____ (n) an important stage in a process or journey

WHILE VIEWING

A ▶ Watch the video. Circle the correct option to complete each sentence.

1. The purpose of the first experiment is to test a child's ability to
   tell when someone is lying / tell white lies.

2. The purpose of the second experiment is to test a child's ability to lie in order to
   cover up a transgression / help another person.

B ▶ Watch the video again. Complete the notes below.

Experiment One—Method	Experiment Two—Method
• Researcher asks child series of questions	• Researcher plays card game with child
• Researcher gives child a prize	• Researcher tells child that if next answer is right, she will get a prize

AFTER VIEWING

A Kang Lee sees the ability to lie as a positive development in a child's life. How do you think a parent should react if their child lies to them? Discuss with a partner.

B Why does Kang Lee say that a world in which no one lies would be a very cruel place? Discuss with a partner.

Writing

EXPLORING WRITTEN ENGLISH

A Read the sentences. How else could the quantities in **bold** be expressed? Discuss with a partner. Then look again at paragraph H of the reading to check your ideas.

NOTICING

1. Lee and his researchers have discovered that **more than 50 percent** of children can't resist peeking.

2. Among two-year-olds who peek, **just over 30 percent** lie about it.

3. Among three-year-olds, **50 percent** lie.

4. By age eight, **about four-fifths** of the children tested claim they didn't peek.

LANGUAGE FOR WRITING Introducing Results and Describing Data

When you refer to numerical data, you can use words and phrases to describe it instead of using numbers. Sometimes using words and phrases rather than numbers and percentages to express data can make it easier for readers to understand the significance of the data. It can also make your writing more interesting and less repetitive.

Some words that express percentages and numerical data include:

1 in 10 = *10 percent*	**two-fifths** = *40 percent*
1 in 5 = *20 percent*	**two-thirds** = *66.6 percent*
a quarter = *25 percent*	**three-quarters** = *75 percent*
a third = *33.3 percent*	**the majority (of)** = *more than 50 percent*
half = *50 percent*	**almost all** = *slightly less than 100 percent*

In addition, you can add modifiers such as *fewer/less than, more than, approximately, nearly, exactly, precisely,* and *just over.*

> **More than a quarter** of those who took part in the study were children.

> **Approximately a third** of those aged 13–17 told no lies over the 24-hour period.

When you summarize a research study or article, you can use certain words and phrases to introduce the results of the study.

Here are some expressions for introducing results. Both the active and passive voice are often used.

> *Researchers found / discovered / saw / observed / noticed that …*
> *It was found / discovered / observed / noticed that …*

B Look back at the infographic on *Lying frequency* in the reading passage. Complete the sentences using words and phrases from the Language for Writing box.

INTRODUCING RESULTS AND DESCRIBING DATA

1. Researchers found that _____ of people aged 60–77 told one to five lies over a 24-hour period.

2. _____ of people aged 45–59 told no lies.

3. _____ children aged 9–12 told at least one lie in 24 hours.

4. _____ of children aged 6–8 told one to five lies.

TRUTH AND DECEPTION **201**

C Write two more sentences describing the data in the infographic. Use words and phrases from the Language for Writing box.

1. _____

    _____

2. _____

    _____

WRITING SKILL Summarizing Research

A research summary covers the main points of a scientific study.

Part 1—Purpose of study: Includes background on the issue and states the question(s) the researchers wanted to answer

Part 2—Method: Explains how the researchers set up the study, what they did, and what they had the participants/subjects do

Part 3—Results: Describes what the researchers found, how the participants behaved, or what happened

Part 4—Conclusion: Explains the significance of the results/what the results of the study indicate regarding the research question

---

D Read the notes for a research summary. Write the letters a–g in the correct places in the outline.

The Stanford Marshmallow Experiment

a. The aim was to find out if children could delay gratification, and how this ability can affect people's lives.

b. About 33 percent of children were able to delay gratification long enough to eat both marshmallows.

c. Researchers took children into a room with a chair, a small desk, two marshmallows, and a bell.

d. About 33 percent of subjects rang the bell and ate one marshmallow immediately after researchers left.

e. People who are able to resist their impulses and delay gratification tend to be more successful in life.

f. Researchers later found that participants who delayed gratification had higher SAT scores and were better able to deal with stress.

g. The researchers left the room after telling the children they could eat both marshmallows if they waited until the researchers came back. The children were told that if they couldn't wait, they could ring the bell and eat one marshmallow. The researchers left the children alone for up to 20 minutes.

Outline

1. Introduction (purpose of study): _____

2. Method: _____ _____

3. Results: _____ _____ _____

4. Conclusion: _____

WRITING TASK

GOAL In this lesson, you are going to write an essay on the following topic:

Write a research summary of a famous study.

A Research some of the experiments listed below. Decide which one you will summarize. Then find two or more articles that give details about the experiment you have chosen.

RESEARCHING

- The Invisible Gorilla Experiment; conducted by Daniel Simons and Christopher Chabris
- The Good Samaritan Experiment; conducted by John Darley and Daniel Batson
- A Class Divided; conducted by Jane Elliott
- Ross's False Consensus Effect Study; conducted by Lee Ross
- Car Crash Experiment; conducted by Elizabeth Loftus and John Palmer
- The Chameleon Effect; conducted by Tanya Chartrand and John Bargh

B Follow these steps to make notes for your summary.

PLANNING

Step 1 Read the articles once to understand the main points of the experiment.

Step 2 Reread the articles and take notes in your own words. Identify the purpose of the study, the method(s), the result(s) of the experiment, and the conclusion suggested by the results. (See Unit 5 for a review of information on avoiding plagiarism.)

Step 3 Use your notes to complete the outline. Make note of where you got your information. Include the references at the end of your research summary.

OUTLINE

Purpose of Study: _____

_____

Method: _____

_____

_____

_____

_____

_____

TRUTH AND DECEPTION **203**

Results: _____

_____

_____

_____

Conclusion: _____

_____

FIRST DRAFT **C** Use the information in your outline to write a first draft of your research summary.

REVISING PRACTICE

The draft below is a model of the type of research summary you are writing. Follow the steps to create a better second draft.

1. Write the sentences or phrases (a–c) in the correct spaces.

   a. If they couldn't wait until the researchers returned, the children could ring the bell and eat one, but not both, of the marshmallows.

   b. The researchers also found that in adulthood, the children who had been able to wait longer for the marshmallows had been able to avoid addictive behaviors, had more stable marriages, and were in better physical health.

   c. Ultimately, however, Mischel transformed his experiment into a longitudinal study (one conducted over several years) to find out how people's ability to delay gratification affects the rest of their lives.

2. Now fix the following problems (a–b) with the summary.

   a. Fix a problem with language for introducing results in the Results section.

   b. Replace a percentage with a word or phrase to avoid repetition at the start of the Results section.

The Stanford Marshmallow Experiment

Purpose of Study

In the 1960s and 1970s, Stanford psychologist Walter Mischel conducted a series of studies with 653 preschool students aged three to five. The original purpose of the study was to determine at what age children develop the ability to resist their impulses and delay their own gratification. _____

Method

In the study, researchers took individual children into a room with nothing but a chair and a small desk. On the desk were two marshmallows and a bell. The researchers told each child that they had to leave for a few minutes. They also told the children that if they waited until the researchers came back, they would win both marshmallows. _____ The researchers then left the children alone with both marshmallows for up to 20 minutes to observe whether or not the children were able to wait.

Results

The researchers found that about 33 percent of the children were able to delay their gratification long enough to win both marshmallows. Approximately 33 percent of the subjects rang the bell and ate one marshmallow immediately after researchers left. Another 33 percent of the subjects tried to wait, covering their eyes, tugging on their ponytails, or making up songs in order to distract themselves. However, they gave in before the researchers returned to the room. The researchers continued to study the children's lives long into adolescence and adulthood. It found that as teenagers, the participants who could delay their own gratification as children had higher levels of self-esteem, higher SAT scores, and were better able to deal with stress than the participants who had not been able to control their impulses. _____

Conclusion

The results of Mischel's longitudinal study demonstrated that people who are able to control their impulses and delay their own gratification tend to be more successful in life.

D Now use the questions below to revise your paragraph.

REVISED DRAFT

☐ Did you explain the purpose of the study?

☐ Did you explain the method clearly and thoroughly?

☐ Did you include the results of the study?

☐ Did you describe the conclusion of the study?

☐ Did you correctly use phrases for introducing results?

☐ Did you use words and phrases to vary the way data is expressed?

In the Stanford Marshmallow experiment, about one third of children were able to resist the temptation to eat the marshmallow.

EDITING PRACTICE

Read the information below. Then find and correct one mistake with words and phrases for describing data in each of the sentences (1–4).

In sentences with words and phrases that describe data, remember:

- the verb usually agrees with the main noun

  e.g. *Two-thirds of the country's drinking <u>water</u> **is** imported from abroad.*
  *A third of all the <u>customers</u> in the survey **were** unhappy with the service they received.*

- include *of* before a noun, after phrases such as a *third, three-quarters*, and *the majority*

- use *fewer than* with plural count nouns and *less than* with noncount nouns

1. A third of the participants was able to delay gratification.

2. The majority of the research were carried out in South America.

3. Around two-thirds the participants weren't able to wait for the two marshmallows.

4. Less than one hundred children took part in the study.

FINAL DRAFT **E** Follow the steps to write a final draft.

1. Check your revised draft for mistakes with words and phrases for referring to results and data.

2. Now use the checklist on page 248 to write a final draft. Make any other necessary changes.

UNIT REVIEW

Answer the following questions.

1. What are two reasons people lie?

_____

_____

2. Why might someone believe a lie that is clearly contradicted by evidence?

_____

_____

3. What are the four main parts of a research summary?

_____

_____

4. Do you remember the meanings of these words? Check (✔) the ones you know. Look back at the unit and review the ones you don't know.

☐ automatically AWL
☐ capacity AWL
☐ cover up
☐ deceitful
☐ deceptive
☐ emergence AWL
☐ fundamental AWL
☐ gullible

☐ impostor AWL
☐ innocence
☐ mislead
☐ prominent
☐ prone to
☐ systematically
☐ thrive

IMAGINING THE FUTURE

10

An architect's vision of the city of London in the future

ACADEMIC SKILLS

READING Identifying literary elements
WRITING Writing an analytical essay
GRAMMAR Using a variety of sentence types
CRITICAL THINKING Reading literature critically

THINK AND DISCUSS

1 How do you think cities of the future will be different to today?
2 What do you think it would be like to leave Earth and live on another planet?

EXPLORE THE THEME

A Look at the information on these pages and answer the questions.

1. What challenges of living on Mars are mentioned in the infographic?
2. What other challenges do you think the first people to visit Mars might have?

B Match the correct form of the words in blue to their definitions.

_____ (v) to create a new permanent home

_____ (n) the main place where you work or live

_____ (v) to land

1 TEMPORARY SHELTER

NASA is testing a flexible life-support structure that recycles all water, air, and waste. It would serve as a base for working astronauts while permanent shelters are assembled.

2 BUILDING MATERIALS

Transporting resources from Earth to Mars would be very expensive. One option for creating permanent shelters would involve using the soil on Mars to create building materials.

FIRST STEPS ON MARS

4

The idea of humans settling on Mars was once an idea restricted to science fiction novels. But the day when human beings touch down on the surface of the red planet for the first time is drawing closer. NASA is already preparing to send humans to set up bases on Mars. However, even with advanced technology, it won't be easy to survive in the harsh Martian environment.

3

3 GETTING AROUND

Pressurized rovers able to carry two people could be used to aid exploration missions on the surface.

4 THE Z-2 SUIT

A special suit is essential to enable astronauts to work outside. They would slide into and out of the Z-2 space suit through a "suit port" in the back, which would attach directly to the outside of a pressurized shelter or rover.

Reading

PREPARING TO READ

BUILDING
VOCABULARY

A The words in **blue** below are used in the reading passage. Match the correct form of each word to its definition.

THE POWER OF SCIENCE FICTION

Ever since people first gazed up at the flickering stars, we have wondered what might be "out there." This fascination with distant worlds is still with us today. When we watch movies such as *Star Trek* or *Star Wars* and their many **sequels**, we can visit worlds that look familiar and strange at the same time. We can also see what beings from other planets might be like. For example, Peter Quill, the human **protagonist** in the *Guardians of the Galaxy* movies works with species from various planets—including a walking, talking tree and a raccoon—to protect the galaxy from a **ruthless** villain with superhuman strength. Science fiction also allows us to imagine the eventual **destiny** of our own planet. The movie *Arrival*, for example, gives us a **glimpse** of a future where **aliens** come to Earth to make contact with humans.

1. A(n) _____ is a being from another planet.

2. A(n) _____ is the main character in a movie, play, or book.

3. If someone is _____, they are very cruel and are willing to make other people suffer to achieve their goals.

4. _____ refers to what will happen in the future, especially when it is thought to be controlled by someone or something else.

5. A(n) _____ of something is a brief experience or view of it.

6. A(n) _____ to a book or a movie continues its story.

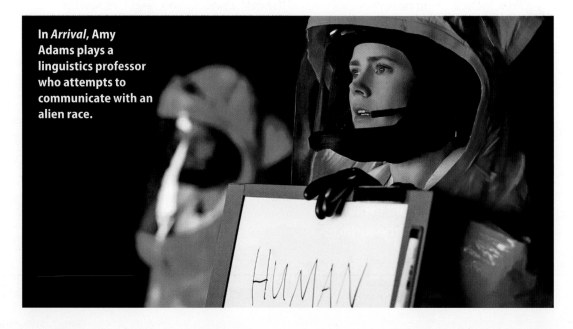

In *Arrival*, Amy Adams plays a linguistics professor who attempts to communicate with an alien race.

B Complete the definitions with the words in the box. Use a dictionary to help you.

| flee | inferior | intellectual | literally | stunned | unimaginable |

1. If you _____ a person or thing, you escape from that person or thing.

2. If you are _____ by something, you are extremely shocked or surprised by it.

3. We use the word "_____" to describe something that deals with knowledge, thought, and understanding.

4. If something is _____, it is lower in status than something else.

5. If something is _____, it is very difficult to create a mental picture of it.

6. We use the word "_____" to show that something we are saying is really true.

C Discuss these questions with a partner.

1. Do you think humans will ever make contact with **aliens**? Why or why not?

2. What do you think is the **destiny** of our own planet? What will it be like 1,000 years from now?

D Note answers to the questions below. Then discuss with a partner.

1. What are some reasons that someone might want to write stories about space exploration?

   _____

2. What are some reasons that humans might want to live on another planet?

   _____

3. What are some reasons aliens might want to come to Earth?

   _____

E Skim the following passages and answer the questions. As you read, check your predictions.

1. What kind of reading is the first passage?

   a. a fictional story

   b. an autobiographical essay

   c. an explanatory article

2. What kinds of readings are the second and third passages?

   a. fictional stories

   b. extracts from an autobiography

   c. explanatory articles

MY MARS

by Ray Bradbury

> "That was the day Mars took me home—and I never really came back."

🎧 2.5

When I was six years old, I moved to Tucson, Arizona, and lived on Lowell Avenue, little realizing I was on an avenue that led to Mars. A It was named for the great astronomer Percival Lowell, who took fantastic photographs of the planet that promised a spacefaring future to children like myself.

Along the way to growing up, I read Edgar Rice Burroughs and loved his Martian books, and followed the instructions of his Mars pioneer John Carter, who told me, when I was 12, that it B was simple: If I wanted to follow the avenue of Lowell and go to the stars, I needed to go out on the summer night lawn, lift my arms, stare at the planet Mars, and say, "Take me home."

That was the day that Mars took me home—and I never really came back. I began writing on C a toy typewriter. I couldn't afford to buy all the Martian books I wanted, so I wrote the **sequels** myself.

When I was 15, a Martian disguised as an American boy went to see the film *Things to Come,* by H. G. Wells, about a dark, war-torn future Earth. In the final scene the **protagonist,** D Cabal, and his friend Passworthy watch the first moon rocket disappear into the heavens carrying their two grown children toward a brighter **destiny.** Cabal looks toward the dust at his feet then up at the stars, saying to Passworthy and to the audience, "Is it this or that? All the universe or nothing? Which shall it be? Which shall it be?"

This Martian staggered out of the theater E inspired to write more stories because I knew we were going to the stars.

Some years later, I made my way to New York City on a Greyhound bus, hoping to find a publisher. I carried a bundle of manuscripts with me, and people would ask, "Is that a novel?" To F which I replied, "No, I write short stories." On my last night in New York, I got a break. I had dinner with an editor from Doubleday who said to me, "I think that without realizing it, you have, in fact, written a novel."

G I asked him what he meant.

He replied, "If you tied all your Martian landscapes together and made a tapestry of them, H wouldn't they make a book that you could call *The Martian Chronicles?*"

I was **stunned.** The small Martian in me hadn't realized that he'd been putting his hands inside my hands and moving the typewriter keys I to write a book. I finished it over the next six months. I was 29—and well on my way to the stars.

In 1976 I was invited to stay overnight at the J Jet Propulsion Laboratory in Pasadena, waiting for news to come back from the *Viking 1* lander, which was going to **touch down** on Mars and take photographs.

K It was incredibly exciting to be there, surrounded by engineers, waiting for the first pictures. There was a tall gentleman standing next to me, who I thought looked familiar. At last, I realized it was none other than Wernher von Braun, the man who had **fled** Germany for America to become the co-inventor of the rocket that took us to the moon and that was now taking us to the planets.

L Early in the morning, the photographs began to arrive. I could hardly believe I was seeing the surface of Mars! At 9:00 a.m., ABC television put me on the air to get my reaction.

M The interviewer said, "Mr. Bradbury, how do you feel about this landing? Where are the Martian cities and where are all the living beings?"

N "Don't be a fool," I said. "WE are the Martians! We're going to be here for the next million years. At long last, WE ARE MARTIANS!"

O That was the end of the interview.

P **I like to think** of the cosmos[1] as a theater, yet a theater cannot exist without an audience, to witness and to celebrate. Robot craft and mighty telescopes will continue to show us **unimaginable** wonders. But when humans return to the moon and put a **base** there and prepare to go to Mars and become true Martians, we—the audience—**literally** enter the cosmic theater. Will we finally reach the stars?

Q A few years ago, I traveled back to my boyhood home in Tucson. I stood out on the lawn and looked up at the night sky—and realized the stars had never looked closer than right there on Lowell Avenue.

[1]The **cosmos** is the universe.

Adapted from "My Mars," by Ray Bradbury: National Geographic Magazine Special Issue "Space," October 2008

Author Ray Bradbury (1920–2012) was one of the most celebrated American writers of the 20th century. He is best known for the award-winning novel *Fahrenheit 451* and his numerous works of science fiction.

A Martian sunset captured by NASA's Spirit rover

FROM *THE MARTIAN CHRONICLES* [1950] BY RAY BRADBURY

At the start of The Martian Chronicles, *humans are beginning to **settle** on Mars. Some go to escape problems, while others go to experience something new. Very few go at first, but eventually many settlers arrive on the new planet and turn Mars into a second Earth, with familiar homes, businesses, and neighborhoods.*

NOVEMBER 2005: THE WATCHERS

They all came out and looked at the sky that night. They left their suppers or their washing up or their dressing for the show and they came out upon their now-not-quite-as-new porches and watched the green star of Earth there. It was a move without conscious effort; they all did it, to help them understand the news they had heard on the radio a moment before. There was Earth and there the coming war, and there hundreds of thousands of mothers or grandmothers or fathers or brothers or aunts or uncles or cousins. They stood on the porches and tried to believe in the existence of Earth, much as they had once tried to believe in the existence of Mars; it was a problem reversed. To all intents and purposes, Earth now was dead; they had been away from it for three or four years. Space was an anesthetic; seventy million miles of space numbed you, put memory to sleep, depopulated Earth, erased the past, and allowed these people here to go on with their work. But now, tonight, the dead were risen. Earth was reinhabited, memory awoke, a million names were spoken: What was so-and-so doing tonight on Earth? What about this one and that one? The people on the porches glanced sidewise at each other's faces.

At nine o'clock Earth seemed to explode, catch fire, and burn.

The people on the porches put up their hands as if to beat the fire out.

They waited.

By midnight the fire was extinguished. Earth was still there.

There was a sigh, like an autumn wind, from the porches.

"We haven't heard from Harry for a long time."

"He's all right."

"We should send a message to Mother."

"She's all right."

"Is she?"

"Now, don't worry."

"Will she be all right, do you think?"

"Of course, of course; now come to bed."

But nobody moved. Late dinners were carried out onto the night lawns and set upon collapsible tables, and they picked at these slowly until two o'clock and the light-radio message flashed from Earth. They could read the great Morse-code flashes which flickered like a distant firefly:

AUSTRALIAN CONTINENT ATOMIZED IN PREMATURE EXPLOSION OF ATOMIC STOCKPILE. LOS ANGELES, LONDON BOMBED. WAR. COME HOME. COME HOME. COME HOME.

They stood up from their tables.

COME HOME. COME HOME. COME HOME.

"Have you heard from your brother Ted this year?"

"You know. With mail rates five bucks a letter to Earth, I don't write much."

COME HOME.

"I've been wondering about Jane; you remember Jane, my kid sister?"

COME HOME.

At three in the chilly morning, the luggage-store proprietor glanced up.

A lot of people were coming down the street.

"Stayed open late on purpose. What'll it be, mister?"

By dawn the luggage was gone from his shelves.

FROM *THE WAR OF THE WORLDS* [1898] BY H. G. WELLS

This excerpt is from the opening chapter of H. G. Wells's novel The War of the Worlds, *published in 1898. This famous story deals with the concept of an* **alien** *invasion of Earth. Wells's work had a huge influence on Ray Bradbury and other 20th century science fiction writers.*

CHAPTER ONE: THE EVE OF THE WAR

No one would have believed in the last years of the nineteenth century that this world was being watched keenly and closely by intelligences greater than man's and yet as mortal as his own; that as men busied themselves about their various concerns they were scrutinised[2] and studied, perhaps almost as narrowly as a man with a microscope might scrutinise the … creatures that swarm and multiply in a drop of water.

And looking across space with instruments, and intelligences such as we have scarcely dreamed of, [the Martians] see … a morning star of hope, our own warmer planet, green with vegetation and grey with water, with a cloudy atmosphere eloquent[3] of fertility,[4] with **glimpses** through its drifting cloud wisps[5] of broad stretches of populous country and narrow, navy-crowded seas.

And we men, the creatures who inhabit this earth, must be to them at least as alien and lowly as are the monkeys and lemurs[6] to us. The **intellectual** side of man already admits that life is an incessant[7] struggle for existence, and it would seem that this too is the belief of the minds upon Mars. Their world is far gone in its cooling and this world is still crowded with life, but crowded only with what they regard as **inferior** animals. To carry warfare sunward is, indeed, their only escape from the destruction that, generation after generation, creeps upon them.

And before we judge of them too harshly we must remember what **ruthless** and utter[8] destruction our own species has wrought,[9] … Are we such apostles[10] of mercy as to complain if the Martians warred in the same spirit?

[2]To **scrutinize** is to look at something carefully.
[3]If things or people are **eloquent**, they express ideas in a clear and fluent manner.
[4]**Fertility** is the ability of living things to reproduce.
[5]**Wisps** are things that appear as long, thin, delicate shapes; for example, smoke or clouds.
[6]A **lemur** is a small primate that lives in Madagascar.
[7]If something is **incessant**, it never stops.
[8]**Utter** is used to emphasize a noun in the same way as "total" or "complete."
[9]If a person has **wrought** destruction, they have caused it to happen.
[10]**Apostles** believe in something strongly and try to get others to believe in it, too.

An illustration depicting the alien invasion in *The War of the Worlds*

DEVELOPING READING SKILLS

> **READING SKILL** Identifying Literary Elements
>
> Literary fiction consists of several elements. These are similar to the elements of a personal narrative.
>
> **Plot** is the action of the story—what the characters do, say, and think. Plot has a beginning, a middle, and an end. Between the beginning and the middle, action rises toward the story's climax, or most intense point. After that, the action falls toward the conclusion, or resolution, of the story.
>
> **Characters** are all of the individuals in the story. These can include people, animals, or any other things that perform action or express thoughts in the story. The main character of a story is called the protagonist.
>
> **Setting** is the time and place. However, the setting is more than just a time and location; it can also set the mood for a story.
>
> **Point of view** is the perspective from which the story is told. Is the story told by a narrator outside of the story? Is it told by a character?
>
> **Theme** is the story's main idea or central message. A story can have more than one theme. Sometimes the theme is stated directly, and other times it is implied.

ANALYZING **A** Match each element below with an example from *The Martian Chronicles*.

Element

1. _____ plot
2. _____ characters
3. _____ setting
4. _____ point of view
5. _____ theme

Example

a. narrator (the writer of the story)

b. human colonists

c. our attachment to home

d. Human settlers on Mars watch the Earth, anticipating a war. Eventually, they see parts of the Earth explode. Worried about their loved ones, they decide to go back to Earth.

e. small towns set up on the surface of Mars

APPLYING **B** Complete the chart with information about a famous story or movie that you know about. Then describe the story to a partner, but don't say the title. Can your partner guess which story or movie you are describing?

Title	
Main Character(s)	
Setting	
Point of View	
Theme(s)	
Plot	

UNDERSTANDING THE READING

A Note answers to the questions about "My Mars." Then share your ideas with a partner.

UNDERSTANDING MAIN IDEAS

1. What events or experiences in Ray Bradbury's childhood led to his writing *The Martian Chronicles*?

   _____

   _____

2. Bradbury writes that "WE are the Martians!" (paragraph N). What does he mean?

   _____

   _____

B Note answers to the questions about "My Mars."

UNDERSTANDING DETAILS

1. Who is John Carter? What influence did he have on Bradbury?

   _____

   _____

2. Why did Bradbury write sequels to the books that he read?

   _____

   _____

3. Why was Bradbury's visit to Pasadena in 1976 significant?

   _____

   _____

C Read the sentences below. Does each one refer to *The Martian Chronicles* excerpt, *The War of the Worlds* excerpt, or both? Write **M** for *The Martian Chronicles,* **W** for *The War of the Worlds,* or **B** for both.

UNDERSTANDING MAIN IDEAS

1. The Martians in the excerpt are humans. _____

2. The Martians in the excerpt are aliens. _____

3. The excerpt deals with the theme of war and destruction. _____

4. The excerpt describes the view of Earth from Mars. _____

D Find and underline the following words and phrases in the reading. Use the context to match each word or phrase with its definition.

CRITICAL THINKING: GUESSING MEANING FROM CONTEXT

1. Paragraph B: **along the way** _____   a. towards the sky

2. Paragraph D: **into the heavens** _____   b. was lucky after a period of effort

3. Paragraph F: **got a break** _____   c. in fact; surprisingly

4. Paragraph K: **none other than** _____   d. during the course of a particular event

5. Paragraph N: **at long last** _____   e. after you have been hoping for it for a long time

> **CRITICAL THINKING**   When you **read literature critically**, you analyze it in more detail than you would when simply reading for pleasure, focusing more on the characters, plot, theme, and use of language. As you read, ask yourself questions: *Why do the characters do the things they do? Are there any consistent themes? What do people and things in the story symbolize? What is the author's message?*

CRITICAL THINKING:
READING LITERATURE
CRITICALLY

E Note answers to the questions below about the excerpts from *The Martian Chronicles* and *The War of the Worlds*. Then discuss your answers in a small group.

THE MARTIAN CHRONICLES: THE WATCHERS

1. What emotions are the colonists experiencing?

2. What is the author referring to when he says, "It was a problem reversed"?

3. What do the colonists decide to do? How do we know this?

THE WAR OF THE WORLDS: THE EVE OF THE WAR

1. Why does the author compare the aliens to "a man with a microscope"?

2. Why does the author mention "monkeys and lemurs"?

3. Why do the Martians want to come to Earth?

4. In the last paragraph, why does Wells warn us not to "judge of them too harshly"?

A panoramic view of a huge crater on Mars captured by NASA's Opportunity Rover

F Read each sentence or phrase from the reading. What is the author saying in each case?

CRITICAL THINKING: INTERPRETING FIGURATIVE LANGUAGE

1. In "My Mars," what does the author mean when he says, "I was on an avenue that led to Mars."

   _____

   _____

2. In *The Martian Chronicles*, why does the author say, "Space was an anesthetic"?

   _____

   _____

3. In *The Martian Chronicles*, what does the author say was like "a distant firefly"?

   _____

   _____

4. In *The War of the* Worlds, what is described as "a morning star of hope"?

   _____

G Note answers to the questions below. Then discuss with a partner.

CRITICAL THINKING: MAKING INFERENCES

1. Based on what Bradbury writes in "My Mars," why do you think he told the kinds of stories that he told?

   _____

   _____

2. What is one message or warning that you think Bradbury was trying to communicate with his stories?

   _____

   _____

3. From his writing in *The War of the Worlds,* what can we infer about the author's attitude to the human race?

   _____

   _____

Video

An orbital view of
Olympus Mons volcano
on Mars

MISSION: MARS

BEFORE VIEWING

DISCUSSION   **A**   If you could stand on the surface of Mars, what do you think you would see? Note your ideas below. Then discuss with a partner.

_____

_____

LEARNING ABOUT
THE TOPIC   **B**   Read the information. Then answer the questions.

Mars, the fourth planet from the sun, is often called "the red planet." With an average temperature of around minus 50 degrees Celsius, Mars is much colder than Earth. Gravity on Mars is also much lower. For example, a person who weighs 150 pounds (68 kilograms) on Earth would weigh about 50 pounds (23 kilograms) on Mars. As on Earth, there are wind storms on Mars. Small ones look like tornadoes, and large ones can cover the entire planet. Mars has some geological features that we are familiar with, such as mountains and canyons, but many are enormous compared to the ones on Earth.

1. What might make life on Mars difficult for humans?

   _____

2. What kinds of things might be easier to do on Mars than on Earth?

   _____

C The words in **bold** below are used in the video. Match the correct form of each word to its definition. Use a dictionary to help.

> Olympus Mons is **colossal**. It is the largest known volcano in our solar system.
>
> During an eruption, **fissures** often appear on the surface of a volcano.
>
> The size of some of the geological features on Mars is truly **astounding**.

1. _____ (n) a deep crack in something, especially in rock or in the ground

2. _____ (adj) very large

3. _____ (adj) amazing; incredible

WHILE VIEWING

A ▶ Watch the video. What is the main purpose? Check (✓) the best answer.

a. ☐ to explain where the best landing sites are on Mars

b. ☐ to show how Mars's low gravity could cause problems for human explorers

c. ☐ to describe the amazing geographical features on Mars

B ▶ Watch the video again. Then answer the questions.

1. How long is the Valles Marineris? How deep is it?

   _____

2. How big is the Valles Marineris when compared to the Grand Canyon?

   _____

3. How much higher is Olympus Mons than Mount Everest?

   _____

4. What is described as "deeper than the canyon itself"?

   _____

AFTER VIEWING

A Imagine that an alien was visiting Earth. Which of Earth's geographical features would you show them? Note your ideas below. Then discuss with a partner.

_____

_____

_____

Writing

EXPLORING WRITTEN ENGLISH

WRITING SKILL Writing an Analysis of Literature

When you write an analysis of a story or novel, it is common to choose one aspect of the story or novel to focus on. Then you state an argument about that aspect, and you use quotes and paraphrases from the story as evidence to support your argument. The argument should be broad enough that you can write several paragraphs about it.

Good argument/question: In *The Martian Chronicles,* Ray Bradbury shows us that when we try to escape from our problems, we do not suddenly have perfect and happy lives.

Weak argument/question: In *The Martian Chronicles,* people decide to go to Mars to escape their problems.

To come up with an argument, consider the theme or themes of your story. Then think of arguments that are related to that theme. For example, one theme of *The Martian Chronicles* is the effects of colonization. Some additional arguments related to this theme include:

Colonization may benefit one society, but it may destroy another.

We can't avoid destroying ourselves, even by moving to another planet, because humans are the cause of destruction.

In each paragraph of your analysis, you can include one or more quotes or paraphrases from the story as your evidence. Then show how each of the quotes or paraphrases is significant. In other words, show how it supports your argument or answer.

CRITICAL THINKING:
EVALUATING

A Check (✓) two statements that are possible topics for analysis of *The Martian Chronicles*.

a. ☐ The actions and feelings of the people in *The Martian Chronicles* are similar to the actions and experiences of people in real life in several ways.

b. ☐ In "November 2005: The Watchers," the people are watching a war on Earth.

c. ☐ Many events in *The Martian Chronicles* are similar to events that occur in real life.

d. ☐ *The Martian Chronicles* is a famous story about space exploration.

CRITICAL THINKING:
EVALUATING

B Check (✓) three statements that are possible topics for analysis of *The War of the Worlds*.

In *The War of the Worlds*, H. G. Wells shows us that …

a. ☐ the struggle for existence is not just a human problem.

b. ☐ Martians have destroyed their own planet and are looking for a new place to live.

c. ☐ it is difficult to criticize others' tendency for destruction if we are just as destructive.

d. ☐ no matter how superior you think you are, you are always inferior to someone else.

e. ☐ humans are special and life in the universe is rare.

C Read the excerpts from "My Mars" and answer the questions.

a. It was named for the great astronomer Percival Lowell, who took fantastic photographs of the planet.

b. On my last night in New York, I got a break.

c. I like to think of the cosmos as a theater, yet a theater cannot exist without an audience, to witness and to celebrate.

1. Which sentence has one independent clause and no dependent clause? _____

2. Which sentence has two independent clauses and no dependent clause? _____

3. Which sentence has one independent clause and one dependent clause? _____

LANGUAGE FOR WRITING Using a Variety of Sentence Types

One way to add interest to your writing is to include a variety of sentence types: simple, compound, and complex.

A simple sentence consists of one independent clause (one subject and verb).

The men went to Mars.

A compound sentence consists of two independent clauses joined by a coordinating conjunction (*for, and, or, but, so, nor, yet*).

People wanted to escape their problems, so they went to Mars.

After they landed on Mars, the men changed the landscape so that it looked like Earth.

A complex sentence consists of at least one independent clause and one or more dependent clauses. Dependent clauses begin with relative pronouns such as *that, who,* or *which,* or with subordinating conjunctions such as *because, although, before, after,* or *when.*

Using only simple sentences can make your writing sound abrupt or choppy. However, if you combine those sentences, your writing will sound smoother.

The men landed on Mars. They changed the landscape. They wanted it to look like Earth.

↓

After they landed on Mars, the men changed the landscape so that it looked like Earth.

D What kind of sentence is each of the following? Write **S** for simple, **CD** for compound, or **CX** for complex.

1. _____ The individuals from Earth go to Mars for various reasons, but many go to leave problems behind such as "bad wives or bad jobs or bad towns."

2. _____ However, some of them eventually find that they're leaving one set of problems for another.

3. _____ In *The War of the Worlds*, because their planet is slowly dying, Martians have to leave Mars and conquer another planet in order to survive.

4. _____ They turn Mars into a second Earth "filled with sizzling neon tubes and yellow electric bulbs."

5. _____ In a sense, they bring their problems with them because they need to be surrounded by familiar things such as "flowerpots and chintz" on this strange new planet.

E The following paragraph has been written using only simple sentences. Rewrite it in the space provided using compound and complex sentence types.

> It was a crisp January morning. Snow topped the distant Aspromonte mountains. Oranges were ripening on the nearby trees. Giuseppe Passarino guided his silver minivan up a curving road. The road went into the hinterlands of Calabria. Calabria is mainland Italy's southernmost region. The road climbed through fruit and olive groves. Passarino chatted with his colleague Maurizio Berardelli. Passarino is a geneticist at the University of Calabria. Berardelli is a geriatrician. They were headed for the small village of Molochio. Molochio had the distinction of numbering four centenarians—and four 99-year-olds—among its 2,000 inhabitants.

_____

_____

_____

_____

_____

_____

_____

_____

_____

_____

_____

_____

_____

_____

_____

_____

_____

_____

_____

_____

F Compare your revised paragraph with paragraph A of the reading passage in Unit 8. How similar or different is your version?

WRITING TASK

GOAL In this lesson, you are going to write an essay on the following topic:

Write an analysis of a piece of literature.

BRAINSTORMING

A Choose a novel or short story that you know well. What arguments could you make about it for a literary analysis? Note any ideas below.

_____

_____

_____

_____

PLANNING

B Follow the steps to make notes for your essay.

Step 1 Write your thesis statement in the outline.

Step 2 Think of three examples or excerpts from your story that support your argument.

Step 3 Write topic sentences for your three body paragraphs.

Step 4 Write notes about evidence from the excerpts that support each topic sentence. For each piece of evidence, write notes about why the evidence is significant.

OUTLINE

Introductory paragraph: What is your argument?

_____

_____

Body paragraph 1: What is one piece of evidence that supports your thesis?

Topic sentence: _____

_____

Evidence and significance of evidence: _____

_____

_____

Body paragraph 2: What is a second piece of evidence that supports your thesis?

Topic sentence: _____

_____

Evidence and significance of evidence: _____

_____

_____

Body paragraph 3: What is a third piece of evidence that supports your thesis?

Topic sentence: _____

_____

Evidence and significance of evidence: _____

_____

_____

Concluding paragraph: Review your main points and your thesis statement.

_____

_____

FIRST DRAFT   **C**   Use the information in your outline to write a first draft of your essay.

REVISING PRACTICE

The draft below is a model of the essay you are writing. Follow the steps to create a better second draft.

1. Write the sentences (a–c) in the correct spaces.

   a. This shows that the migrants are creating new problems for themselves as they try to escape their old problems.

   b. Another problem that the migrants experience is the ugliness of their own invasion of Mars.

   c. In *The Martian Chronicles*, Ray Bradbury shows us that when we try to escape from our problems, we don't suddenly have perfect and happy lives.

2. Now fix the following problems (a–b) with the essay.

   a. Use a conjunction to combine two sentences in paragraph A.

   b. Use *even though* to combine two sentences in paragraph C.

A

The Martian Chronicles is a novel about a time when humans on Earth start moving to and colonizing the planet Mars. The individuals from Earth go to Mars for various reasons. Many go to leave problems behind such as "bad wives or bad jobs or bad towns." Some of them find that they're leaving one set of problems for another. _____

B

The first problem that moving to Mars causes for the migrants is a disease called "The Loneliness." As the narrator explains in "August 2001: The Settlers," "this disease was called The Loneliness, because when you saw your home town dwindle to the size of your fist . . . you felt you had never been born, there was no town, you were nowhere, with space all around, nothing familiar, only other strange men." _____ At least on Earth, people were surrounded by familiarity—a town they knew, people they knew, and people who knew them. On their way to Mars, the "Lonely Ones" become nothing and are surrounded by nothing.

C

_____ In "February 2002: The Locusts," as more rockets land on their new home planet, they burn the planet's trees and melt the rock and sand. Many of the migrants come to Mars to escape their lives on Earth. They end up recreating some of the less appealing things from their home planet. They turn Mars into a second Earth "filled with sizzling neon tubes and yellow electric bulbs." This demonstrates that in a sense, they bring their problems with them because they need to be surrounded by familiar things such as "flowerpots and chintz" on this strange new planet.

D

In "November 2005: The Watchers," the migrants learn that they really can't escape their own problems or their own lives. For a while, they are able to forget about Earth. After being on Mars for three or four years, "Earth now was dead" to them. However, as they watch Earth seem to "explode, catch fire, and burn" at the start of a war, they are reminded of the people and the lives they left behind. They start to wonder and worry about them. When they receive a message telling them to "COME HOME. COME HOME. COME HOME," they feel that they have to. This supports the idea that their problems haven't disappeared. They need to go back to Earth and reclaim the lives that they abandoned.

E

Through the actions and words of the characters in the story, Ray Bradbury's *The Martian Chronicles* shows the reader that even if you go to another planet, you can't forget about who you are or live a problem-free life. No matter where you go, you bring your problems with you, or you create new ones.

D Now use the questions below to revise your essay.   REVISED DRAFT

☐ Is your argument broad enough so you could write several paragraphs about it?

☐ Did you provide evidence from your story in your body paragraphs?

☐ Did you explain the significance of your evidence in your body paragraphs?

☐ Did you use a variety of sentence types?

☐ Does the concluding paragraph review the main points of the essay?

EDITING PRACTICE

Read the information below. Then find and correct one mistake with each of the sentences (1–4).

When you use compound or complex sentences, remember to:

- use an appropriate coordinating conjunction (*for, and, or, but, so, nor, yet*).
- use a comma before a coordinating conjunction that joins two independent clauses.
- use an appropriate relative pronoun (*that, who, which*).
- use a comma if the dependent clause comes before the independent clause.

1. When it was first published in 1897 *The War of the Worlds* was generally well-received by critics.

2. *The War of the Worlds* was one of the earliest stories to describe a conflict between humans and an alien race so its impact at the time is hard for us to appreciate now.

3. Wells got the idea for *The War of the Worlds* from his brother, which had raised the topic of an alien invasion of Earth during a casual conversation.

4. In the novel, the planet Mars is dying, yet the Martians need to find a new home.

FINAL DRAFT **E** Follow the steps to write a final draft.

1. Check your revised draft for sentence variety.

2. Now use the checklist on page 248 to write a final draft. Make any other necessary changes.

UNIT REVIEW

Answer the following questions.

1. How did Ray Bradbury and H. G. Wells imagine Mars differently?

_____

_____

2. What are two interesting geological features on Mars?

_____

_____

3. What are three sentence types?

_____

_____

4. Do you remember the meanings of these words? Check (✓) the ones you know. Look back at the unit and review the ones you don't know.

- ☐ alien
- ☐ base
- ☐ destiny
- ☐ flee
- ☐ glimpse
- ☐ inferior
- ☐ intellectual
- ☐ literally
- ☐ protagonist
- ☐ ruthless
- ☐ sequel
- ☐ settle
- ☐ stunned
- ☐ touch down
- ☐ unimaginable

VOCABULARY EXTENSION   UNIT 1

For adjectives, the suffix *-ic* means "having the characteristics of." For example, *dramatic* means that something has the characteristics of a drama. To change an *-ic* adjective into an adverb, add *-ally*.

A Complete the chart. Use a dictionary to check your spelling.

Noun	Adjective	Adverb
academy		
	artistic	
athlete		
		atmospherically
	dramatic	
energy		
		linguistically

WORD PARTNERS *dramatic* + noun

Collocations are words that often go together. Here are some common collocations with the adjective *dramatic*.

dramatic **change**	*dramatic* **decline**
dramatic **increase**	*dramatic* **improvement**
dramatic **effect**	*dramatic* **action**
dramatic **moment**	*dramatic* **difference**

B Circle the best option to complete each sentence.

1. The world's governments need to take dramatic **action** / **change** to halt climate change.

2. The most dramatic **difference** / **moment** came towards the end of the movie.

3. Unfortunately, the past year has seen a dramatic **decline** / **increase** in our company's profits.

4. Studying philosophy had a dramatic **change** / **effect** on the way I thought about life.

5. There is a dramatic **difference** / **improvement** between the lives of the richest and poorest people on Earth.

VOCABULARY EXTENSION UNIT 2

Here are some adjectives that collocate with the noun *priority*.
high priority
low priority
first / top / number one priority
urgent / immediate priority

Below are some verbs that also collocate with *priority*. Read the definitions.
*If you **give priority** to something, you make it the most important thing.*
*If you **identify priorities**, you decide on the most important things to do.*
*If one thing **takes priority** over another, it's more important.*

A Circle the best option to complete each sentence.

1. Many parents tell their children that doing homework should **identify / take** priority over playing video games.

2. For most businesses, customer satisfaction is a **high / low** priority.

3. When boarding a plane, airlines often **give / take** priority to families with young children.

4. Before a hurricane strikes, evacuating residents in the hurricane's path is the **first / high** priority.

5. Compared to math and science, the teaching of arts is a **first / low** priority for many publicly-funded schools.

6. To manage your workload, **give / identify** priorities that are urgent versus ones that are less important.

7. As a parent, my **number one / low** priority in life is taking care of my son.

B Complete the sentences about yourself.

1. My number one priority in life is _____
   _____.

2. For me, _____
   takes priority over _____.

3. Next week, _____
   is an urgent priority.

VOCABULARY EXTENSION   UNIT 3

WORD FORMS Nouns, Verbs, Adjectives, and Adverbs

Some words can be formed into nouns, verbs, adjectives, and adverbs. For example:
depression (noun), **depress** (verb), **depressing** (adjective), **depressingly** (adverb).

A Complete the chart below. Use a dictionary to check your answers.

Noun	Verb	Adjective	Adverbs
color		colorful	colorfully
depression	depress	depressing / depressed	depressingly
perfection		perfect	perfectly
proportion	proportion		proportionally
	satisfy	satisfactory	satisfactorily
style	style	stylish	

B Complete each sentence with one of the words in the chart above. More than one word may be possible.

1. Vincent Van Gogh's paintings are recognized for their bright, _____ palettes.

2. His earlier paintings were quite dark, but he developed a lighter, brighter _____ in his later work.

3. Van Gogh painted pictures of cypress trees. He remarked that the tall, thin shape of the trees gave them similar _____ to ancient Egyptian pillars.

4. Van Gogh was often _____ and spent several months in hospital for treatment.

5. *The Starry Night* is one of Van Gogh's most famous paintings. Many people think it _____ captures the bright night sky.

VOCABULARY EXTENSION   UNIT 4

A   Circle the best option to complete each sentence.

1. Gucci and Armani are examples of expensive, **high-end** / **low-end** clothing brands.

2. In economic theory, an increase in **demand** / **supply** for a product usually leads to an increase in prices.

3. Many companies reinvest their **profits** / **losses** to help their business grow.

4. A company is in financial difficulty if its **expenditure** / **revenue** exceeds its **expenditure** / **revenue**.

5. A **shortage** / **surplus** of crude oil usually leads to a rise in the price drivers pay at the gas pump.

B   Complete each sentence with one of the nouns or adjectives in the box above.

1. In economics, a monopoly is a market where there is no _____.

2. The data that financial consultants provide to a business can be very _____.

3. The rise of online shopping has been _____ to many small and medium-sized stores that struggle to compete.

4. On learning that there was a serious fault in their new product, the company needed to decide quickly upon what _____ action to take.

5. During the 2008 financial crisis, many governments took prompt _____ to stabilize the financial markets.

VOCABULARY EXTENSION   UNIT 5

The prefixes *co-*, *com-*, and *col-* usually mean "with" or "together." For example, *cooperate* means to "work (or, operate) together."

A   Match the words in **bold** (1–5) with the correct definitions (a–e).

1. At a party last night, I was wearing the exact same T-shirt as another guy. What a **coincidence**! _____

2. To make pancakes, **combine** eggs, flour, milk, and butter. Then heat the mixture in a pan. _____

3. Politicians and business leaders should **coordinate** to improve the conditions for workers. _____

4. There was heavy traffic yesterday following a **collision** between two vehicles. _____

5. The best meals have flavors, textures, and colors that **complement** each other. _____

a. to put together to make a whole

b. to go well together

c. to organize and work together in a systematic way

d. a situation where two similar events occur at the same time by chance

e. a situation where two or more objects crash into each other

B   Circle the best option to complete each sentence. Use a dictionary to help.

1. My best friend owns a **collection** / **comparison** of rare postage stamps.

2. I recently **collaborated** / **combined** with my neighbors to start a fundraising project for local homeless people.

3. A quick **collection** / **comparison** of the two essays showed that it was a clear case of plagiarism.

4. The company's poor sales, **collaborated** / **combined** with its increased overheads, led to a terrible year financially.

VOCABULARY EXTENSION   UNIT 6

A Write the opposite form of the words. Use *ir-*, *im-*, or *il-*. Check any unknown words in a dictionary.

1. responsible   _____

2. literate   _____

3. plausible   _____

4. moral   _____

5. practical   _____

6. measurable   _____

7. legal   _____

8. logical   _____

9. mature   _____

10. reversible   _____

B Choose six words from exercise **A**. Write a sentence with each one.

1. _____

2. _____

3. _____

4. _____

5. _____

6. _____

VOCABULARY EXTENSION   UNIT 7

WORD PARTNERS Adjective + *economy*

Here are some adjectives that collocate with the noun *economy*. Check any phrases you don't know in a dictionary.

booming *economy*   **developing** *economy*   **global** *economy*
service-based *economy*   **stable** *economy*   **weak** *economy*

A Complete each sentence with one of the word partners in the box above.

1. A _____ economy relies heavily on industries such as hospitality and retail.

2. Countries with _____ economies are moving from more traditional lifestyles to more modern ones.

3. Some economists blame a _____ economy for the low growth in wages.

4. The _____ economy suffered greatly during the 2009 economic crisis. The United States, countries in the EU, and Japan all suffered significant drops in their GDPs.

5. Our country has a _____ economy. We haven't seen growth like this for over a hundred years!

WORD PARTNERS *distinct* + noun

Here are some nouns that collocate with the adjective *distinct*. Check any phrases you don't know in a dictionary.

distinct **advantage**   *distinct* **possibility**   *distinct* **groups**
distinct **difference**   *distinct* **pattern**   *distinct* **smell**

B Complete each sentence with one of the word partners in the box above.

1. The United States is a nation made up of immigrants—over the centuries, a number of distinct _____ of people have moved to the U.S. to start a new life.

2. Historically, there have been distinct _____ of immigration to the U.S. For example, in the early 1900s most immigrants were from Southern and Eastern Europe. More recently, most immigrants are from Mexico.

3. There is a distinct _____ between people who immigrate legally to a country and those that enter a country illegally.

4. Many economists think that countries with large immigrant populations have a distinct _____ over other countries, particularly in terms of entrepreneurship and innovation.

5. With many people around the world wanting to emigrate, there is a distinct _____ that immigration levels will continue to rise in the future.

VOCABULARY EXTENSION   UNIT 8

Here are some words and phrases that include or commonly partner with *life*, such as *life span*:

life expectancy (n) how long animals are expected to live on average

life story (n) the history of someone's life

private life (n) a person's social, personal, or family life

lifetime (n) the length of someone's life

lifelong (adj) lasting all one's life

life-threatening (adj) endangering life

real-life (adj) happening in the real world

A Complete each sentence with a word or phrase in the box above.

1. For some elderly people, getting the flu can be _____.

2. Many people in the public eye avoid talking about their _____. They want to keep the focus away from their family.

3. In 2016, the actor Jackie Chan received an Academy Award for a _____ of achievement in the film industry.

4. Near the end of their careers, many celebrities publish a book with their _____.

5. My grandfather had a _____ interest in photography.

The prefix *re-* usually means "again." For example, when you *reconstruct* events from your past you "construct" them again from your memory. Here are some more examples:

rebuild	**rediscover**	**regrow**
renew	**reunite**	**rewrite**

B Complete each sentence with the correct form of a word in the box above.

1. The student wasn't happy with the first paragraph of his essay, so he _____ it.

2. After Hurricane Katrina devastated New Orleans, the government and many local volunteers helped to _____ many parts of the city.

3. In India, people over the age of 50 have to pass a medical exam in order to _____ their driver's license.

4. After being divided for over 40 years, East and West Germany finally _____ in 1990.

5. Salamanders, like many amphibians, have the ability to _____ their tails if they lose them to predators.

VOCABULARY EXTENSION   UNIT 9

The suffixes *-ence* and *-ance* indicate a noun form and are often made from adjectives ending in *-ent* or *-ant* (e.g., *emergent—emergence*). In addition, *-ance* can be added to some verbs to create nouns (e.g., *appear—appearance*).

A Write the correct noun form using *-ence* or *-ance*. Check your answers in a dictionary.

1. independent _____

2. intelligent _____

3. dominant _____

4. resist _____

5. attend _____

6. prominent _____

The word *deceit* can be formed into the following parts of speech:
  deceive (v)   **deceit** (n)   **deceitful** (adj)   **deceitfully** (adv)

B Complete each sentence with the correct form of *deceit*.

1. Frank Abagnale Jr.'s most elaborate_____ was probably his impersonation of an airline pilot.

2. By using a fake employee ID, he _____ an airline operator into thinking he was a pilot. He flew over one million miles.

3. Abagnale also became an attorney using a fake degree from Harvard Law School. One of his colleagues—a Harvard graduate—thought Abagnale was behaving _____ and started to investigate him.

4. Abagnale believes that he got away with these acts largely because people are generally very trusting and do not expect _____ behavior from others.

VOCABULARY EXTENSION UNIT 10

Here are some adjectives and their antonyms that can be used to describe the qualities of a book or movie:

realistic	—	*far-fetched*
well-developed	—	*under-developed*
memorable	—	*forgettable*
lively	—	*monotonous*
fast-moving	—	*slow-paced*

A Complete each sentence with one of the adjectives in the box above. More than one word may be possible.

1. If a book is _____, you keep thinking about it after you've read it.

2. If a plot is _____, the characters and story are not very well thought out.

3. If a plot is _____, it doesn't seem believable.

4. If a story is _____, exciting events happen in quick succession.

5. If a writing style is _____, it is fun to read.

WORD PARTNERS Phrasal Verbs with *down*

Some phrasal verbs, such as *touch down*, have a literal meaning. There are many other phrasal verbs with the preposition *down* where the meaning is more idiomatic.

B Choose the best meaning of each phrasal verb in **bold**. Use a dictionary to help.

1. The original manuscript for the first *Harry Potter* book was **turned down** by many publishers before J. K. Rowling finally got a contract.

   a. revised   b. rejected   c. reduced

2. One characteristic of Harry Potter, the main protagonist, is his modesty. He often **plays down** his achievements.

   a. talks continuously about   b. tells everyone about   c. gives little importance to

3. Rowling and her publishers have been in several legal disputes over the years. They have **cracked down on** local companies selling unauthorized *Harry Potter* merchandise.

   a. stopped   b. broken   c. promoted

4. One of the characters, Ron, struggles to **live down** a number of embarrassing incidents.

   a. make people forget   b. make people believe   c. make up

5. The *Harry Potter* movies **let down** some fans of the books. These fans complained that the movies did not follow the plots of the books closely enough.

   a. excited   b. disappointed   c. surprised

Independent Student Handbook

TIPS FOR READING FLUENTLY

Reading slowly, one word at a time, makes it difficult to get an overall sense of the meaning of a text. As a result, reading becomes more challenging and less interesting. In general, it is a good idea to first skim a text for the gist, and then read it again more closely so that you can focus on the most relevant details. Use these strategies to improve your reading speed:

- Read groups of words rather than individual words.

- Keep your eyes moving forward. Read through to the end of each sentence or paragraph instead of going back to reread words or phrases.

- Skip functional words (articles, prepositions, etc.) and focus on words and phrases carrying meaning—the content words.

- Use clues in the text—such as **bold** words and words in *italics*—to help you know which parts might be important and worth focusing on.

- Use section headings, as well as the first and last lines of paragraphs, to help you understand how the text is organized.

- Use context clues, affixes, and parts of speech—instead of a dictionary—to guess the meaning of unfamiliar words and phrases.

TIPS FOR READING CRITICALLY

As you read, ask yourself questions about what the writer is saying, and how and why the writer is presenting the information at hand.

Important critical thinking skills for academic reading and writing:

- **Analyzing:** Examining a text in close detail in order to identify key points, similarities, and differences.

- **Applying:** Deciding how ideas or information might be relevant in a different context, e.g., applying possible solutions to problems.

- **Evaluating:** Using evidence to decide how relevant, important, or useful something is. This often involves looking at reasons for and against something.

- **Inferring:** "Reading between the lines"; in other words, identifying what a writer is saying indirectly, or *implicitly*, rather than directly, or *explicitly*.

- **Synthesizing:** Gathering appropriate information and ideas from more than one source and making a judgment, summary, or conclusion based on the evidence.

- **Reflecting:** Relating ideas and information in a text to your own personal experience and viewpoints.

TIPS FOR NOTE-TAKING

Taking notes will help you better understand the overall meaning and organization of a text. Note-taking also enables you to record the most important information for future uses— such as when you are preparing for an exam or completing a writing assignment. Use these techniques to make your note-taking more effective:

- As you read, underline or highlight important information such as dates, names, and places.

- Take notes in the margin. Note the main idea and supporting details next to each paragraph. Also note your own ideas or questions about the paragraph.

- On a separate piece of paper, write notes about the key points of the text in your own words. Include short headings, key words, page numbers, and quotations.

- Use a graphic organizer to summarize a text, particularly if it follows a pattern such as cause-effect, comparison-contrast, or chronological sequence.

- Keep your notes brief by using these abbreviations and symbols. Don't write full sentences.

approx.	approximately	→	leads to / causes
e.g./ex.	example	↑	increases / increased
i.e.	that is / in other words	↓	decreases / decreased
etc.	and others / and the rest	& or +	and
Ch.	Chapter	*b/c*	because
p. (pp.)	page (pages)	*w/*	with
re:	regarding, concerning	*w/o*	without
incl.	including	=	is the same as
excl.	excluding	>	is more than
info	information	<	is less than
yrs.	years	~	is approximately / about
para.	paragraph	∴	therefore

TIPS FOR LEARNING VOCABULARY

You often need to use a word or phrase several times before it enters your long-term memory. Here are some strategies for successfully learning vocabulary:

- Use flash cards to test your knowledge of new vocabulary. Write the word you want to learn on one side of an index card. Write the definition and/or an example sentence that uses the word on the other side.

- Use a vocabulary notebook to note down a new word or phrase. Write a short definition of the word in English and the sentence where you found it. Write another sentence of your own that uses the word. Include any common collocations (see *Word Partners* in the Vocabulary Extensions).

- Use memory aids, or mnemonics, to remember a word or phrase. For example, if you want to learn the idiom *keep an eye on someone*, which means "to watch someone carefully," you might picture yourself putting your eyeball on someone's shoulder so that you can watch the person carefully. The stranger the picture is, the more likely you will remember it!

- Make word webs or word maps. See the example below.

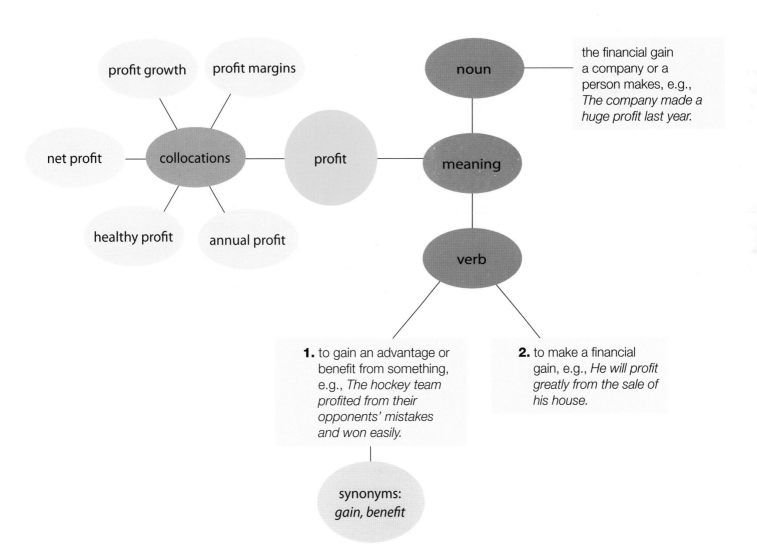

Common Affixes

Some words contain an affix at the start of the word (*prefix*) and/or at the end (*suffix*). These affixes can be useful for guessing the meaning of unfamiliar words and for expanding your vocabulary. In general, a prefix affects the meaning of a word, whereas a suffix affects its part of speech. See the examples below.

Prefix	Meaning	Example
com-	with	compile
con-	together, with	constitute
em- / en-	making, putting	empower, endanger
ex-	away, from, out	explode
im- / in-	not	imperfect, independent
inter-	between	interact
mis-	wrongly	mislead
mono-	one, only	monotonous
pre-	before	preview
pro-	forward, outward	prominent
re-	back, again	restore
trans-	across	transfer
un-	not	unclear
vid- / vis-	seeing	video, vision

Suffix	Part of Speech	Example
-able / -ible	adjective	affordable, feasible
-al	adjective	traditional
-ary	adjective	evolutionary
-ate	verb	generate
-ed	adjective	dedicated
-ent / -ant	adjective	confident, significant
-er	noun	researcher
-ful	adjective	harmful
-ic	adjective	nostalgic
-ical	adjective	hypothetical
-ism	noun	mechanism
-ity	noun	minority
-ive	adjective	inventive
-ize	verb	criticize
-ly	adverb	definitely
-ment	noun	replacement
-tion	noun	determination

TIPS FOR ACADEMIC WRITING

There are many types of academic writing (descriptive, argumentative/persuasive, narrative, etc.), but most types share similar characteristics. Generally, in academic writing, you should:

- write in full sentences.
- use formal English. (Avoid slang or conversational expressions such as *kind of*.)
- be clear and coherent—keep to your main point; avoid technical words that the reader may not know.
- use signal words or phrases and conjunctions to connect your ideas. (See examples below.)
- have a clear point (main idea) for each paragraph.
- use a neutral point of view—avoid overuse of personal pronouns (*I*, *we*, *you*) and subjective language such as *nice* or *terrible*.
- use facts, examples, and expert opinions to support your argument.
- avoid using abbreviations or language used in texting. (Use *that is* rather than *i.e.*, and *in my opinion*, not *IMO*.)
- avoid using contractions. (Use *is not* rather than *isn't*.)
- avoid starting sentences with *or*, *and*, or *but*.

Signal Words and Phrases

Use signal words and phrases to connect ideas and to make your writing more academic.

Giving personal opinions	Giving details and examples	Linking ideas
In my opinion, …	An example of this is …	Furthermore, …
I (generally) agree that …	Specifically, …	Moreover, …
I think/feel (that) …	For instance, …	In addition, …
I believe (that) …		Additionally, …
It is my personal view that …		

Presenting similar ideas	Presenting contrasting views	Giving reasons
Similarly, …	On the other hand, …	This is because (of) …
Both … and …	In contrast, …	This is due to …
Like … , …	Conversely, …	One reason (for this) is …
Likewise, …	Despite the fact that …	This is a consequence of …
	Even though …	

Describing effects	Describing a process	Concluding
Therefore, …	First (of all), …	In conclusion, …
As a result, …	Then / Next / After that, …	In summary, …
Because of this, …	As soon as …	To conclude, …
If … , then …	Once …	To summarize, …
	Finally, …	

Writing Citations

Below are some examples of how to cite print sources according to the American Psychological Association Style.

Guidelines	Reference entry	In-text citation
For an **article**, include the author's name, year and month of publication, article title, the name of the magazine/journal, and page references.	White, M. (2011, June). Brimming pools. *National Geographic*, 100–115.	(White, 2011) White (2011) says …
For a **book**, include the author's name, year of publication, title of the book, the location of the publisher (if known), and the name of the publisher.	Hawking, S. (1988). *A brief history of time*. New York, NY: Bantam.	(Hawking, 1988) Hawking (1988) says …
If there are **two authors**, use & to list their names.	Sherman, D., & Salisbury, J. (2008). *The west in the world: Renaissance to present*. New York, NY: McGraw-Hill.	(Sherman & Salisbury, 2008) Sherman and Salisbury (2008) say …
For a **book that is not the first edition**, include the edition number after the title.	Turnbull, C. M. (2009). *A history of modern Singapore, 1819–2005*, (3rd ed.). Singapore: NUS Press.	(Turnbull, 2009) According to Turnbull (2009), …

TIPS FOR EDITING

Capitalization

Remember to capitalize:

- the first letter of the word at the beginning of every sentence.

- proper nouns such as names of people, geographical names, company names, and names of organizations.

- days, months, and holidays.

- the word *I*.

- the first letter of a title such as the title of a movie or a book.

- the words in titles that have meaning (content words). Don't capitalize *a, an, the, and*, or prepositions such as *to, for, of, from, at, in*, and *on*, unless they are the first word of a title (e.g., *The Power of Creativity*).

Punctuation

- Use a period (.) at the end of any sentence that is not a question. Use a question mark (?) at the end of every question.

- Exclamation marks (!), which indicate strong feelings such as surprise or joy, are generally not used in academic writing.

- Use commas (,) to separate a list of three or more things. (*She speaks German, English, and Spanish.*)

- Use a comma after an introductory word or phrase. (*However, William didn't let that stop him.*)

- Use a comma before a combining word—*and, but, so, or*—that joins two sentences. (*Black widow spider bites are not usually deadly for adults, but they can be deadly for children.*)

- Use an apostrophe (') for showing possession. (*James's idea came from social networking websites.*)

- Use quotation marks (" ") to indicate the exact words used by someone else. (*"Our pleasures are really ancient," says psychologist Nancy Etcoff.*)

Other Proofreading Tips

- Print out your draft and read it out loud.

- Use a colored pen to make corrections on your draft so you can see them easily when you write your next draft.

- Have someone else read your draft and give you comments or ask you questions.

- Don't depend on a computer's spell-check. When the spell-check suggests a correction, make sure you agree with it before you accept the change.

- Check the spelling and accuracy of proper nouns, numbers, and dates.

- Keep a list of spelling and grammar mistakes that you commonly make so that you can be aware of them as you edit your draft.

- Check for frequently confused words:

  - *there, their*, and *they're*
  - *its* and *it's*
  - *your* and *you're*
  - *then* and *than*

  - *to, too*, and *two*
  - *whose* and *who's*
  - *where, wear, we're*, and *were*
  - *affect* and *effect*

EDITING CHECKLIST

Use the checklist to find errors in the second draft of your writing task for each unit.

	Unit				
	1	2	3	4	5
1. Did you use capitalization correctly, e.g., for the first word of a sentence, for proper nouns, etc.					
2. Do your subjects and verbs agree?					
3. Are commas and other punctuation marks used correctly?					
4. Have you used an appropriate level of formality?					
5. Is the spelling of places, people, and other proper nouns correct?					
6. Did you check for frequently confused words? (see examples in the *Tips for Editing* section)					
7. Did you use appropriate signal words and phrases to introduce and connect ideas? (see examples in the *Tips for Academic Writing* section)					
8. For essays that require research and the use of information from external sources, did you cite all sources properly? (see examples in the *Writing Citations* section)					

	Unit				
	6	7	8	9	10
1. Did you use capitalization correctly, e.g., for the first word of a sentence, for proper nouns, etc.					
2. Do your subjects and verbs agree?					
3. Are commas and other punctuation marks used correctly?					
4. Have you used an appropriate level of formality?					
5. Is the spelling of places, people, and other proper nouns correct?					
6. Did you check for frequently confused words? (see examples in the *Tips for Editing* section)					
7. Did you use appropriate signal words and phrases to introduce and connect ideas? (see examples in the *Tips for Academic Writing* section)					
8. For essays that require research and the use of information from external sources, did you cite all sources properly? (see examples in the *Writing Citations* section)					

WRITING REFERENCE

UNIT 3

Restrictive and Nonrestrictive Adjective Clauses

There are two types of adjective clauses. One type gives essential information about the noun. These are called **restrictive adjective clauses**. Do not use commas with restrictive adjective clauses.	I saw a photograph **that** illustrated all of Griffiths's aesthetic principles. I read the essay on photography **that** Annie Griffiths wrote.
The other type of adjective clause gives extra, or nonessential, information about the noun. These are called **nonrestrictive adjective clauses.** Commas always set off nonrestrictive adjective clauses.	Photography, **which** is a relatively recent invention, influenced our notions of beauty. Susan Sontag, **who** was a noted essayist, wrote a book on photography. Japonaiserie, **which** is also referred to as Japonism, is an artistic movement from the mid-1800s. Vincent van Gogh, **who/whom** many people consider one of the greatest Impressionists, was influenced by Japanese woodblock prints.

UNIT 4

Initial Phrases

You can use initial phrases (prepositional, time, and verbal phrases) to avoid short, choppy sentences. Using initial phrases is also a way to vary your sentence style and to show the relationship between ideas.

Prepositional phrases	**In Africa**, Nigeria is the most populous country. **At a distance of 4.3 light-years**, Alpha Centauri is the nearest star outside our Solar System. **Just opposite this building**, you can find a really good restaurant.
Time phrases	**Since I was a young child**, I've had a keen interest in science. **When she first started the business**, there were many problems to deal with. **Once I met her**, I realized why she'd been so successful in life.
Verbal phrases	**Starting in Peru**, the Amazon River runs through seven separate countries. **Concerned about the increasing workload**, he decided to look for a new job. **Painted by Leonardo da Vinci**, the *Mona Lisa* is one of the most valuable paintings in the world.

Inversion with Negative Adverb Phrases

In formal writing, when certain negative adverb phrases are used at the start of a sentence, the subject and auxiliary verb of the main clause must be inverted (switched). Look at the examples on the right.	**Never before** <u>have I</u> found a book so difficult to put down. **Not since** I went to New Zealand <u>have I</u> seen such amazing scenery. **Not until** I arrived at the shop <u>did I</u> realize I'd forgotten my wallet.

WRITING REFERENCE

UNIT 5

Paraphrasing

When you want to report what someone else wrote, but you don't want to quote the person directly, you can paraphrase. Paraphrasing is using your own words to express another person's idea. Paraphrasing is different from summarizing. For example, when you summarize a paragraph, you restate the main points of the paragraph. When you paraphrase a paragraph, you restate all of the ideas of the paragraph.

Follow these steps to help you paraphrase successfully:

1. Read the original passage that you want to paraphrase several times to make sure that you understand the meaning. Look up any words that you don't understand.

2. Without looking at the original passage, write notes about it on a piece of paper. Don't write complete sentences.

3. Use your notes to write a paraphrase. Don't look at the original passage.

4. Compare your paraphrase with the original passage. Make sure that your paraphrase expresses the same meaning as the original. If your paraphrase looks too much like the original, check your sentence structures and word choices. Make sure that your sentence structures are different from the original. Also, try to use synonyms for the content words (like nouns and verbs) in the original passage.

Here's an example of a paraphrase:

Original Passage:

Between 1960 and 2000, Seoul's population increased from fewer than three million to almost ten million people. In the same period, South Korea went from being one of the world's poorest countries, with a per capita GDP of less than $100, to being richer than some countries in Europe.

Paraphrase:

The population of Seoul grew a lot between 1960 and 2000. In 1960, there were fewer than three million people in Seoul. By 2000, just under 10 million people were living there. In 1960, the per capita GDP of South Korea was less than $100, and the country was one of the poorest in the world. However, by 2000, South Korea was wealthier than some European countries.

WRITING REFERENCE

UNIT 7
Referring to Sources

According to and *say* are two of the most commonly used reporting verbs/phrases. Here are some additional verbs and phrases to help you vary your style when referring to sources. Consider the meaning you intend to convey when choosing a reporting verb.

according to	emphasize	predict
acknowledge	estimate	propose
admit	explain	recommend
allege	express	report
argue	feel	say
ask	indicate	speculate
assert	insist	state
believe	iterate	stress
claim	maintain	suggest
conclude	mention	think
deny	note	warn
determine	point out	write

Past Simple and Past Participle Forms of Commonly Used Irregular Verbs

become—became—become	eat—ate—eaten	mean—meant—meant
begin—began—begun	fall—fell—fallen	meet—met—met
bend—bent—bent	feel—felt—felt	pay—paid—paid
bet—bet—bet	fight—fought—fought	put—put—put
bite—bit—bitten	find—found—found	quit—quit—quit
bleed—bled—bled	fly—flew—flown	read—read—read
blow—blew—blown	forget—forgot—forgotten	run—ran—run
break—broke—broken	get—got—gotten	say—said—said
bring—brought—brought	give—gave—given	see—saw—seen
build—built—built	go—went—gone	send—sent—sent
buy—bought—bought	grow—grew—grown	sleep—slept—slept
catch—caught—caught	have—had—had	speak—spoke—spoken
choose—chose—chosen	hear—heard—heard	spend—spent—spent
come—came—come	hide—hid—hidden	stand—stood—stood
cost—cost—cost	hold—held—held	steal—stole—stolen
cut—cut—cut	hurt—hurt—hurt	take—took—taken
deal—dealt—dealt	keep—kept—kept	teach—taught—taught
dive—dove—dove	know—knew—known	tell—told—told
do—did—done	lead—led—led	think—thought—thought
draw—drew—drawn	leave—left—left	wear—wore—worn
drink—drank—drunk	lie—lay—laid	win—won—won
drive—drove—driven	lose—lost—lost	write—wrote—written

VOCABULARY INDEX

Word	Unit	CEFR	Example sentence / definition
accomplish	5	C1	
acknowledge*	2	C1	
alien	10	-	
annual*	7	B1	
apparel	4	-	
apparently*	2	B2	
assess*	2	B2	
associate (v)	7	C1	
atmosphere	1	B2	
authority*	2	C2	
automatically*	9	B2	
balance (n)	3	B2	
base (n)	10	C2	
beyond	8	B2	
brand	4	B2	
capability*	5	C1	
capacity*	9	B2	
captivated	6	-	
collectively	5	-	
competitive	4	B2	
competitor	4	B1	
complementary*	5	-	
complex* (adj)	5	B2	
composition	3	C2	
concept*	1	B2	

Word	Unit	CEFR	Example sentence / definition
consequence*	1	B2	_____
context*	3	B2	_____
contradictory*	8	C2	_____
conversely*	8	-	_____
coordinate*	5	-	_____
cover up	9	C1	_____
criteria*	1	C1	_____
crops	7	B1	_____
crucial*	3	B2	_____
cryptic	6	-	_____
current	1	B2	_____
deceitful	9	-	_____
deceptive	9	C2	_____
declare	5	B2	_____
dedicated*	2	C1	_____
defense	5	-	_____
definitively*	6	-	_____
deny*	7	B2	_____
depression*	3	B2	_____
destiny	10	C1	_____
devoted to*	1	B2	_____
distinct*	7	C1	_____
dramatic*	1	B2	_____
economic*	7	B2	_____
eliminate*	1	C1	_____

Word	Unit	CEFR	Example sentence / definition
emergence*	9	-	_____
emergent*	5	-	_____
erosion*	1	C1	_____
essentially	1	B2	_____
ethics*	3	C2	_____
evidently*	6	B2	_____
evolutionary*	7	-	_____
exclude*	6	C1	_____
executive	4	C1	_____
expose to*	3	B2	_____
feasible	2	C1	_____
fertilizer	1	-	_____
flee	10	C1	_____
found*	4	B2	_____
fundamental*	9	C2	_____
gain insight*	8	C1	_____
geometric	3	-	_____
glimpse	10	C1	_____
gullible	9	-	_____
headquarters	4	B2	_____
hypothetical*	2	-	_____
imperfect	3	C1	_____
implication*	8	C1	_____
impostor*	9	-	_____
inferior	10	C1	_____

Word	Unit	CEFR	Example sentence / definition
innocence	9	C2	_____
insight*	3	C1	_____
intact	8	C2	_____
integral*	6	C1	_____
intellectual	10	B2	_____
investment*	7	B2	_____
irresistible	6	-	_____
lethal	2	C2	_____
life span	8	C2	_____
literally	10	B2	_____
livestock	7	-	_____
longevity	8	C2	_____
manipulate*	5	-	_____
marketing	4	B2	_____
mechanisms*	8	C1	_____
merchandise	4	-	_____
metaphor	6	C2	_____
minority	7	B2	_____
mislead	9	C1	_____
monotonous	6	C1	_____
multiple	6	C1	_____
nostalgic	6	C2	_____
notion*	3	C1	_____
on the contrary*	6	C1	_____
orientation*	7	C2	_____

Word	Unit	CEFR	Example sentence / definition
outcome*	8	C1	_____
outnumber	8	C1	_____
outsource	4	-	_____
perspective*	1	C1	_____
poaching	2	-	_____
precisely*	5	B2	_____
predator	2	C1	_____
prey	2	C2	_____
principle*	3	C1	_____
priority*	2	B2	_____
profit	4	B2	_____
profound	1	C2	_____
project* (v)	2	-	_____
prominent	9	C1	_____
prone to	9	C2	_____
proportion*	3	C1	_____
prosper	7	C2	_____
protagonist	10	C2	_____
pursue*	3	C1	_____
ratio*	8	C1	_____
realistically*	5	C1	_____
reconstruct*	8	C1	_____
relevant*	5	B2	_____
resolve*	2	C1	_____
restriction*	8	C1	_____

Word	Unit	CEFR	Example sentence / definition
retail	4	C1	_____
revenue*	7	C1	_____
rival	4	C1	_____
ruthless	10	C2	_____
satisfy	1	B2	_____
secretive	2	-	_____
sequel	10	-	_____
settle	10	B2	_____
shortage	4	B2	_____
simulation*	5	C1	_____
simultaneously	6	B2	_____
straightforward*	6	B2	_____
stunned	10	C2	_____
substantial	6	B2	_____
supply chain	4	-	_____
systematically	9	C2	_____
tensions*	7	B2	_____
thereby*	7	C1	_____
thrive	9	C1	_____
touch down	10	-	_____
transform*	1	B2	_____
undermine	8	C2	_____
unimaginable	10	C2	_____
unpredictable*	5	B2	_____
violate*	3	C2	_____

*These words are on the Academic Word List (AWL). The AWL is a list of the 570 most frequent word families in academic texts. It does not include the most frequent 2,000 words of English.

ACKNOWLEDGMENTS

The Authors and Publisher would like to acknowledge the teachers around the world who participated in the development of the second edition of *Pathways*.

A special thanks to our Advisory Board for their valuable input during the development of this series.

ADVISORY BOARD

Mahmoud Al Hosni, Modern College of Business and Science, Oman; **Safaa Al-Salim**, Kuwait University; **Laila Al-Qadhi**, Kuwait University; **Julie Bird**, RMIT University Vietnam; **Elizabeth Bowles**, Virginia Tech Language and Culture Institute, Blacksburg, VA; **Rachel Bricker**, Arizona State University, Tempe, AZ; **James Broadbridge**, J.F. Oberlin University, Tokyo; **Marina Broeder**, Mission College, Santa Clara, CA; **Shawn Campbell**, Hangzhou High School; **Trevor Carty**, James Cook University, Singapore; **Jindarat De Vleeschauwer**, Chiang Mai University; **Wai-Si El Hassan**, Prince Mohammad Bin Fahd University, Saudi Arabia; **Jennifer Farnell**, University of Bridgeport, Bridgeport, CT; **Rasha Gazzaz**, King Abdulaziz University, Saudi Arabia; **Keith Graziadei**, Santa Monica College, Santa Monica, CA; **Janet Harclerode**, Santa Monica Community College, Santa Monica, CA; **Anna Hasper**, TeacherTrain, UAE; **Phoebe Kamel Yacob Hindi**, Abu Dhabi Vocational Education and Training Institute, UAE; **Kuei-ping Hsu**, National Tsing Hua University; **Greg Jewell**, Drexel University, Philadelphia, PA; **Adisra Katib**, Chulalongkorn University Language Institute, Bangkok; **Wayne Kennedy**, LaGuardia Community College, Long Island City, NY; **Beth Koo**, Central Piedmont Community College, Charlotte, NC; **Denise Kray**, Bridge School, Denver, CO; **Chantal Kruger**, ILA Vietnam; **William P. Kyzner**, Fuyang AP Center; **Becky Lawrence**, Massachusetts International Academy, Marlborough, MA; **Deborah McGraw**, Syracuse University, NY; **Mary Moore**, University of Puerto Rico; **Raymond Purdy**, ELS Language Centers, Princeton, NJ; **Anouchka Rachelson**, Miami Dade College, Miami, FL; **Fathimah Razman**, Universiti Utara Malaysia; **Phil Rice**, University of Delaware ELI, Newark, DE; **Scott Rousseau**, American University of Sharjah, UAE; **Verna Santos-Nafrada**, King Saud University, Saudi Arabia; **Eugene Sidwell**, American Intercon Institute, Phnom Penh; **Gemma Thorp**, Monash University English Language Centre, Australia; **Matt Thurston**, University of Central Lancashire, UK; **Christine Tierney**, Houston Community College, Houston, TX; **Jet Robredillo Tonogbanua**, FPT University, Hanoi.

GLOBAL REVIEWERS

ASIA

Antonia Cavcic, Asia University, Tokyo; **Soyhan Egitim**, Tokyo University of Science; **Caroline Handley**, Asia University, Tokyo; **Patrizia Hayashi**, Meikai University, Urayasu; **Greg Holloway**, University of Kitakyushu; **Anne C. Ihata**, Musashino University, Tokyo; **Kathryn Mabe**, Asia University, Tokyo; **Frederick Navarro Bacala**, Yokohama City University; **Tyson Rode**, Meikai University, Urayasu; **Scott Shelton-Strong**, Asia University, Tokyo; **Brooks Slaybaugh**, Yokohama City University; **Susanto Sugiharto**, Sutomo Senior High School, Medan; **Andrew Zitzmann**, University of Kitakyushu.

LATIN AMERICA AND THE CARIBBEAN

Raul Bilini, ProLingua, Dominican Republic; **Alejandro Garcia**, Colegio Marcelina, Mexico; **Humberto Guevara**, Tec de Monterrey, Campus Monterrey, Mexico; **Romina Olga Planas**, Centro Cultural Paraguayo Americano, Paraguay; **Carlos Rico-Troncoso**, Pontificia Universidad Javeriana, Colombia; **Ialê Schetty**, Enjoy English, Brazil; **Aline Simoes**, Way To Go Private English, Brazil; **Paulo Cezar Lira Torres**, APenglish, Brazil; **Rosa Enilda Vasquez**, Swisher Dominicana, Dominican Republic; **Terry Whitty**, LDN Language School, Brazil.

MIDDLE EAST AND NORTH AFRICA

Susan Daniels, Kuwait University, Kuwait; **Mahmoud Mohammadi Khomeini**, Sokhane Ashna Language School, Iran; **Müge Lenbet**, Koç University, Turkey; **Robert Anthony Lowman**, Prince Mohammad bin Fahd University, Saudi Arabia; **Simon Mackay**, Prince Mohammad bin Fahd University, Saudi Arabia.

USA AND CANADA

Frank Abbot, Houston Community College, Houston, TX; **Hossein Aksari**, Bilingual Education Institute and Houston Community College, Houston, TX; **Sudie Allen-Henn**, North Seattle College, Seattle, WA; **Sharon Allie**, Santa Monica Community College, Santa Monica, CA; **Jerry Archer**, Oregon State University, Corvallis, OR; **Nicole Ashton**, Central Piedmont Community College, Charlotte, NC; **Barbara Barrett**, University of Miami, Coral Gables, FL; **Maria Bazan-Myrick**, Houston Community College, Houston, TX; **Rebecca Beal**, Colleges of Marin, Kentfield, CA; **Marlene Beck**, Eastern Michigan University, Ypsilanti, MI; **Michelle Bell**, University of Southern California, Los Angeles, CA; **Linda Bolet**, Houston Community College, Houston, TX; **Jenna Bollinger**, Eastern Michigan University, Ypsilanti, MI; **Monica Boney**, Houston Community College, Houston, TX; **Nanette Bouvier**, Rutgers University – Newark, Newark, NJ; **Nancy Boyer**, Golden West College, Huntington Beach, CA; **Lia Brenneman**, University of Florida English Language Institute, Gainesville, FL; **Colleen Brice**, Grand Valley State University, Allendale, MI; **Kristen Brown**, Massachusetts International Academy, Marlborough, MA; **Philip Brown**, Houston Community College, Houston, TX; **Dongmei Cao**, San Jose City College, San Jose, CA; **Molly Cheney**, University of Washington, Seattle, WA; **Emily Clark**, The University of Kansas, Lawrence, KS; **Luke Coffelt**, International English Center, Boulder, CO; **William C. Cole-French**, MCPHS University,

Boston, MA; **Charles Colson**, English Language Institute at Sam Houston State University, Huntsville, TX; **Lucy Condon**, Bilingual Education Institute, Houston, TX; **Janice Crouch**, Internexus Indiana, Indianapolis, IN; **Charlene Dandrow**, Virginia Tech Language and Culture Institute, Blacksburg, VA; **Loretta Davis**, Coastline Community College, Westminster, CA; **Marta Dmytrenko-Ahrabian**, Wayne State University, Detroit, MI; **Bonnie Duhart**, Houston Community College, Houston, TX; **Karen Eichhorn**, International English Center, Boulder, CO; **Tracey Ellis**, Santa Monica Community College, Santa Monica, CA; **Jennifer Evans**, University of Washington, Seattle, WA; **Marla Ewart**, Bilingual Education Institute, Houston, TX; **Rhoda Fagerland**, St. Cloud State University, St. Cloud, MN; **Kelly Montijo Fink**, Kirkwood Community College, Cedar Rapids, IA; **Celeste Flowers**, University of Central Arkansas, Conway, AR; **Kurtis Foster**, Missouri State University, Springfield, MO; **Rachel Garcia**, Bilingual Education Institute, Houston, TX; **Thomas Germain**, University of Colorado Boulder, Boulder, CO; **Claire Gimble**, Virginia International University, Fairfax, VA; **Marilyn Glazer-Weisner**, Middlesex Community College, Lowell, MA; **Amber Goodall**, South Piedmont Community College, Charlotte, NC; **Katya Goussakova**, Seminole State College of Florida, Sanford, FL; **Jane Granado**, Texas State University, San Marcos, TX; **Therea Hampton**, Mercer County Community College, West Windsor Township, NJ; **Jane Hanson**, University of Nebraska – Lincoln, Lincoln, NE; **Lauren Heather**, University of Texas at San Antonio, San Antonio, TX; **Jannette Hermina**, Saginaw Valley State University, Saginaw, MI; **Gail Hernandez**, College of Staten Island, Staten Island, NY; **Beverly Hobbs**, Clark University, Worcester, MA; **Kristin Homuth**, Language Center International, Southfield, MI; **Tim Hooker**, Campbellsville University, Campbellsville, KY; **Raylene Houck**, Idaho State University, Pocatello, ID; **Karen L. Howling**, University of Bridgeport, Bridgeport, CT; **Sharon Jaffe**, Santa Monica Community College, Santa Monica, CA; **Andrea Kahn**, Santa Monica Community College, Santa Monica, CA; **Eden Bradshaw Kaiser**, Massachusetts International Academy, Marlborough, MA; **Mandy Kama**, Georgetown University, Washington, D.C.; **Andrea Kaminski**, University of Michigan – Dearborn, Dearborn, MI; **Eileen Kramer**, Boston University CELOP, Brookline, MA; **Rachel Lachance**, University of New Hampshire, Durham, NH; **Janet Langon**, Glendale Community College, Glendale, CA; **Frances Le Grand**, University of Houston, Houston, TX; **Esther Lee**, California State University, Fullerton, CA; **Helen S. Mays Lefal**, American Learning Institute, Dallas, TX; **Oranit Limmaneeprasert**, American River College, Sacramento, CA; **Dhammika Liyanage**, Bilingual Education Institute, Houston, TX; **Emily Lodmer**, Santa Monica Community College, Santa Monica, CA; **Ari Lopez**, American Learning Institute, Dallas, TX; **Nichole Lukas**, University of Dayton, Dayton, OH; **Undarmaa Maamuujav**, California State University, Los Angeles, CA; **Diane Mahin**, University of Miami, Coral Gables, FL; **Melanie Majeski**, Naugatuck Valley Community College, Waterbury, CT; **Judy Marasco**, Santa Monica Community College, Santa Monica, CA; **Murray McMahan**, University of Alberta, Edmonton, AB, Canada; **Deirdre McMurtry**, University of Nebraska Omaha, Omaha, NE; **Suzanne Meyer**, University of Pittsburgh, Pittsburgh, PA; **Cynthia Miller**, Richland College, Dallas, TX; **Sara Miller**, Houston Community College, Houston, TX; **Gwendolyn Miraglia**, Houston Community College, Houston, TX; **Katie Mitchell**, International English Center, Boulder, CO; **Ruth Williams Moore**, University of Colorado Boulder, Boulder, CO; **Kathy Najafi**, Houston Community College, Houston, TX; **Sandra Navarro**, Glendale Community College, Glendale, CA; **Stephanie Ngom**, Boston University, Boston, MA; **Barbara Niemczyk**, University of Bridgeport, Bridgeport, CT; **Melody Nightingale**, Santa Monica Community College, Santa Monica, CA; **Alissa Olgun**, California Language Academy, Los Angeles, CA; **Kimberly Oliver**, Austin Community College, Austin, TX; **Steven Olson**, International English Center, Boulder, CO; **Fernanda Ortiz**, University of Arizona, Tucson, AZ; **Joel Ozretich**, University of Washington, Seattle, WA; **Erin Pak**, Schoolcraft College, Livonia, MI; **Geri Pappas**, University of Michigan – Dearborn, Dearborn, MI; **Eleanor Paterson**, Erie Community College, Buffalo, NY; **Sumeeta Patnaik**, Marshall University, Huntington, WV; **Mary Peacock**, Richland College, Dallas, TX; **Kathryn Porter**, University of Houston, Houston, TX; **Eileen Prince**, Prince Language Associates, Newton Highlands, MA; **Marina Ramirez**, Houston Community College, Houston, TX; **Laura Ramm**, Michigan State University, East Lansing, MI; **Chi Rehg**, University of South Florida, Tampa, FL; **Cyndy Reimer**, Douglas College, New Westminster, BC, Canada; **Sydney Rice**, Imperial Valley College, Imperial, CA; **Lynnette Robson**, Mercer University, Macon, GA; **Helen E. Roland**, Miami Dade College, Miami, FL; **Maria Paula Carreira Rolim**, Southeast Missouri State University, Cape Girardeau, MO; **Jill Rolston-Yates**, Texas State University, San Marcos, TX; **David Ross**, Houston Community College, Houston, TX; **Rachel Scheiner**, Seattle Central College, Seattle, WA; **John Schmidt**, Texas Intensive English Program, Austin, TX; **Mariah Schueman**, University of Miami, Coral Gables, FL; **Erika Shadburne**, Austin Community College, Austin, TX; **Mahdi Shamsi**, Houston Community College, Houston, TX; **Osha Sky**, Highline College, Des Moines, WA; **William Slade**, University of Texas, Austin, TX; **Takako Smith**, University of Nebraska – Lincoln, Lincoln, NE; **Barbara Smith-Palinkas**, Hillsborough Community College, Tampa, FL; **Paula Snyder**, University of Missouri, Columbia, MO; **Mary Evelyn Sorrell**, Bilingual Education Institute, Houston, TX; **Kristen Stauffer**, International English Center, Boulder, CO; **Christina Stefanik**, The Language Company, Toledo, OH; **Cory Stewart**, University of Houston, Houston, TX; **Laurie Stusser-McNeill**, Highline College, Des Moines, WA; **Tom Sugawara**, University of Washington, Seattle, WA; **Sara Sulko**, University of Missouri, Columbia, MO; **Mark Sullivan**, University of Colorado Boulder, Boulder, CO; **Olivia Szabo**, Boston University, Boston, MA; **Amber Tallent**, University of Nebraska Omaha, Omaha, NE; **Amy Tate**, Rice University, Houston, TX; **Aya C. Tiacoh**, Bilingual Education Institute, Houston, TX; **Troy Tucker**, Florida SouthWestern State College, Fort Myers, FL; **Anne Tyoan**, Savannah College of Art and Design, Savannah, GA; **Michael Vallee**, International English Center, Boulder, CO; **Andrea Vasquez**, University of Southern Maine, Portland, ME; **Jose Vasquez**, University of Texas Rio Grande Valley, Edinburgh, TX; **Maureen Vendeville**, Savannah Technical College, Savannah, GA; **Melissa Vervinck**, Oakland University, Rochester, MI; **Adriana Villarreal**, Universidad Nacional Autonoma de Mexico, San Antonio, TX; **Summer Webb**, International English Center, Boulder, CO; **Mercedes Wilson-Everett**, Houston Community College, Houston, TX; **Lora Yasen**, Tokyo International University of America, Salem, OR; **Dennis Yommer**, Youngstown State University, Youngstown, OH; **Melojeane (Jolene) Zawilinski**, University of Michigan – Flint, Flint, MI.

CREDITS

Photos

Cover, iii Robbie Shone/National Geographic Creative, **iv** (from top to bottom) © Edward Burtynsky, Michael Nichols/National Geographic Creative, Francois Nel/Getty Images, View Pictures/UIG/Getty Images, Matthias Hangst/Getty Images, **vi** (from top to bottom) Mark Peterson/Redux, © Mark Henley/Panos, Amble Design/Shutterstock, Alex Hyde/NPL, © Tsvetan Toshkov, **1** © Edward Burtynsky, **2** sunlow/Getty Images, **3** (tl) Chris Gray/National Geographic Creative, (tr) Robytravel/Alamy Stock Photo, **4** Xinhua News Agency/Getty Images, **6** Paul Chesley/National Geographic Creative, **9** © Edward Burtynsky, **10–11** (spread) Jim Richardson/National Geographic Creative, **11** (br) © Nicholas Whitman, **13** National Geographic Creative, **16** Frans Lanting/National Geographic Creative, **18–19** (spread) National Geographic Creative, **23** National Geographic Creative, **25** Michael Nichols/National Geographic Creative, **26** Janette Hill/National Geographic Creative, **27** (cr) (bl) (tl) Joel Sartore/National Geographic Creative, **28** James R.D. Scott/Getty Images, **30** Steve Winter/National Geographic Creative, **32** Steve Winter/National Geographic Creative, **34** (b) Steve Winter/National Geographic Creative, (cr) Evan Agostini/Getty Images, **38** Konrad Wothe/Minden Pictures, **40** Joel Sartore/National Geographic Creative, **42** Dmitrij Skorobogatov/Shutterstock, **45** National Geographic Creative, **47** Francois Nel/Getty Images, **48–49** (spread) FineArt/Alamy Stock Photo, **50** (bl) Bridgeman Images, (br) Interfoto/Alamy Stock Photo, **52** Raymond Gehman/National Geographic Creative, **54** Sam Abell/National Geographic Creative, **55** James L. Stanfield/National Geographic Creative, **56** Michael Melford/National Geographic Creative, **57** (t) Annie Griffiths/National Geographic Creative, (br) Araya Diaz/Getty Images, **59** O. Louis Mazzatenta/National Geographic Image Collection, **61** © Brian Yen, **66** Richard Nowitz/National Geographic Creative, **71** View Pictures/UIG/Getty Images, **72–73** (spread) National Geographic Creative, **72** (bl) Richard Boll/Getty Images, **74** (b) AP Images/Lee Jin-man, **76** Newscast/Eyevine/Redux, **78–79** (spread) Xurxo Lobato/Getty Images, **80** (tr) © Mike Peng, (bl) Jock Fistick/Bloomberg via Getty Images, **83** Miguel Riopa/Getty Images, **84** Christopher Goodney/Bloomberg/Getty Images, **93** Matthias Hangst/Getty Images, **94–95** (spread) David Ramos/Getty Images, **98** Frans Lanting/National Geographic Creative, **100** Mauricio Handler/National Geographic Creative, **101** Mark Thiessen/National Geographic Creative, **102–103** (spread) Kenneth Whitten/Design Pics/National Geographic Creative, **103** (br) © Peter Miller, **108** Anand Varma/National Geographic Creative, **114–115** (spread) Kathleen Reeder Wildlife Photography/Getty Images, **117** Mark Peterson/Redux, **120** Helen Sessions/Alamy Stock Photo, **122** Macduff Everton/National Geographic Creative, **125** (t) M&N/Alamy Stock Photo, (br) Macduff Everton/National Geographic Creative, **130** National Geographic Creative, **133** Mark Peterson/Redux, **139** © Mark Henley/Panos, **144–145** (spread) © Kees Veenenbos, **146** Chris Johns/National Geographic Creative, **147** Frans Lanting/National Geographic Creative, **148–149** (spread) Pascal Maitre/National Geographic Creative, **149** Agence Opale/Alamy Stock Photo, **153** Hemis/Alamy Stock Photo, **158** EQRoy/Shutterstock, **163** Amble Design/Shutterstock, **164** Paul Nicklen/National Geographic Creative, **165** (tl) Robbie George/National Geographic Creative, (bl) Joel Sartore/National Geographic Photo Ark, (br) Images & Stories/Alamy Stock Photo, **167** Yuriko Nakao/Getty Images, **169** Fritz Hoffman/National Geographic Creative, **171** Fritz Hoffman/National Geographic Creative, **172** © Rick Rickman, **173** © Stephen S. Hall, **175** Gianluca Colla/National Geographic Creative, **178** View Stock/Alamy Stock Photo, **187** Alex Hyde/NPL, **188** (bl) Tim McDonagh/National Geographic Creative, (br) Tim McDonagh/National Geographic Creative, **189** (t) Ryan Morris/National Geographic Creative, (br) Tim McDonagh/National Geographic Creative, **191** AF archive/Alamy Stock Photo, **192** National Geographic Creative, **194** Ryan Morris/National Geographic Creative, **195** © Yudhijit Bhattacharjee, **199** National Geographic Creative, **205** © University of Rochester, **207** © Tsvetan Toshkov, **208–209** (spread) Stephan Martiniere/National Geographic Creative, **210** Pictorial Press Ltd/Alamy Stock Photo, **212** © NASA/JPL-Caltech, **214** (b) NASA, (cr) Ulf Andersen/Getty Images, **216–217** (spread) Mark Garlick/Alamy Stock Photo, **220–221** (spread) © NASA/JPL-Caltech/Cornell Univ./Arizona State Univ., **222** Historical/Getty Images, **228** © NASA/JPL-Caltech, **241** Jim Richardson/National Geographic Creative

Texts/Sources

6–11 Adapted from "The Age of Man," by Elizabeth Kolbert: NGM March 2011; **30–34** Adapted from "A Cry for the Tiger," by Caroline Alexander: NGM December 2011; **52–57** Adapted from the Introduction to *Simply Beautiful Photographs* pp. 25–31, by Annie Griffiths: National Geographic Books, 2010; **72–73** Based on information from "Global Fashion Industry Statistics":

www.fashionunited.com; "The World's Largest Apparel Companies 2016": www.forbes.com; "Who Spends the Most on Apparel": www.wwd.com; "The Impact of a Cotton T-Shirt": www.worldwildlife. org; **76–80** Adapted from "Zara Excels in Marketing and Supply Chain Management," by Mike W. Peng: *Global Business 4th Edition* © Cengage Learning 2015; **98–103** Adapted from "Swarm Theory," by Peter Miller: NGM July 2007; **122–125** Adapted from "The Secret Language" by Daisy Zamora: reprinted with permission of the National Geographic Society from the book *How I Learned English*. Edited by Tom Miller. Copyright © 2007 Tom Miller; **144–149** Adapted from "The Shape of Africa," by Jared Diamond: NGM September 2005; **160–161** Based on information from "Singapore's total fertility rate dipped to 1.20 in 2016": www.straitstimes.com, "Census of Population 2010": Singapore Department of Statistics, "Rapid Growth in Singapore's Immigrant Population Brings Policy Challenges": www.migrationpolicy.org; **164–165** Based on information from www.nationalgeographic.com/animals; "Life Spans of the Animal Kingdom": www.dailyinfographic.com; **169–173** Adapted from "On Beyond 100," by Stephen S. Hall: NGM May 2013; **188–189**, **192–195** Adapted from "Why We Lie," by Yudhijit Bhattacharjee: NGM June 2017; **212–214** Adapted from "My Mars," by Ray Bradbury: NGM Special Issue "Space," October 2008; **215** Excerpt from *The Martian Chronicles* by Ray Bradbury (1950); **216** Excerpt from *The War of the Worlds* by H. G. Wells (1898)

NGM = National Geographic Magazine

Maps and Infographics

2–3 National Geographic Maps; **33** Virginia W Mason/National Geographic Creative; **72** 5W Infographics; **140–141** National Geographic Maps; **164–165** 5W Infographics

INDEX OF EXAM SKILLS AND TASKS

The activities in *Pathways Reading, Writing, and Critical Thinking* develop **key reading skills** needed for success on standardized tests such as TOEFL® and IELTS. In addition, many of the activities provide useful exam practice because they are similar to **common question types** in these tests.

Key Reading Skills	IELTS	TOEFL®	Page(s)
Recognizing vocabulary from context	✓	✓	14, 17, 18, 26, 36, 39, 59, 62, 63, 81, 85, 104, 109, 127, 130, 154, 155, 176, 179, 196, 200, 219, 223
Identifying main ideas	✓	✓	12, 35, 58, 81, 104, 126, 150, 175, 196, 219
Identifying supporting ideas	✓	✓	12, 35, 58, 81, 104, 126, 150, 175, 176, 196, 219, 220, 221
Scanning for details	✓	✓	12, 35, 82, 105, 126, 151, 196, 219
Making inferences	✓	✓	39, 85, 127, 168, 221
Recognizing pronoun references	✓	✓	15, 19
Understanding charts and infographics	✓		2, 13, 72, 82, 118, 140, 164, 177, 178, 188, 201, 202, 208

Common Question Types	IELTS	TOEFL®	Page(s)
Multiple choice	✓	✓	20, 39, 75, 81, 83, 110, 154, 177, 179, 211, 223
Completion (notes, diagram, chart)	✓		13, 14, 17, 35, 60, 82, 105, 154, 176, 200
Completion (summary)	✓		150, 196
Short answer	✓		12, 39, 58, 85, 106, 109, 126, 151, 175, 219, 220, 221, 223
Matching headings / information	✓		35, 36, 62, 104, 106, 126, 128, 218
Categorizing (Matching features)	✓	✓	62, 132, 150, 154, 219
True / False / Not Given	✓		17
Prose summary		✓	110, 111
Rhetorical purpose		✓	126, 127, 152, 220, 221

Level 4 of *Pathways Reading, Writing, and Critical Thinking* also develops **key writing skills** needed for exam success.

Key Writing Skills	Unit(s)
Writing a strong introduction and conclusion	1, 2
Expressing and justifying opinions	1, 2, 3, 6, 8, 10
Giving reasons and examples	1, 2, 3, 4, 6, 7, 8, 9, 10
Paraphrasing / Summarizing	4, 5, 7, 9, 10
Making comparisons	4
Describing problems and solutions	1, 2, 8
Explaining a process	9
Expressing agreement and disagreement	3, 8
Describing a graph or chart	9

Pathways	CEFR	IELTS Band	TOEFL® Score
Level 4	**C1**	**6.5–7.0**	**81–100**
Level 3	B2	5.5–6.0	51–80
Level 2	B1–B2	4.5–5.0	31–50
Level 1	A2–B1	0–4.0	0–30
Foundations	A1–A2		